T0381094

KING NEBUCHADNEZZAR
The First Biblical Werewolf

by

CONSTANCE LEE

authorHOUSE®

AuthorHouse™
1663 Liberty Drive
Bloomington, IN 47403
www.authorhouse.com
Phone: 1-800-839-8640

First published by AuthorHouse 10/6/2011

ISBN: 978-1-4567-3281-3 (sc)

Library of Congress Control Number: 2011908005

Printed in the United States of America

This book is dedicated to:
My Family

Preface

"Behold, I will do a new thing; now it shall spring forth; shall ye not know it? I will even make a way in the wilderness and rivers in the desert.

The beast of the field shall honor me, the dragons and the OWLS: *because I give waters in the wilderness and rivers in the desert to give drink to my people, my chosen.*

This people have I formed for myself; they shall shew forth my praise."

(Isaiah 43:19-21)

This story is being introduced and narrated by animals that met a *real live* wolf man.

One day (in the forest of ancient Babylon) the animals met a man named,

KING **NEBUCHADNEZZAR**
@ 604-562 B.C.

(The Land to Rest)

(Exodus 23:10-11)

"And six years thou shalt sow thy land, and shalt gather in the fruits thereof: But the seventh year thou shalt let it rest and lie still; that the poor of thy people may eat: and what they leave the beasts of the field shall eat. In like manner thou shalt deal with thy vineyard, and with thy oliveyard."

(Chastisement)

(Leviticus 26:18-22)

"And if you will not yet for all this hearken unto me, then I will punish you seven times more for your sins. And I will break the pride of your power; and I will make your heaven as iron, and your earth as brass: And your strength shall be spent in vain: for your land shall not yield her increase neither shall the trees of the land yield their fruits. And if ye walk contrary unto me, and will not hearken unto me; I will bring seven times more plagues upon you according to your sins. I will also send wild beasts among you, which shall rob you of your children, and destroy your cattle, and make you few in number; and your high ways shall be desolate."

(Leviticus 26:23-26)

"And if ye will not be reformed by me by these things, but will walk contrary unto me; Then will I also walk contrary unto you, and will punish you yet seven times for your sins. And I will bring a sword upon you that shall avenge the quarrel of my covenant: and when

ye are gathered together within your cities, I will send the pestilence among you; and ye shall be delivered into the hand of the enemy. And when I have broken the staff of your bread, ten women shall bake your bread in one oven, and they shall deliver you your bread again by weight: and ye shall eat, and not be satisfied."

(Curses)

(Leviticus 26:27-39)

"And if ye will not for all this hearken unto me, but walk contrary unto me; then I will walk contrary unto you also in fury; and I even I, will chastise you seven times for your sins. And ye shall eat the flesh of your sons, and the flesh of your daughters shall ye eat. And I will destroy your high places, and cut down your images, and cast your carcases upon the carcases of your idols, and my soul shall abhor you. And I will make your cities waste, and bring your sanctuaries unto desolation, and I will not smell the savour of your sweet ordours. And I will bring the land into desolation; and your enemies which dwell therein shall be astonished at it. And I will scatter you among the heathen, and will draw out a sword after you: and your land shall be desolate, and your cities waste. Then shall the land enjoy her Sabbaths, as long as it lieth desolate, and ye be in your enemies' land; even then shall the land rest, and enjoy her Sabbaths. As long as it lieth desolate it shall rest; because it did not rest in your Sabbaths, when ye dwelt upon it. And upon them that are left alive of you I will send a faintness into their hearts in the lands of their enemies; and the sound of a shaken leaf shall chase them; and they shall flee, as fleeing from a sword; and they shall fall when none pursueth. And they shall fall one upon another, as it were before a sword, when one pursueth: and ye shall have no power to stand before your enemies. And ye shall perish among the heathen, and the land of your enemies shall eat you up. And they that are left of you shall pine away in their

iniquity in your enemies' lands; and also in the iniquities of their fathers shall they pine away with them."

(Confess Iniquities: Covenant Renewed)

(Leviticus 26:40-46)
"If they shall confess their iniquity, and the iniquity of their fathers, with their trespass which they trespassed against me, and that also they have walked contrary unto me; And that I also have walked contrary unto them, and have brought them into the land of their enemies; if then their uncircumcised hearts be humbled, and then they accept of the punishment of their iniquity: Then will I remember my covenant with Jacob, and also my covenant with Isaac, and also my covenant with Abraham, will I remember; and I will remember the land. The land also shall be left of them, and shall enjoy her Sabbaths, while she lieth desolate without them: and they shall accept of the punishment of their iniquity: because, even because they despised my judgments, and because their soul abhorred my statutes. And yet for all that, when they be in the land of their enemies, I will not cast them away, neither will I abhor them to destroy them utterly, and to break my covenant with them: for I am the Lord their God. But I will for their sakes remember the covenant of their ancestors, whom I brought forth out of the land of Egypt in the sight of the heathen, that I might be their God: I am the Lord. These are the statutes and judgments and laws, which the Lord made between him and the children of Israel in mount Sinai by the hand of Moses."

Contents

Chapter 1

Kurt ~ the Erzurum wolf

Background ~ Erzurum Village

Kurt was the leader of the most *ferocious* pack of wolves that lived in a city called, **Erzurum** *(Eastern Anatolia Region, TURKEY)*. The Erzurum wolves had rival cousins living in a nearby city, **Hakkari**. [1] The mountainous territory and plains were huge but the food supply was too small for the wolves. The Erzurum and Hakkari wolves were in great competition with other wild animals *(black bears and leopards)* as well as the two-legged *human residents* searching for *red meat to sustain them in the freezing winter months.*

---

1   Hakkari is a village in Turkey also known as the home of many Assyrian tribes.

Kurt – *the leader* of the Erzurum wolf pack

Erzurum pack of wolves migrating to Babylon

Due to the scarcity of food, the wolves were forced to attack the villagers, small innocent children playing in the open fields, livestock, and pets for food. So, the people decided to do something about the wolves. Revenge, hatred, and the need to survive forced the villagers to kill and drive-off countless packs of wolves from Erzurum, Hakkari, and other villages. The best fighting men joined together to hunt down the wolves, bears, and leopards. Every night, they built up soaring walls of protective fires, set baited traps, and employed large ferocious dogs to force the wild predators out of their mountains.

Kurt in Babylon

As stated, two forces drove off the **Erzurum** wolves: angry villagers (their forceful campaigns to drive away all man-eating beasts) and other carnivorous animals competing for the same cuisine. The insufferable treatment from the villagers forced the wolves to relocate. According to Kurt, the wolves lived and hunted the way they were biologically created to do. From the *wolves' viewpoint*, the villages were insane! Kurt said that when he saw something that looked delicious, he ate it! So, the **Erzurum wolves** migrated from Eastern Turkey to Antioch (near Tarsus [2]) and even to further sites like, Babylon. Although there was a better supply of "red meat" in the Antioch Mountains, it snowed heavily and the wolves *were not* the only ones hunting for food. Again, driven by competition, hatred, and rage from the Antioch villagers, many of the **Erzurum** wolves migrated from the Antioch Mountains to better hunting grounds hundreds of miles away (down the Euphrates River) to the forest in Babylon. And that's how Kurt (the Erzurum wolf) came to live in Babylon.

Kurt Sees the Man-like-Beast

One day (after devouring a small gazelle), Kurt was peacefully resting

_____
2   Tarsus: the birthplace of Apostle Paul (A.K.A. Saul of Tarsus) and the capital of Cilicia. Acts 9:11

under a Juniper tree in the forest of Babylon. Afterwards, Kurt decided to take a lunchtime nap. Out of the *clear* blue sky, there appeared a naked human being running around on his hands and feet in a bizarre way. Like fish out-of-water, *the man-like-animal was out-of-his mind!* Even worse, there was still some kind of metaphysical change taking place.

Of course, this was not the first time Kurt laid eyes on a naked human. Kurt *(the Erzurum wolf)* led packs of wolves that attacked groups of human beings. Sometimes the wolves caught people off-guard while they were swimming, changing clothes, playing, or walking through the fields. *When its time to eat, hungry wolves don't care about clothes!* The ruthless wolves aggressively shredded the clothing of their victims. In other words, the carnivorous pack consumed the hunted and ate them down to the bone.

But this was the first time Kurt *(the Erzurum wolf)* witnessed a metamorphosis-taking place *(except for butterfly pupas emerging from their chrysalides)* before his eyes. The unknown human (still undergoing changes) was taking on animal-like instincts, behavior, and physical features resembling a wolf. In Kurt's presence, the man was being transformed from man to animal!

Immediately, Kurt howled (so loudly) as if he'd lost his mind! Just like a four-legged wild animal, the man was traveling on his hands and feet. At the end of the man's arms, the palms of both hands seemed *slightly arched* to the ground and the fingers *slightly flattened* (facilitating better leaps and running speed). Genetically, how was this possible? The man no longer had regular fingernails. Instead, the man's finger nails were two and one-half (2 ½) inches long, curved, and thick like bird claws enabling him to *viciously* defend himself, dig for food, rip things apart, as well as climb trees.

There seemed to be an arch in the beast's back. This allowed the hands and feet to be compressed to the ground. His legs were strong and muscular like the hind legs of an animal. The joints of his anklebones, legs, feet, and heels were *altered* pressing his toes flush to the ground. He was naked (no use for clothes) and his animal-like hair was his *new* outward garment. His hair was now so long, thick, and feathery (completely covering his bare skin from the elements). From his head to toe – ***there was no bare skin in sight!*** Considering the new environment and his new physique, the regent had no use for kingly luxuries such as palaces, meetings, elaborate decorations, temples, ziggurats, tables, campaigns, governorship, councils, chairs, beds, couches, silverware, servants, dancing, feasts, banquets, drunken parties, wine toasting, etc. In fact, all former ways of living were passed away and placed on hold for the moment.

At first, Kurt thought he was dreaming with his eyes wide open! So he stood on his hind legs to get a good scent of the new man-like-beast! Kurt elevated his nose and took a whiff of the air to make sure this creature was an animal and not a human. Nope! There was no error with Kurt's superb 20 by 20 vision or his power to discern scents. This creature did not smell like the other humans Kurt attacked and devoured!

Still, Kurt was not satisfied with this outrageous and unclassified creature in the animal kingdom. Inwardly, Kurt thought, "My Mama told me there would be days like this but I did not believe her." Still, Kurt ran down to the river and jumped in hoping to awaken himself from the horrible nightmare! The river water was cold and it sharpened Kurt's understanding and wits. Emerging from the water, Kurt realized this was no nightmare *– **this is reality.***

The Buzzz

By this time, all of animals in the forest were buzzing around and spreading the headline:

"A new man-like-beast (fully-grown) appeared from no where without the mating

of natural parents (male and female animals of the same species) and without emerging from the womb of a female animal of the same species."

Instead, this "thing" just appeared in the forest obviously resembling the male species and a crossbreed between a human and beast! Certainly, this fusion is an unnatural calamity! To date, there was no other creature on earth like this man who was *originally* created in the image of God but now changed into an animal! So, where, when, and how did this man become *a beast* with long feathers and claws?

Because of all the excitement, *the man-like-beast* ran away to hide inside a cave. No one believed Kurt's citing, because he reacted so *rickety*. Just the same, the news traveled through the forest on the wings of the wind, the birds, and all of nature *(even the ants were on the march)*. In fact, the trees whispered from treetop to treetop about the new creature in the forest! However, *the man-beast* was extremely shy and reserved so he remained hidden! This forced Kurt to publish a transcript of his findings and paste it on the trees in the forest.

Kurt's Affidavit

Kurt turned to Freddie *(the fox) saying,*
" **I Kurt *(the Erzurum wolf)* make the following statement of my own free will. Man you should have seen this human's transformation. It made me gag so hard that my tongue rolled to the back of my throat and back again!**

I'd just finished lunch! I ate a miniature gazelle and I couldn't run! My legs felt like four tons of brick, one ton per leg. And you know, Freddie, I'm built like my Daddy (short and muscular)! My legs are not that long and my stomach (being so full) just sat down on the ground. In fact, I felt like a rocking chair *or whatever!* O-o-o-h *my* Brother, [3] the hair from the gazelle gave me incredible gas! I

---

3   Up until this point, Kurt never called Freddie *(the fox)* his brother.

couldn't even bend over to pick up extras droppings of the gazelle's meat on the ground!

To make matters worse that animal-like-man just <u>FELL</u> out on the ground right in front of me! It was as if somebody shot me with a stung-gun! I was crippled with fear! I couldn't remember my name. *Believe me!* Really, I wanted to run but I could not move one muscle. I couldn't even scream – my vocal cords were paralyzed!!

My next statement will blow you away! Since I witnessed this phenomenon, I knew that history was being made. In a way, I felt honored to be there. To be more exact, I felt like a brand new-daddy facing a real-life birth of an ugly duckling offspring, but *I'm not a Daddy!*

My biggest question and nightmare was would this beast or *what-you-may-call-it* call me Daddy or Mamma? Or, will it bond with me in an awkward way and follow me wither I go? Or, will it attack me, kill me and/or eat me alive? If I survive, what will I tell my fiancée? What will I tell the other Erzurum wolves and animals in the forest? What will I tell my MAMA? Did this *fantastical* creature fall out of space? The fact is I'm facing a real-life trauma! I'm stressing out! Oh, Dear God! I need a Tylenol aspirin!"

The Other Animals and Insects

(Koos, Sinjop, Charlie Jr., Koos' parents, and Mrs. Beavers' comments)

There was a cute little *humming bird*, Koos, who fainted when he spotted the man-like-beast. Just before Koos fell to the ground, there was a *fat, furry* squirrel (Sinjop) hanging on a branch and Sinjop (with his extra-elongated bushy tail) caught the little humming bird. Sinjop used his long tail as a slingshot to thrust Koos back into the air while shouting, "Snap out of it, *Koos-Koos!*" Again, Sinjop shouted, "Snap out of it, *Koos-Koos!* Wake up Koos-Koos!"

Flying like a baseball, Koos *(the little humming bird)* still unconscious sailed through the air. Luckily, Charlie, Jr. (the wasp), was flying by so he stung Koos in the butt! Well, let me tell you, Koos snapped out of his unconscious state-of-mind real fast. He yelled out to Charlie, Jr. and Sinjop, "Gee, thanks you guys." Up, up, and away Koos flew to his family's home to spread the news about the *new man-like-beast* in the forest. But Koos' parents were already in the air on their way to see the new beast. They flew right past Koos who yelled out, "Hey Dad and Mom, stop I have something to tell you." But Koos' parents answered, "Son, we already know about the new monster in the forest! Mrs. Beaver pounded the drums all morning about the buzzz."

Finally, Koos' parents were suspended in the air looking down at the monster. Being mature adult humming birds, they were prepared for the unexpected. Yet, this was the first time they looked upon a genuine man-like-beast! Koos' Dad was amazed and Koos' Mom was astonished! They had never seen anything like it and they swirled in circles in the air with the other birds for three hours looking down at the man-like-beast.

(Wild Horses)

Violently, a herd of wild horses galloped up over the mountains to see *the man-like beast.* They were the most beautiful horses in Babylon and the world! The wind carried the news about the new forest creature and the wild horses were determined to get a first hand look. From the air, the birds watched the horses crossing the fields, streams, and rivers. In fact, they didn't even stop to drink water! There was a cloud of dust hovering over the horses' heads and that made it difficult to see them run. The dust cloud totally covered the herd of horses. Finally, the dust cloud stopped and (it seemed as if) the horses emerged out of the dust cloud.

(Beygir's comments)

Beygir *(the lead horse, a Black Stallion)* yelled out, "Stop! There he is! Man, I've never seen anything like that in my lifetime. BUT, What is it?" Without hesitation, the herd circled *the man-like-beast* who was astonished to see the attention he was getting. Up to this point, *the man* never got the chance to look at his reflection in a puddle, river, or lake but he was quite aware of his transformation from man to animal.

The horses completely encircled *the man-like-beast* and all the animals in the forest came-a-running to see the wonder! The entire forest were eyewitnesses to this spectacular event! The mass swarms of birds and flying critters hovering in the air blocked the sunlight! Normal life in the forest was turned upside down. The animals were bewildered. Worst of all, there were no treatment centers or veterinarians to help the animals to deal with this unnatural trauma.

(Comments: Macy and Charlie Jr.)
Macy was a *little honeybee* and she kept yelling, "The world is coming to an end...the world is coming to an end...the world is coming to an end." Then, Charlie, Jr. (*the wasp*) slapped Macy on her rump. Charlie said, "Macy, Macy get a hold of yourself, girl! Do you think I'd still be here flapping my wings (in mid air) and talking to you, if the world is about to suddenly end? You know that I've prepared a place to hide in the cave over yonder? I done asked you to join me, so don't worry your pretty little self about that *stupid* fish man." Irritably, Macy said, "Charlie Jr., you are not paying attention and you need to put on your spectacles because that "man is a beast" not a "fish." Why Charlie Jr., do you see any water? Is the man flapping around like a fish out-of-water?" THAT MAN IS A BEAST! So, Charlie said, "Macy, he's like a fish out of water! That's why I said it because he is out of his own natural habitat! Now, do you understand?"

(Wedding Bells for Macy and Charlie)
In a feminine and flirtatious voice, Macy's mood changed (360 degrees) and she said, "C-h-a-r-l-i-e *honey* you're right about one thing. We must protect ourselves. So, I accept your invitation but, *firstly*, we *must* get married before we can live together in the cave." Macy continued, " My

Mother told me you've got to live right!" Being a gentleman, Charlie Jr. said, "If you really want to marry me, I've got my minister ready right now. All I have to do is ask Mrs. Beaver to pound a message on the drums." With a great big smile, Macy said, ***"I do!"***

(Forest Animals in Unison)

All the other animals in the forest sighed with tears in their eyes and said, **"Congratulations, you two!"**

(Keci's comments)

But, Keci *(the old goat)* said, "Never minds thems two little stupid bugs! Yawl need to come back to REE-ALI-TY and check out the man-likes-beast."

(Esek's comments)

Then, Esek *(the donkey)* hee-hawed so loudly that it cracked one of Macy's *little* wings! Esek told Keci, "Amigo, you need to take an Anglish class because the right word is man-like-beasta not man-likes-beast. Are you stupid? You justa said that the man-likes beast and it doesn't make sense."

(Keci's comments)

So, Keci *(the old goat)* said, "Yous the stupid one fer callin hims a beasta likes hims a pasta dish yous fixin to eat!

(Esek's comments)

Answering, Esek *(the donkey)* said, "Amigo, you wronga! I meanna no harm!"

(Keci's comments)

Well, Keci *(the old goat)* got real mad and told Esek, "Man what's yawls' problem! Yawls' alweys correcting me in front of my home-boys! This the ways ah alweys talks and (if yawl don't like it) don't listen!"

Positive Closure

(Macy's comments)

Macy *(the cute little honeybee)* said, "Gentlemen, I have every right to speak up (after all, Esek cracked my little wing with his loud hee-hawing. Lets try to get along because you two are long time friends. There is no reason to quarrel. Esek, you have a black belt in hind-leg kicking. And Keci, you are a natural champion. So, can't we all just get through this ordeal without fighting each other?"

(Esek's comments)

So, Esek said, "Amigo, I'm sorry, Keci, please forgive me."

(Keci's comments)

Keci looked around to see that all eyes were upon him and he said, "Yo, Man it's cool, no problem."

Chapter 2

Nebuchadnezzar's Testimony

The True Story

This story is not make-believe! A "real live" man was transformed into an "animal!" Kurt *(the Erzurum wolf)* was the first animal to look upon the man-like-beast that did not have a name or at least he thought. From the beginning of time, this "creature" was unknown to man and beast. There wasn't another like him on earth — ***the first Biblical <u>werewolf</u>.***

(Nebuchadnezzar's Testimony)

Being center stage, the wolf-man *(werewolf)* stood upward on his two legs *(now functioning like hind legs)* and he opened his mouth saying, **"I am Nebuchadnezzar II!"**

Mother Nature's Reaction

At that point, the forest became violent! The wind blew fiercely through the tree tops as if the trees would snap into pieces; the birds were chirping; the squirrels were hopping from tree limb to tree limb; the rabbits were running into each other on the ground; the ants were *scurrying in circles*; judging from the buzzing sound, the honey bees lost their *harmonious* rhythm; the bears stood up on their hind legs to sniff the air; the wolves were *fierce-fully* howling; the wild horses *ran* through the meadows *fanatically leaping* over bushes and downed trees; the donkeys *hee-hawed* in stress; the spiders began *spinning* outrageous webs; and the ground hogs asked, "What day is this?"

Suddenly, the forest just shutdown to a dead silence! The animals were angry and bewildered! <u>There was complete silence!</u>

(Nebuchadnezzar continues)

Again, the *what-you-may-call-it* said, **"<u>Really, I am Nebuchadnezzar II.</u>"** Please allow me to tell my story and explain my physical condition. I can speak in the language of all forest animals. By some miracle, I am speaking in the language of the wolves but you will hear and interpret it in your own ancestral language. This means, if you are a squirrel, rabbit, donkey, bird, or whatever, you will hear with the understanding of your own species.

The GOD OF HEAVEN has brought "righteous" judgment upon me. Please, take a seat and get comfortable. This may take a little time. It all started with a dream!

(Kurt's response to Nebuchadnezzar)

Speechless, Kurt stared at the wolf-like-man for about five to ten minutes. Kurt looked around at the other animals and their faces were stunned beyond belief. Again, Kurt *(the Erzurum wolf)* presented himself as the moderator. Then, Kurt said, "That's quite a story *Mr. Neb-u-chad-nezzie...I mean Mr. Wolf-man...or whatever you call yourself.* BUT, I believe you because there's *no other* explanation for such a disaster! Obviously, something supernatural happened to you – you weren't born like that!

Unconsciously, Kurt *(the wolf)* approached the *what-you-may-call-it* and sniffed around Nebuchadnezzar (from head to toe) and said, "You smell like a wolf, therefore, you must be a wolf."

(Keci's comments)

Naturally, Keci *(the old goat)* blurted out, "Well what was yer before yer come to the forest? Ah hopes yer don't mind my next question. Is yer planning to eat me?"

(Nebuchadnezzar's response)

"Well now," said Nebuchadnezzar, "Keci *(you old goat)* No! I'm not a meat eater because God ordered me to eat grass like the oxen! Besides, I had a great supper last night in my palace but this morning (as you can see) is a different matter!

MOVING ON, this whole nightmare started with a dream. In fact, I want all of you to take notice because what I have to tell you is extremely important and true!"

Chapter 3

Ancient Babylon & Nebuchadnezzar II

Ancient Babylon 101 (about 2300 B.C.)

(The Professor's comments)

By now, Professor Baykus (*the old Hittite owl*) stretched his long feathered-wings, cracked his knuckles (*well owls can have knuckles in this story*) and set straight up because *now* he was wide-awake! He was ready to jump knee-deep (*with his little short legs*) into Babylon's history! Hopping down to a lower branch, he said, "If I get too excited, I won't have far to fall!" The Professor had that twinkle in his eyes as if he knew exactly what to say and when to say it!

So, the Professor said that way, way, way, way, way before kings Nabopolassar and Nebuchadnezzar, Babylon was one of the oldest and ancient cities in the world and the Babylonians *ironically* dubbed it "the holy city." But it wasn't a *holy city* it was *The Mother of Harlots and Abominations*! The Professor said, "Originally, Babylon was founded by Nimrod (the wicked son of Cush, the son of Ham, the son of Noah)."

Professor Baykus said that Jerusalem is The Holy City not Babylon, **"Awake, awake: put on thy strength, O Zion [Jerusalem]; put on thy beautiful garments, O Jerusalem, the holy city: for henceforth there**

15

shall no more come unto thee the uncircumcised and the unclean." (Isaiah 52:1) The Professor said, "Just read the following ***Books of the Bible*** and you will see." (Isaiah 48:2; Nehemiah 11:1, 18; Daniel 9:16; Matthew 4:5; 27:53; and New Jerusalem [4] = The Holy City in the Book of Revelation 21:2.

(Sweet-pea Interrupts the Professor)

Then, the most outrageous thing happened! **Sweet-pea (a little tick who lived under the Professor's feathered arm-pit) spoke up and said, "SO WHAT!"**

(The Professor's comments)

The Professor got so mad that he dropped his spectacles and said, "All insects should be muzzled especially if they talk badly to the host they feed on! I've seen talking animals (like Balaam's donkey, Miss Chamora) [5] in the Bible but not insects! Be quiet, Sweet-pea, or else, I'll start charging you a fee for the free drink. I am not the Red Cross!"

(Keci's comments)

The *old goat* said, "Does theys menufacteurs muzzles that small fer bugs?"

(Sweet-pea's comments)

The little tick said, "Gee-whiz Keci! And, I'm really sorry, *Professor-Sir*!"

(Keci's comments)

Then, old Keci *(the mean old goat)* said, "Youse right Mister-Professor-Sir that's telling Sweet-pea! In fact, Ah told them other animals to quit fussing over them *two little stupid bugs* (Macy and Charlie, Jr.) that done

---

4   ***"And I John saw the holy city, New Jerusalem coming down from God out of heaven, prepared as a bride adorned for her husband."*** (Revelation 21:2)
5   See book entitled: ALL of The ANIMALS Are TALKING ABOUT IT! By Constance Lee

got engaged! We's talking about this here man *(Nebuchedder)* who went through a change like a worm cums out the cocoon. Only thang, him was a man and now him's a wolf. But, them other animals started talking about the engagement between that little cute honeybee (Macy) and that bad-tempered, stanging wasp (Charlie, Jr.)! I just can't imagine what theys' baby bugs will look like, we'll probably call em "waspbees."

They done got me so mad! I told thems animals to get a grip on REE-ALI-TY! Even the little tick, Sweet-pea (thats sucken yose blood) is talking out the sides of his'm neck! Ah ain't got no ed-j-u-ma-ca-t-i-o-n and Ah shows ain't no scholar, but I gots planty common sense. It's a strange world, Mister- Professor-Sir."

(The Professor's comments)

The Professor said, "Keci, that's O.K. most of the educated ones are plastic and spineless. It's better to be simple, honest, poor, and real *than to be men pleasers.* But I must tell you the correct pronunciation is Nebuchadnezzar not *Nebuchedder, which sounds like the name of a cheese!* Anyhow, let us move on!"

Nimrod the Great Builder (about 2300 B.C.)

The *wise old Hittite owl* said, **"And the sons of Ham: Cush, Mizraim, Phut, and Canaan. And Cush begat Nimrod, a mighty one in the earth and a mighty hunter before the Lord. And the beginning of his kingdom was BABEL, Erech, Accad, and Calneh in the land of Shinar."** (Genesis 10:6-10) Nimrod *(the son of Cush, the son of Ham, the son of Noah) means = rebel or we shall rebel.* Nimrod was a wicked, awful, and controlling man! As a great hunter of animals, Nimrod exceeded in sport and skill above all other men *on the face of the earth.* Nimrod's need to dominate the animal world spilled over into his bizarre need to dominate and terrorize men. So, Nimrod did as Nimrod wanted. He forced his way of living and beliefs upon others and he looked for ways to keep people in line! He purposefully started **false religions and false**

worship to separate the people from the **Living God.** In doing so, Nimrod instituted certain mandates, rituals, orgies, and sacrifices to gain power over the people! The deeper the people sinned, the further away they got from God! Obviously, their lives were in moral and spiritual decay because they were separated from **"The Almighty God."**

Nimrod was a *"flamboyant sinner"* who greatly opposed the **Lord GOD** by calling Babylon *"the holy city."* THAT WAS ONE OF THE MOST STUPIDEST THINGS NIMROD DID BECAUSE HE ANGERED THE GOD OF HEAVEN. To make matters worse, Nimrod *(the son of Cush, the son of Ham, the son of Noah)* personally knew his great, great grandfather, NOAH,[6] who told him ALL about the **ONE TRUE Living GOD,** his visits and talks with **GOD**, and the Flood (A.K.A. Noah's Deluge)!

Imagine, Nimrod had the opportunity to speak with the one man **(Noah)** who found *"grace and mercy"* with God. Moreover, Noah's favor with God saved his entire family from the flood upon the earth. To make it clear, Nimrod got it straight from the horse's mouth: **Noah was the first Biblical Talk Master!**[7] As commanded and commissioned by The Almighty GOD, **Noah (The Preacher)** taught *120 years* before the flood and another *350 years* (after the flood) about morals, devoutness, obedience, righteousness, and worship to all of his relatives, grandchildren *(including little Nimrod and Assur)*, neighbors, travelers, and to many others living

---

6   The Flood ended exactly one year on the first month & day after Noah entered the Ark. (Genesis 8:13) **Noah** lived to see the births of many nations (including his grandchildren). As little **Nimrod** sat on his great, great grandfather's (Noah) knee, he listened to marvelous stories about the Almighty God who said, **"...all flesh wherein is the breath of life from under heaven and every thing that is in the earth shall die"** in the **Flood**. And, God said to Noah, **"But with thee will I establish my covenant; and thou shalt come into the ark, thou and thy sons, and thy wife, and thy sons' wives with thee. And of every thing that is of all flesh, two of every sort shalt thou bring into the ark, to keep them alive with thee; they shall be male and female..."** (Genesis 6:17-18)

7   So, tell that to FM 95.5!

around him. Once a preacher, always a preacher! Yet, Nimrod still refused to live righteously!

The Professor said that Nimrod's rebellion and disobedience was premeditated and an outrage against Noah, and especially, against the **Lord GOD**! Considering his heritage, Nimrod should have been a faithful grandson and a godly follower *like his great, great grandfather, Noah, who was a model citizen as well as a justified leader for his family.* Nimrod should have realized that his many gifts and heritage were from the **True Living GOD** who blessed him! Instead, Nimrod led the people astray and they (like idiots) *willingly* followed Nimrod into idolatry rather than serve **"The Almighty God!"** Truly this was a negative reflection on Nimrod's character.

Babylon = BABEL

The LAND OF SHINAR refers to all the cities of Nimrod mentioned in Genesis 10:8-11. ***"And the whole earth was of one language, and of one speech."*** (Genesis 10:1) But Nimrod and his people [8] chose Babylon for a special site, ***"And it came to pass, as they journeyed from the east, they found a plain in the land of Shinar and they dwelt there. And they said one to another, Go to, let us make brick, and burn them thoroughly. And they had brick for stone, and slime had they for mortar. And they said, Go to, let us build us a city and a tower, whose top may reach unto heaven; and let us make us a name, lest we be scattered abroad upon the face of the whole earth."*** (Genesis 11:2-4)   The latter statement was extremely prophetic. They built themselves a city, **a huge worship center** (the Ziggurat of Babel that reached up to heaven), and made themselves famous throughout the land, ***"so they would not be scattered abroad upon the face of the whole earth."*** (Genesis 11:4) However, the city's patron (Marduk) was no match for **Yahweh**!

---

[8]   ***"And the whole earth was one language, and of one speech."*** (Genesis 11:1)

However, the Jews call Babylon, BABEL, [9] ***"And the Lord came down to see the city and the tower, which the children of men built. The Lord said, Behold the people are one and they have all one language; and this they begin to do: <u>and now nothing will be restrained from them, which they have imagined to do.</u>***

Go to, let us go down and there confound their language, that they may not understand one another's speech. So the Lord scattered them abroad from thence upon the face of all the earth: and they left off to build the city. Therefore is the name of it called Babel; because the Lord did there confound the language of all the earth: and from thence did the Lord scatter them abroad upon the face of all the earth." (Genesis 11:5-9)

Furthermore, GOD turned their own words against them! The very thing they tried to prevent was executed in judgment against them! Why? They were pagans, rebellious heathens, and they boasted, ***"…we will not be scattered abroad…"*** GOD did just the opposite and He scattered them abroad upon the face of the whole earth. GOD **broke up the chain-gang. In fact, God broke the chains, the gangs, and the links!** When GOD got through with them, no body understood a word the other person was saying! And so, they regrouped into smaller clans (according to their new languages) and went their separate ways! Question: **I wonder what Nimrod said?** Answer: **He probably said, "I'll be a monkey's uncle!"**

(Old Keci's remarks)

"WOW WEE, WEE!" said old Keci *(the mean old goat)*, "Thems peoples left off building because the **Lord GOD** was madder than a stanging donkey-bee! And God done comp-founded theys language and theys don't know whuts theys own Pappy wuz saying! You know that's like somebody from Chinna speaking in Chinnessee to me, and <u>Ah peaks</u>

---

9   According to the ***Bible***, the word Babel means = to confuse (confusion).

20

perfect Anglash with an Afro-Merry-caine-Anglash twist! Ah tells you this world's a mess!"

(Esek's comments)

Then, Esek *(the donkey)* told old Keci *(the goat)* "Amigo, you talking too muchie since the monster-wolfa-man arrive in the foresta! Why you no take-a-break? The Professor knows more about everything and I wanta to hear what him has to say."

(The Professor's comments)

However, Professor Baykus *(the old Hittite owl)* said that king Nebuchadnezzar (the wolf-man) is the most qualified one to tell the story. Moreover, it is his exclusive story to share.

Nebuchadnezzar 101

Mr. Wolf-man said, "Once upon a time, I was the king of Babylon, and I was ruthless, worldly, and a wicked king, Nebuchadnezzar II." As a conqueror of nations, my eyes witnessed many things. I was *the* undisputed ruler, dictator, murderer, egotist, warlord, successful businessman, politician, strategist, victorious builder, suppressor, tormenter, full of fury, rage, and revenge, promoter of false religion and false worship, and false accuser among many other things. Even worse, I lusted and craved for others to worship me as a god!"

"I will speak the truth about my father, Babylon's independence, her major enemy *(Assyria)*, and a few very critical prophecies concerning Assyria and Babylon. *I may deviate a little but it's important for me to bring forth certain elements to flavor the story as a cook spices foods.*"

Nabopolassar, king of Babylon

The wolf-man continued, "I must pay homage to my *earthly* father,

Nabopolassar (the *king of Babylon* about 626-604 B.C.) means = may the god Nabu protect my son. The Assyrians fought many wars against the Babylonians and greatly distressed them for nearly two hundred years. One day, Nabopolassar (the great and powerful general) and his army overthrew Assyrian rule (under the last Assyrian king, Ashurbanipal [10]) about 626 B.C. As the founder and liberator of the Neo-Babylonian Chaldean [11] Empire, Nabopolassar appointed himself <u>king</u> and made <u>Babylon</u> his capital. As a victor, Nabopolassar thrived to bring down Assyria to the ground. On or about 612 B.C. *(at the Battle of Nineveh)*, the king of Babylonia and the king of the Media *united* to overthrew Nineveh, *capital of Assyria.*

(Nabopolassar, Visionary and Builder)

As a *religious visionary*, Nabopolassar built the Etemenanki (a huge ziggurat) a seven-story temple dedicated to Marduk, Babylonia's *great lord* and it was one of Nabopolassar's greatest constructions. Nabopolassar may have patterned the Etemenanki of Babylon (on a smaller scale) after the Ziggurat of Babel, built by Nimrod, in the plain *(in the land of Shinar)*. As a *political visionary*, Nabopolassar united Babylonia to Media through the marriage of his son, Nebuchadnezzar to Amytis *(daughter of king Astyages, son of king Cyaxares)*. As a *military visionary*, Nabopolassar led and participated in wars and was an excellent example for his successors. Prior to his death, Nabopolassar named Nebuchadnezzar II *(his eldest and favorite son)* Commander-in-Chief over the Babylonian army!

Nebuchadnezzar, king of Babylon

Nebuchadnezzar means = may the god Nabu defend. Nebuchadnezzar and his army fought and defeated the Egyptian army at the infamous *Battle of Carchemish* (about 605 B.C.). Also, they made Syria and Phoenician subject to Babylon. After word came of Nabopolassar's death,

---

10   King Ashurbanipal (about 668 to 629 B.C.) has variant spellings: Assurbanipal, Osnappar and Asnapper, and Sardanapalus).
11   Chaldea or Babylonia was located in the lower Tigris and Euphrates Valleys.

Nebuchadnezzar returned to Babylon and became king about 605-562 B.C. Although king Nabopolassar *did not* die on the battlefield, he passed away honorably and from natural causes. He was remembered as a great king and not a coward for giving up his throne to his rightful son and heir, Nebuchadnezzar.

About 597 B.C., Nebuchadnezzar captured Jerusalem and placed Jerusalem in the care of *General Nebuzaradan (of the Babylonian army)* executed many nobles, burned the city and its temples, left the lower classes to live in houses and to attend the fields, and took the upper class captives (about twelve thousand and more) to Babylon. Without Nebuzaradan's generosity *(permitted by God's mercy)*, the villagers would never have the chance to own houses or fields. Frankly, the upper class coveted everything. More importantly, *General Nebuzaradan gave special care to Jeremiah and freed him from prison.* (Jeremiah 39:11-12)

(The Professor's comments)

Professor Baykus said that Nebuchadnezzar continued the pursuits and aspirations of his late father, king Nabopolassar! Under Nebuchadnezzar's watch, Babylon became the Center of the World. There was no other place in ancient Mesopotamia or on earth with such splendor and greatness! The Professor said that Nebuchadnezzar started rebuilding, constructing, and transforming Babylon on a monumental scale. Like his father, Nebuchadnezzar continued his own building campaign and constructed one of the most famous gates in the world, the *notorious* Ishtar Gate [12] (on the main avenue) which was just *one* of the *eight* gates within ancient Babylonia. Among other building projects, Nebuchadnezzar is revered for the waterways, beautiful lakes, *hidden* irrigation systems and water conduits (from the Euphrates River into the city and throughout the terraced Garden), and above all the *infamous* Hanging Gardens of Babylon.

---

12   The scattered remains and bricks of the Ishtar Gate, cuneiform tablets (wedge-shaped tablets with ancient inscriptions in Akkadian, Assyrian, Babylonian, and Persian) and many other relics were excavated and taken to Germany from 1899 to 1917.

The Hanging Gardens of Babylon

(The Professor's comments)

King Nebuchadnezzar married *the beautiful and exotic* Amytis of Media *(the daughter of Astyages who reigned about 584-550 B.C.; and the granddaughter of Cyaxares who reigned about 625 to 585 B.C.).* Cyaxares *(of Kurdish ancestry and the son of king Phraortes, the son of Deioces)* was the *first king* of the ancient Kurdish [13] state, Media. [14] The marriage of Nebuchadnezzar to Amytis was a *political union and it solidified the alliance between king Nabopolassar of Babylonia* (Nebuchadnezzar's father) *and king Cyaxares of Media* (Amytis' grandfather).

The Professor said that Nebuchadnezzar's concern for Amytis' enjoyment led to the building of the Hanging Gardens (about 600 B.C.). Amytis dearly missed her homeland and made it her business to describe her *native gardens* (the beautiful flowers, scents, plants, exotic birds, various trees, and waterways) to her *politically correct* husband, king Nebuchadnezzar. Obviously, king Nebuchadnezzar *actively* listened to his wife and he felt it was his duty to make his wife happy. Therefore, it gave king Nebuchadnezzar great pleasure to create a beautiful playground for his wife. In doing so, king Nebuchadnezzar copied the Median/Persian gardens **on a colossal scale** and the Hanging Gardens of Babylon became one of the seven wonders of the ancient world.

For sure, the construction of the Hanging Gardens prove that king Nebuchadnezzar was a great visionary, builder, art lover, and so forth.

---

13   Today, the Kurdish people are without a state and fighting for their independence and rights in the Middle East *(these countries include Turkey, Syrian, Iraq, and Iran).* The Kurds are considered the largest ethnic group (about twenty-five million plus) without a recognized homeland. The Turkish military is greatly opposed to the Kurdish people receiving a state of their own. To date, there is a great deal of fighting between the two groups, Turks vs. Kurds.

14   Media is the region known today as, Iran. After the collapse of the Bronze Age, The Medes were among the first Iranian tribes who lived in the northwestern segment of Iran. **Cyaxares** was the first king of Media (about 625-585 B.C.); **Astyages** (his son) ruled (about 584-550 B.C.); **Cyrus the Great** (king of Persia) ruled (about 550 B.C.) after three years of fighting.

Also, he was compassionate to the needs of his wife that proves him to be a great negotiator, politician because he knew how to keep a happy, stress free, and peaceful home life. **More than likely, the broom stayed locked up in the closet!**

Without any questions, the Hanging Gardens of Babylon is one of the Seven Wonders of antiquity. There is definite proof of its existence from the remaining physical evidence [15] and eyewitness reports from foreign visitors, Greek historians, military troops, and many other travelers who carried great stories abroad about Babylon the Great. But, there is much controversy about the structure and dimensions of the Hanging Gardens. Some say that the Hanging Gardens was approximately 100 long by 100 feet wide; or 200 feet long by 200 feet wide; or 300 feet long by 300 feet wide; or 400 feet long by 400 feet wide. Most agree that the garden was quadrangular in shape, built up in tier levels, and the top tier rising to about seventy-five (75) feet. The Hanging Gardens of Babylon were built upon massive stone slabs, columns, and cement to strengthen the foundation. The walls were said to be approximately twenty-six feet to thirty-two feet in thickness to support, bond, and strengthen the weight of the ascending terraces. The structure was graced with arches, massive beams and columns (perhaps as tall as seventy-four feet or more in length). The builders fortified the walls with heavy tar, thoroughly baked bricks, asphalt, cement, and gigantic screws among other materials. In fact, the builders thought of every thing! The engineers brought in water from the Euphrates River to water each terrace of the Hanging Garden and they made it transparent to the public. And, they also used the Euphrates to water the city. *In fact, the irrigation system was a wonder by itself!*

Thousands of exotic flowers and humongous trees of sorts were imported and planted in the soil beds on each terrace. Tons and tons of dirt were brought in to make sure every tree was well planted. On every terrace level, there was color and creativity: huge ascending stairways, balconies, promenades, art galleries, varieties of shops, tucked away dens of sins, paintings, huge planters for the trees, assorted designs, ornamentations, and a gorgeous roof top for worshippers (strollers, foreign and prominent

---

15   The Medes and Persians conquered Babylon. About the second century B.C., a few earthquakes destroyed the city. Today, a few mounds and tells represent ancient Babylon.

Constance Lee

visitors, idolaters, prostitutes, and lovers) overlooking the entire city from every direction.

The king and his advisors selected the best architects, builders, experts in various fields and machinery, artists, painters, decorators, workers, and others.

Nebuchadnezzar's Spiritual Failure

The Professor said that king Nebuchadnezzar got beside himself. He said that it was just a matter of time before the king revealed his true face. Baykus said, "One day, the inevitable occurred." The king ordered his subjects to make a solid golden statue (about one hundred and twenty-five feet tall) for the people to worship. Apparently, Nebuchadnezzar was introducing a new World religion!

Chapter 4

The Three Hebrew Boys & Daniel

(Nebuchadnezzar's comments)

King Nebuchadnezzar said, "There are two things I must say. Firstly, I must tell you about the Southern Kingdom of Judah's frame-of-mind during their captivity in Babylon and the unhappy predictions for Edom and Babylon. And secondly, I will talk about four *extraordinary* children who were filled with *godly* wisdom, knowledge, and understanding. They were the choicest of the Hebrew children and I captured them. But I did not conquer them."

Judah's Testimony, Prayers, Prophecy, & Babylonia Captivity

(Nebuchadnezzar's comments)

The Hebrews were very unhappy and they lost their melodies,

(Psalm 137:1-6)

"By the rivers of Babylon, there we sat down, yea, we wept, when we remembered Zion. We hanged our harps upon the willows in the midst thereof. For there they that carried us away captive required of us a song and they that wasted us required of us mirth, saying, sing us one of the songs of Zion. How shall we sing the Lord's song in a strange land? If I forget thee, O Jerusalem, let my right hand forget *her cunning. If I do not remember thee, let my tongue cleave to the roof of my mouth; if I prefer not Jerusalem above my chief joy."*

(Specific points of Judah's Melancholy)
After reviewing Psalm 137:1-9, the following summary can be made:

1. Israel sat down;
2. Israel wept;
3. Israel remembered Zion (Jerusalem);
4. Israel hung their harps (instruments) on the willows;
5. Israel refused to sing songs of Zion;
6. Israel vowed not to forget Jerusalem (God's Holy City);
7. Israel prayed for vengeance upon its enemies; and
8. Babylon's fall was predicted.

(Prayer for Revenge Against Edom)
When Jerusalem fell, the children of Esau (Edom, their brother) rejoiced over their destruction!

"Remember, O Lord, the children of Edom [Esau] in the day of Jerusalem; who said, Rase it, rase it, even to the foundation thereof." (Psalm 137:7)

(Prophecy Against Babylon)
"O daughter of Babylon, who are to be destroyed; happy shall he be, that rewardeth thee as thou hast served us. Happy shall he be, that taketh and dasheth thy little ones against the stones." (Psalm 137:8)

The Three Hebrew Boys

This chronicle is about *certain* children (*The Three Hebrew Boys & Daniel*) and the Southern Tribe of Judah taken to Babylon. More specifically, the lives of these specific *Hebrew* children is a story all by itself. Yes! They were among the captives, but the **_Bible_** gives us a window into their daily lives! Their names are recorded in the Book of Daniel: Hananiah *(means = the Lord is gracious and/or the grace of the Lord)*; Mishael *(means = who is what God is and/or or He that is the strong God)*; and Azariah *(means = the Lord has helped and/or the Lord is a help)*; and Daniel *(means = God is my judge or God is Judge)*.

Ashpenaz (master of the eunuchs) ordered name changes (Daniel 1:7) for the Hebrew Boys, but most likely, Melzar (a eunuch given charge over the Hebrew Boys, *see* Daniel 1:11) executed the plan[16] as follows: Hananiah renamed Shadrach *(means = command of Aku, the moon god and/or inspiration of the sun because the Chaldeans worshipped the sun god as well)*; Mishael renamed Meshach *(meaning unknown) was named after the goddess Shach (i.e., Venus was worshipped under this name)*; and Azariah renamed Abednego *(means = servant of Nebo [17] and/or the servant of the shining fire because the Chaldeans worshipped fire)*. Daniel was renamed **Belteshazzar** (after Bel, the *god* of the Babylonians) which *means = may Bel protect his life*. (Daniel 1:7)

There is no reference that the Hebrew Boys including Daniel protested to their name changes, but Daniel made a big fuss over the food, ***"Daniel purposed in his heart that he would not defile himself with the portion of the king's meat, nor the wine which he drank: therefore he requested of the prince of the eunuchs that he might not defile himself."*** (Daniel 1:8) And, they refused to eat the daily provisions of the king's meat and wine. However, **Yahweh** gave Daniel favor with the prince of the eunuchs. At the same time, the prince of the eunuchs was not a fool and said, ***"I fear the lord the king who hath appointed your meat and your drink; for why should he see your faces worse liking than the children which are of your sort? Then shall ye make me endanger my head to the***

---

16   However, it was customary for conquerors to change the names of the defeated people. (Daniel: 1:6-7)

17   Per Babylonian history, Nebo is the scribe of heavenly and earthly events. Prophet Isaiah mocked their gods, ***"Bel boweth down and Nebo stoopeth, their idols were upon the beasts and upon the cattle: your carriages were heavy loaden; they are a burden to the weary beast. They stoop, they bow down together; they could not deliver the burden, but themselves are gone into captivity."*** (Isaiah 46:1-2)

king." (Daniel 1:10) So, Daniel used the eunuch's statement as a spin around. He challenged the prince of the eunuchs to give them time to prove the diet of the Hebrews was healthier and superior to the table of the king.

"Prove thy servants, I beseech thee, <u>ten days</u> and let them give us pulse to eat and water to drink. Then let our countenance be looked upon before thee, and the countenance of the children that eat of the portion of the king's meat: and as thou seest, deal with thy servants. So he consented to them in this matter, and proved them ten days. And at the end of ten days their countenance appeared fairer and fatter in flesh than all the children which did eat the portion of the king's meat. Thus Melzar took away the portion of their meat, and the wine that they should drink and gave them pulse." (Daniel 1:12-16)

Superiority of the Hebrew Boys & Daniel

There was none like the Three Hebrew Boys and Daniel in Babylon. Although these boys were foreigners, they were superior candidates *(by Twentieth-First Century A.D. standards)* for Harvard, Stanford, and Yale Universities. All of their spiritual, physical, and mental superiority was attributed to (1) their faithfulness and obedience to true living God; (2) their upbringing; and (3) their diet and daily exercise. In fact, king Nebuchadnezzar had long talks with them. Without question, the king had every right to exalt them over his subjects in Babylon.

(None like the Hebrew Boys & Daniel)
"Now at the end of the days that the king had said he should bring them in, then the prince of the eunuchs brought them in before Nebuchadnezzar.

<u>And the king communed with them; and among them all was found none like Daniel, Hananiah, Mishael, and Azariah; therefore stood they before the king.</u>

And in all matters of wisdom and understanding, that the king enquired of them, he found them ten times better than all the magicians and astrologers that were in all his realm." (Daniel 1:17-20)

(The Hebrew Boys & Daniel Honored)

Look how king Nebuchadnezzar honored the Hebrew Boys and Daniel. The king praised the Hebrew Boys (Daniel 1:19) and spent a great deal of time communicating with them (more than his own counselors) in his throne room. He called them by their birthright names (Daniel, Hananiah, Mishael, and Azariah) rather than by their Babylonian names (Belteshazzar, Shadrach, Meshach, and Abednego). **Without realizing it, the king gave honor to the God of the Hebrews!** This fact alone is more rewarding than all the others. The Babylonians tried to extract the Hebrews' faith in God. These young men represented the entire Hebrew Nation. If the king could break their code of ethics, he could break the Hebrew Nation's code as well! Although the Hebrew Boys (including all of the upper class captives) were isolated from the Temple Worship in Jerusalem (now sacked and burned). There was no were to pray, study the law, or make daily sacrifices to **Yahweh.** But somehow, the Hebrew Boys (and there were probably other Jews as well) found a way to eat the right things, pray, and worship in their own ways (without the Temple)! **True worship was in their hearts and bones and no one could take that away!**

(The Hebrew Boys & Daniel Denied Human Rights)

The Babylonians robbed the Hebrew Boys of their manhood. **They castrated these fine young boys (including others) and made them to be eunuchs!** The ***Bible*** does not give the specifics about the castration: the surgery or cutting procedures, the physicians, sickness or fevers that accompany *this particular* surgery, medicines applied, recovery time, healing, emotional, physical, and the psychological traumas associated with the mutilations. YET, none of these things stopped the Hebrew Boys and Daniel from trusting in **Yahweh**. One might say that these Boys didn't know any better because they never had a woman. That fact is secondary to their *immediate* pain and suffering. Besides, they could not talk about something they never tried. Since they never had it, they didn't know what they were missing. Its simple logic! But, these Boys weren't blind. Physically, they could see the beauty around them, extraordinary women, men and women being affectionate, traditional families, and the splendor of Babylon. They lived in the king's palace, ate at the king's table, and communed with the king in his throne room. They watched parades of caravans entering and leaving Babylon with more beauties for the harems.

31

They walked through the corridors of the palace and the Hanging Gardens filled with exotic flowers and beautiful women.

Moreover, their memories were not erased! *Although they were in captivity and deprived of their manhood,* the Hebrew Boys (including Daniel) had not forgotten their past lives, families, aunts, uncles, cousins, fabulous homes, personal possessions, nobility rights, servants at their *beck and call,* education, and privileges. As princes (before captivity), the Hebrew Boys received lessons in Hebrew religion, customs, and lifestyles. During their captivity, they were educated in Babylonian ways customs, *poor* nutrition, mathematics, sciences, arts, and languages by the best scholars. This does not mean that the Hebrews were better than the Babylonians! Neither one of these societies were Utopias!

God is a rewarder to those who diligently seek Him. As stated, the Hebrew Boys (including Daniel) lost their manhood but they stayed faithful to the Almighty. Therefore, **Yahweh** rewarded and compensated them in other areas with wisdom, knowledge, understanding, high rank, riches, and much more. This is an excellent lesson for all generations of believers *(young, old, Jew or Gentile).* No matter what happens, TRUST IN THE LORD AND LEAN NOT TO YOUR OWN UNDERSTANDING. When one door closes, the **Lord GOD** opens another door! Likewise, if the **Lord GOD** closes the door, no man can open the door!

What more could king Nebuchadnezzar say or do to the Hebrew Boys? **PLENTY!** There is ONE more torturous reward awaiting these young Hebrews, THE BURNING FIERY FURNACE.

Chapter 5

Nebuchadnezzar's First Forgotten Dream

Nebuchadnezzar's 1st Dream

(The Professor's comment)

The old Hittite owl said, "Nebuchadnezzar, you need a break! Everyone can see that you are plum tuckered-out from talking and exhausted from the weather! However, I recommend that you make an official news release admitting your guilt, anger, selfishness, and provocations against your own kingdom! At least, you admitted that you forgot your own dream. And that (my friend) is no one's fault but yours!! Moreover, I don't give a hoot if my statements make you mad! Your own absent-mindedness contributed to your inability to remember. Perhaps, it was God's Will that made you forget the dream so Daniel could use his gifts to reveal God's Glory. *Yet, you threatened to kill your magicians, astrologers, sorcerers, soothsayers, and the Chaldeans because you forgot your own dream!*

(Babylon's Psychics Summoned)

(Daniel 2:1-3)

"In the second year of the reign of Nebuchadnezzar, Nebuchadnezzar

dreamed dreams wherewith his spirit was troubled, and his sleep brake from him.

Then the king commanded to call the magicians, and the astrologers, and the sorcerers, and the Chaldeans, for to shew the king his dreams. So they came and stood before the king.

And the king said unto them, I have dreamed a dream, and my spirit was troubled to know the dream."

(Psychics' Reply)

(Daniel 2:4)
Then spake the Chaldeans to the king in Syriack, O king, live for ever: tell thy servants the dream, and we will shew the interpretation."

(The king's Reward, Death)

(Daniel 2:4-5)
"The king answered and said to the Chaldeans, <u>The thing is gone from me: if ye will not make known unto me the dream, with the interpretation thereof, ye shall be cut in pieces, and your houses shall be made a dunghill</u>."

Certainly, (after reviewing king Nebuchadnezzar's statement), he was a prime candidate for anger management classes!

(The king's Alternative Reward, Gifts)

(Daniel 2:6)
"<u>But if ye shew the dream, and the interpretation thereof, ye shall receive of me gifts and rewards and great honour</u>: therefore shew me the dream, and the interpretation thereof."

(The Psychics' Procrastination and the king's Reply)

(Daniel 2:7-9)
"They answered again and said, Let the king tell his servants the

dream, and we will shew the interpretations of it. The king answered and said, I know of certainty that ye would gain the time, because ye see the thing is gone from me.

But if ye will not make known unto me the dream, there is but one decree for you: for ye have prepared lying and corrupt words to speak before me, till the time be changed: therefore tell me the dream, and I shall know that ye can shew me the interpretation thereof.

(The Psychics' Inability to Reconstruct the king's Dream)
(Daniel 2:10-11)
The Chaldeans answered before the king, and said, <u>There is not a man upon the earth that can shew the king's matter: therefore there is no king, lord, nor ruler, that asked such things at any magician, or astrologer, or Chaldean.</u>

And it is a rare thing that the king requireth, and <u>there is none other that can shew it before the king, except the gods, whose dwelling is not with flesh.</u>"

(The king's Decree)
I, Nebuchadnezzar II, am solely responsible for the havoc and chaos the decree caused in my kingdom. Because of my anger, I wanted to destroy all of the incompetent Babylonian wise men and soothsayers, *"And the decree went forth that the wise men should be slain..."* (Daniel 2:13a) However, my anger triggered them to react negatively toward Daniel and the Three Hebrew Boys. The Babylonian wise men and soothsayers wanted to destroy four innocent Boys, *"...<u>and they sought Daniel and his fellows to be slain.</u>"* (Daniel 2:13b)

However, I did not tell the wise men to seek the lives of Daniel and the other Hebrew Boys! The incompetence, arrogance, and jealousy of Babylonian wise men and soothsayers sought to destroy Daniel and his companions. The king said that he only wanted somebody to tell him what he dreamed. Also, the king asserted *full* power and authority over his kingdom and constituents. Frankly, king Nebuchadnezzar did not value the lives or property of others. Just the same, the king Nebuchadnezzar set the tone and pace of the *uncaring atmosphere* in his kingdom – *eye for eye and tooth for tooth.* Therefore, it should not surprise the king that his constituents (who were about to die) would seek the lives of others including Daniel and the Hebrew Boys!

Chapter 6

God Reveals Nebuchadnezzar's Dream To Daniel

Daniel

(The Professor's comments)

One of the most courageous and gifted youths in the **_Bible_** was a young man named Prince *Daniel* of the House of Judah (the son of a noble and wealthy family). ***"And the king spake unto Ashpenaz the master of his eunuchs, that he should bring certain of the children of Israel, and of the king's seed, and of the princes..."*** (Daniel 1:3) In Hebrew, Daniel means *"God is my judge"* or *"God is Judge."* However, *Daniel and his three companions* were taken captives (brought from Jerusalem to Babylon by king Nebuchadnezzar) and given new names. The most critical reasons for the change of names was to show the world that Babylon had complete dominion over her captives and to force their captives to forget their *nationality, as Hebrews.*

More importantly, the Babylonians hoped to make the Jews forget their faith in the **_One True God_**, **Yahweh.** The problem is that this plan did not work on all of the Jewish captives! The Babylonian's changed the name of the Three Hebrew Boys and Daniel, but the boys still served the Living God! Daniel's name was changed to Bel-te-shazzar that means, *"preserve thou O Bel his life"* or *"protect the life of the king."* Daniel was named after the principle god of the Babylonians, *Bel*. In spite of these facts, Daniel still prayed three times a day! Therefore, none of these things altered Daniel's *faithfulness* to **Yahweh.** One more time, Daniel's *faithfulness* is a role model for all Christian believers! Don't let nothing and nobody separate you from the Love of God!

There were many atrocities imposed on Daniel and his three Jewish companions. As stated earlier, one of the worst inhumane acts was the castration forced upon the young lads who became eunuchs! The worst sin was to deny Daniel and the Three Hebrew Boys the right to worship as they pleased! There is no excuse for such cruelty.

Prophet Isaiah prophesied [18] to king Hezekiah, ***"Behold, the days come, that all that is in thine house, and that which thy fathers have laid up in store until this day, shall be carried to Babylon: nothing shall be left, saith the Lord. And of thy sons that shall issue from thee, which thou shalt beget, shall they take away; and they shall be eunuchs in the palace of the king of Babylon..."*** (Isaiah 39:6-7)

Because of Daniel's (including the Hebrew Boys) misfortune, God was good and extra-sensitive to them. As mentioned earlier, the Lord atoned for their losses by rewarding all of them ***"in all matters of wisdom, knowledge, and understanding."*** (Daniel 1:17-20) More importantly, Daniel (and his companions) was faithful to God! For some reason, God gave Daniel a double portion, ***"in all matters of wisdom, knowledge, and understanding and Daniel had understanding in all visions and dreams."*** (Daniel 1:17-20) Daniel had much favor with God!

---

18   At the time of the prophecy, king Hezekiah did not have male heir to the throne! King Hezekiah became very ill; so he prayed to God. As a result, the king's life was extended for fifteen (15) years. Later (about 710 B.C. three years into the 15 years), king Hezekiah's wife (Hephzibah) produced a son, Manasseh.

Furthermore, Daniel was given a high post in the kingdom of Babylon, ***"Then the king [Nebuchadnezzar] made Daniel a great man, and gave him many great gifts, and made him ruler over the whole province of Babylon, and chief of the governors over all the wise men of Babylon."*** (Daniel 2:48) What is more, Daniel continued active in the courts and councils of Babylon's great monarchs: Nebuchadnezzar (604-562 B.C.); Nabonidus (555-539 B.C., and his son, Belshazzar); Persian Invasion: Cyrus (539-529 B.C.); Cambyses (529-522 B.C.); and Darius I (522-486 B.C.). However, there is a black out and no mention of Daniel during the following reigns: (1) Evil-Merodach (561-560 B.C.); Neriglissar (559-555 B.C.); and Labashi-Marduk (555 B.C.).

Daniel's Strategy

One day (during the reign of king Nebuchadnezzar), there was such a commotion in the palace in Babylon that it caused everyone to run and hide. People were in fear of losing their heads! Arioch *(captain of the king's guard)* was on his way to slay the wise men of Babylon! So, Daniel asked Arioch about king Nebuchadnezzar's decree to slay all of the wise men (magicians, astrologers, and soothsayers and their[19] endeavors to slay Daniel and his companions - Hananiah, Mishael, and Azariah). Immediately, Daniel requested an audience with the king to seek "a stay of execution." Daniel was a "perfect" diplomat: full of wisdom, knowledge, understanding and humility! Because Daniel had favor, the king agreed to see him and ***"Daniel went in and desired of the king that he would give him time, and that he would shew the king the interpretation of the king's dream."*** (Daniel 2:16)

Daniel's Prayer to God

There is only one-way to get immediate help, *RUN TO GOD!* He may not come when you want Him, *but He is always on time!* Whenever

---

19 The wise men (magicians, astrologers, and soothsayers) planned to slay Daniel and his companions.

Constance Lee

one's life or the lives of others are on the line, the fastest way to achieve help is to seek the face of the Lord. <u>So, Daniel called his prayer partners,</u> "*That they would desire mercies of the God of heaven concerning this secret; that Daniel and his fellows [Hananiah, Mishael, and Azariah] should not perish with the rest of the wise men of Babylon.*" (Daniel 2:18) Question: Is this a selfish prayer? Answer: **Yes and so what!** Why should Daniel and the Three Hebrew Boys perish with the false prophets, astrologers, or sinners? That's ridiculous![20]

Nebuchadnezzar's 1st Dream Revealed to Daniel

(1) The Bible states,

(Daniel 2:19-23)
"*Then was the secret revealed unto Daniel in a night vision. Then Daniel blessed the God of heaven. Daniel answered and said, Blessed be the name of God for ever and ever: for wisdom and might are his. And he changeth the times and the seasons: he removeth kings, and setteth up kings: he giveth wisdom unto the wise, and knowledge to them that know understanding: He revealeth the deep and secret things: he knoweth what is in the darkness, and the light dwelleth with him. I thank thee, and praise thee, O thou God of my fathers, who hast given me wisdom and might, and Hast made known unto me now what we desired of thee: for thou hast now made known unto us the king's matter.*"

---

20   Furthermore, why should you perish with unbelievers and why are you hanging out with people out-of- line with **God's WORD**? There is no justification or reason for God's *elect* to: decrease their faith because others refuse to increase theirs; coward like mice; tip around on their tippy-toes; play themselves downward just to blend in with the crowd as men pleasers; perish and go to hell. The ***Bible*** declares that God's people are more than conquerors!

(2) Daniel before king Nebuchadnezzar,

(Daniel 2:24-26)

"Therefore Daniel went in unto Arioch [caption of the king's guard] whom the king had ordained to destroy the wise men of Babylon: he went and said thus unto him; Destroy not the wise men of Babylon: bring me in before the king, and I will shew unto the king the interpretation.

Then Arioch brought in Daniel before the king in haste, and said thus unto him, I have found a man of the captives of Judah, that will make known unto the king the interpretation.

The king answered and said to Daniel, whose name was Belteshazzar, Art thou able to make known unto me the dream which I have seen and the interpretation thereof?"

(3) Daniel praises God,
(Daniel 2:27-30)

"Daniel answered in the presence of the king and said, The secret which the king hath demanded cannot the wise men the astrologers, the magicians, the soothsayers, shew unto the king;

"<u>But there is a God in heaven that revealeth secrets and maketh known to the king Nebuchadnezzar what shall be in the latter days</u>. Thy dream, and the visions of thy head upon thy bed, are these;

As for thee, O king, thy thoughts came into thy mind upon thy bed what should come to pass hereafter: and he that revealeth secrets maketh known to thee what shall come to pass.

<u>But as for me, this secret is not revealed to me for any wisdom that I have more than any living</u>, but for their sakes that shall make known the

interpretation to the king, and <u>**that thou mightest know the thoughts of thy heart.**</u>

(4) Daniel reveals the 1st Dream,

(Daniel 2:31-35)

"Thou O king sawest and behold a great image. This great image, whose brightness was excellent, stood before thee, and the form thereof was terrible.

This image's head was of fine gold, his breast and his arms of silver, his belly and his thigh of brass, His legs of iron, his feet part of iron and part of clay.

Thou sawest till that a stone was cut out without hand, which smote the image upon his feet that were of iron and clay, and brake them to pieces.

Then was the iron, the clay, the brass, the silver, and the gold, broken to pieces together, and became like the chaff of the summer threshing floors; and the wind carried them away, that no place was found for them: and the stone that smote the image became a great mountain, and filled the whole earth."

Chapter 7

Daniel Interprets Nebuchadnezzar's First Dream

The Interpretation

"This is the dream; and we will tell the interpretation thereof before the king. Thou, O king art a king of kings: for the God of heaven hath given thee a kingdom, power, and strength, and glory." (Daniel 2:36)

<u>[Golden head = king Nebuchadnezzar/ kingdom of Babylon]</u>

(Daniel 2:32)
<u>"This image's head was of fine gold…"</u>

(Daniel 2:38)
"And, wheresoever the children of men dwell, the beasts of the field and the fowls of the heaven hath he given into thine hand, and hath made thee ruler over them all. ***<u>Thou art this head of gold</u>.***" (See: Daniel 7:4; Isaiah 13:1)

[Breast and arms of silver = kingdom of Medo-Persia]

(Daniel 2:32)
"...his breast and his arms of silver..."

(Daniel 2:39a)
"And after thee shall arise another kingdom inferior to thee."
(See: Daniel 5:25-31; 7:5; 8:20; 11:1-2; Isaiah 13:17; 21:2; 45:1; Jeremiah 51:11)

[Belly and thighs of brass = kingdom of Grecia [21]]

(Daniel 2:32)
"...his belly and thighs of brass..."

(Daniel 2:39b)
"...and another third <u>kingdom of brass</u> which shall bear rule over all the earth." (See: Daniel 7:6; 8:21; 11:1-4; Joel 3:6; Zechariah 9:13; Revelation 13:1-2; 17:3, 16-17)

[Legs of iron = kingdom of Rome]

(Daniel 2:33)
"His legs of iron..."

(Daniel 2:40)
"And the fourth kingdom shall be strong as iron: forasmuch as iron breaketh in pieces and subdueth all things: and as iron that breaketh all these, shall it break in pieces and bruise." (See Daniel 7:7, 17-24; 9:26; Luke 2:1; John 11:48)

---

21   Grecia = kingdom of Greece.

[Latter days: Roman/World Empire = feet & toes [22] (clay & iron)]

(Daniel 2:33)
"...his feet part of iron and part of clay..."

(Daniel 2:41-43)
"And whereas thou sawest the feet and toes, part of potters' clay, and part of iron, the kingdom shall be divided; but there shall be in it of the strength of the iron, forasmuch as thou sawest the iron mixed with miry clay [mud]. And as the toes of the feet were part of iron, and part of clay, so the kingdom shall be partly strong, and partly broken. And whereas thou sawest iron mixed with miry clay [mud], they shall mingle themselves with the seed of men but they shall not cleave one to another, even as iron is not mixed with clay."

[Stone Empire = Kingdom of Heaven, the Messiah on Earth [23]]

(Daniel 2:34)
"Thou sawest: till that a stone was cut out without hands, which smote the image upon his feet that were of iron and clay, and brake them to pieces."

(Daniel 2:44-45)
"And in the days of these kings shall the God of heaven set up a kingdom which shall never be destroyed and the kingdom shall not be left to other people, but it shall break in pieces and consume all these kingdoms and it shall stand for ever. Forasmuch as thou sawest that the stone was cut out of the mountain without hands, and that it brake in pieces the iron, the brass, the clay, the silver, and the gold;

---

22   Ten toes = ten kingdoms.

23   Futuristic: Messiah's 2nd advent – Isaiah 9:7 *"Of the increase of his government and peace there shall be no end upon the throne of David, and upon his kingdom, to order it, and to establish it with judgment and with justice from henceforth even for ever. The zeal of the Lord of hosts will perform this."* (Also see Jeremiah 23; 30; 33; Daniel 2:44; 7:13-14; Zechariah 14; Luke 1:33; Revelation 20)

the great God hath made known to the king what shall comet to pass hereafter: and the dream is certain, and the interpretation thereof sure."

(Nebuchadnezzar's comments)

Nebuchadnezzar said that he gave more honor to Daniel than God! Looking back, king Nebuchadnezzar said that he was a fool and heathen. He said that all the honor and glory belongs: (1) to the God of Heaven; and (2) honor to whom honor is due. Being a fool, the king said that God is the God of gods and Lord of kings, then, he made a humongous image of gold for everyone to worship! How stupid is that!!

Nebuchadnezzar's Idolatry

"*Then the king Nebuchadnezzar **fell upon his face and worshipped Daniel** and commanded that they should offer an oblation and sweet odors unto him.*

*The king answered unto Daniel and said, **Of a truth it is, that your God is a God of gods, and a Lord of kings**, and a revealer of secrets, seeing thou couldest reveal this secret.*

Then the king made Daniel a great man, and gave him many great gifts, and made him ruler over the whole providence of Babylon and chief of the governors over all the wise men of Babylon." (Daniel 2:46-48)

Daniel's Companions Promoted

Naturally, Daniel needed his own personal and spiritual backup team, so he requested the king to promote his prayer partners and companions.

"Then Daniel requested of the king, and he set Shadrach, Meshach, and Abednego over the affairs of the province of Babylon: but Daniel sat in the gate of the king." (Daniel 2:49)

Nebuchadnezzar's Golden Image

So, Professor Baykus said that king Nebuchadnezzar established a new world religion and order of worship upon completion of the image of gold including the death penalty for refusing to worship the golden image! In fact, the king wanted everyone to assemble (before the golden image), bow down, and worship it. What indignation, what idolatry, and what a slap this was in the face to the Living God who just blessed him as a king of kings with honor, glory, and riches among many things!

(Daniel 3:1-7)
"Nebuchadnezzar the king made an image of gold, whose height was three score cubits and the breadth thereof six cubits [approximately 12 ½ by 125 feet]. He set it up in the plain of Dura in the province of Babylon.

Then Nebuchadnezzar the king sent to gather together the princes, the governors, and the captains, the judges, the treasurers, the counselors, the sheriffs, and all the rulers of the provinces, to come to the dedication of the image which Nebuchadnezzar the king had set up.

Then the princes, the governors, and the captains, the judges, the treasurers, the counselors, the sheriffs, and all the rulers of the provinces, were gathered together unto the dedication of the image that Nebuchadnezzar the king had set up and they stood before the image that Nebuchadnezzar had set up.

<u>*Then a herald cried aloud,*</u> To you it is commanded, O people, nations, and languages, *That at what time ye hear the sound of the cornet, flute, harp, sackbut, psaltery, dulcimer, and all kinds of musick, ye fall down and worship the golden image that Nebuchadnezzar the king hath set up:* <u>*And whoso falleth not down and worshippeth shall the same hour be cast into the midst of a burning fiery furnace.*</u> *Therefore at that time, when all*

the people heard the sound of the cornet, flute, harp, sackbut, psaltery, and all kinds of musick, all the people, the nations, and the languages, fell down and worshipped the golden image that Nebuchadnezzar the king had set up."

The Golden Image a Conflict of Interest

Immediately, Daniel and the Hebrew Boys knew that Nebuchadnezzar's golden image was in conflict with their faith and belief in **Yahweh**! *"Ye shall make you no idols or graven image, neither rear you up a standing image, neither shall ye set up any image of stone in your land, to bow down unto it: for I am the Lord you God."* (Leviticus 26:1) They had three choices to make: (1) disobey the king's degree and be cast into Babylonia's fiery furnace; (2) disobey **Yahweh** and be cast into hell's fire; or (3) copy the attitude of the other Hebrew captives who probably bowed down because of the escape clause, *"...neither shall ye set up any image of stone in your land to bow down unto it..."* Frankly, the Hebrews were not in their land, they were captives in Babylonia!

Chapter 8

Nebuchadnezzar's Second Dream

(The Professor's comments)

Imagine, a great and mighty king who conquered many nations (as the Assyrians and the Egyptians) being afraid of a little dream. Yet king Nebuchadnezzar was so afraid, puzzled, and confused. He remembered this dream but he had no understanding of it.

One fine day, king Nebuchadnezzar was resting in his palace. There was a nice breeze blowing through the window and his servants were attentive to his every command. Soft music played in the court below the king's window and there was a harem filled with the most beautiful women from every corner of the world. Yet, the king was disturbed!

Nebuchadnezzar's 2nd Dream

I had a second dream, but the wise men in my kingdom could not explain my dream,

(Daniel 4:4-6)

"I saw a dream which made me afraid, and the thoughts upon my bed and the visions of my head troubled me. Therefore, I made

a decree to bring in all the wise men of Babylon before me, that they might make known unto me the interpretation of the dream."

(The king's 2nd Dream)

(Daniel 4:10-18)

"Thus were the visions of mine head in my bed; I saw and behold a tree in the midst of the earth, and the height thereof was great. The tree grew and was strong, and the height thereof reached unto heaven, and the sight thereof to the end of all the earth:

The leaves thereof were fair, and the fruit thereof much, and in it was meat for all: the beasts of the field had shadow under it, and the fowls of the heaven dwelt in the boughs thereof, and all flesh was fed of it. I saw in the visions of my head upon my bed, and, behold a watcher and an holy one came down from heaven; He cried aloud, and said, thus Hew down the tree, and cut of his branches, shake off his leaves, and scatter his fruit: let the beasts get away from under it, and the fowls from his branches: Nevertheless leave the stump of his roots in the earth even with a band of iron and brass, in the tender grass of the field; and let it be wet with the dew of heaven, and let his portion be with the beasts in the grass of the earth: Let his heart be changed from man's, and let a beast's heart be given unto him; and let seven times pass over him. This matter is by the decree of the watchers, and the demand by the word of the holy ones: to the intent that the living may know that the most High ruleth in the kingdoms of men, and giveth it to whomsoever he will, and setteth up over it the basest of men. This dream, I king Nebuchadnezzar have seen. Now thou, O Belteshazzar, declare the interpretation thereof, forasmuch as all the wise men of my kingdom are not able to make known unto me the interpretation: but thou art able: for the spirit of the holy gods is in thee."

Powerless Magicians

(Daniel 4:7)

"*Then came in the magicians, the astrologers, the Chaldeans, and the soothsayers: and I told the dream before them; but they did not make known unto me the interpretation thereof.*"

Amazingly, these magicians, astrologers, Chaldeans, and soothsayers were the wisest men in the world. In fact, they were the same group that could not interpret the king's first dream. Luckily for them, Daniel prayed to **Yahweh** for the revelation of the king's first dream. Yet, the king summoned them to his throne room. Once more, these magicians could not interpret the king's second dream. But, Daniel had the Spirit of the Living God in him, and he gave the interpretation to king Nebuchadnezzar.

Again, the True and Living God, showed the Babylonians and the world that there is none like HIM!

Chapter 9

Daniel Interprets Nebuchadnezzar's Second Dream

Nebuchadnezzar Summons Daniel

(Nebuchadnezzar's comments)
   So I called in someone else to interpret my dream,

(Daniel 4:8)
   "But at the last Daniel came in before me, *whose name was Belteshazzar, according to the name of my god, and in whom is the spirit of the holy gods: and before him I told the dream saying,*

Nebuchadnezzar Reveals His Dream To Daniel

(Daniel 4:9-18)
   "O Belteshazzar, master of the magicians, *because I know that the spirit of the holy gods is in thee, and no secret troubleth thee, tell me the visions of my dream that I have seen, and the interpretation thereof.*

   Thus were the visions of mine head in my bed; I saw and behold a tree in the midst of the earth, and the height thereof was great.

The tree grew and was strong, and the height thereof reached unto heaven, and the sight thereof to the end of all the earth:

The leaves thereof were fair, and the fruit thereof much, and in it was meat for all: the beasts of the field had shadow under it, and the fowls of the heaven dwelt in the boughs thereof, and all flesh was fed of it.

<u>I saw in the visions of my head upon my bed, and, behold a watcher and an holy one came down from heaven;</u>

He cried aloud, and said, thus Hew down the tree, and cut of his branches, shake off his leaves, and scatter his fruit: let the beasts get away from under it, and the fowls from his branches:

Nevertheless leave the stump of his roots in the earth even with a band of iron and brass, in the tender grass of the field; and let it be wet with the dew of heaven, and let his portion be with the beasts in the grass of the earth:

Let his heart be changed from man's, and let a beast's heart be given unto him; and let seven times pass over him.

This matter is by the decree of the watchers, and the demand by the word of the holy ones: to the intent that the living may know that the most High ruleth in the kingdoms of men, and giveth it to whomsoever he will, and setteth up over it the basest of men.

This dream, I king Nebuchadnezzar have seen. Now thou, O Belteshazzar, declare the interpretation thereof, forasmuch as all the wise men of my kingdom are not able to make known unto me the interpretation: but thou art able: for the spirit of the holy gods is in thee."

Daniel's Interpretation

(Daniel 4:19-26)

"*Then Daniel who name was Belteshazzar, was astonied for one hour, and his thoughts troubled him. The king spake, and said, Belteshazzar, let not the dream, or the interpretation thereof, trouble thee. Belteshazzar answered and said, My lord, the dream be to them that hate thee, and the interpretation thereof to thine enemies.*

The tree that thou sawest which grew, and was strong, whose height reached unto the heaven, and the sight thereof to all the earth:

Whose leaves were fair, and the fruit thereof much and in it was meat for all: under which the beasts of the field dwelt, and upon whose branches the fowls of the heaven had their habitation:

It is thou, O king, that art grown and become strong: for thy greatness is grown, and reacheth unto heaven, and thy dominion to the end of the earth.

And whereas the king saw a watcher and an holy one coming down from heaven, and saying, Hew the tree down, and destroy it: yet leave the stump of the roots thereof in the earth, even with a band of iron and brass, in the tender grass of the field; and let it be wet with the dew of heaven, and let his portion be with the beasts of the field, till seven times pass over him:

This is the interpretation, O king, and this is the decree of the most High, which is come upon my lord the king:

That they shall drive thee from men, and thy dwelling shall be with the beasts of the field, and they shall make thee to eat grass as oxen, and they shall wet thee with the dew of heaven, and seven times shall pass over thee, till thou know that the most High ruleth in the kingdom of men, and giveth it to whomsoever he will.

And whereas they commanded to leave the stump of the tree roots; thy kingdom shall be sure unto thee, after that thou shalt have known that the heavens do rule."

Daniel's Advice

Daniel told the king to **repent**,

(Daniel 4:27)
"Wherefore, O king, let my counsel be acceptable unto thee, and break off thy sins by righteousness, and thine iniquities by shewing mercy to the poor; if it may be lengthening of thy tranquility."

Nebuchadnezzar Reject's Daniel's Advice

However, king Nebuchadnezzar was conceited, lifted in pride, and refused to listen to Daniel,

(Daniel 4:28-30)
"All of this came upon the king Nebuchadnezzar. At the end of twelve months he walked in the palace of the kingdom of Babylon. The king spake, and said, Is not this great Babylon, that I have built for the house of the kingdom by the might of my power, and for the honour of my majesty?

The Dream Fulfilled

(Daniel 4:31-33)
"While the word was in the king's mouth, there fell a voice from

heaven, saying, O king Nebuchadnezzar, to thee it is spoken; The kingdom is departed from thee.

And they shall drive thee from men, and thy dwelling shall be with the beasts of the field; they shall make thee to eat grass as oxen, and seven times shall pass over thee, until thou know that the most High ruleth in the kingdom of men, and giveth it to whomsoever he will.

The same hour was the thing fulfilled upon Nebuchadnezzar: and he was driven from men, and did eat grass as oxen, and his body was wet with the dew of heaven, till his hairs were grown like eagles' feathers, and his nails like bird's claws."

(The Professor's comments)

The *wise old Hittite* [24] *owl* said that if ever there was a *puffed-up-daddy*, king Nebuchadnezzar fit the mold and broke the mold! Basically, Daniel told king Nebuchadnezzar, "You-the-man" (no matter where you go in the world (among men, beasts, and the fowls of the air), YOU ARE THE HEAD! Daniel's deduction came from the interpretation of the king's first dream, "And, wheresoever the children of men dwell, the beasts of the field and the fowls of the heaven hath he given into thine hand, and hath made thee ruler over them all. Thou art this head of gold." (Daniel 2:38)

That same day, king Nebuchadnezzar was driven from his palace, God gave the king the heart of a beast, but even in the wild, Nebuchadnezzar had dominion over the beasts of the field and the fowls of the air! (Daniel 2:38)   **Furthermore, Nebuchadnezzar's kingdom was not taken from him during his seven years in the wild!!!!!!!   We know this because God said so in His Word!** "*...Hew down, and destroy it; <u>yet leave the stump of the roots thereof in the earth even with a band of iron and brass</u>...*" (Daniel 4:23)

---

24   Turkish.

Chapter 10

King Nebuchadnezzar's Restoration

(The Professor's comments)

All of the animals and insects in the forest were actively listening and talking about Nebuchadnezzar's story in their own language. It was quite the Buzzz! They were overwhelmed and the story was out-of-this-world! Better yet, the wolf-man's dilemma *made them delirious!*

Nebuchadnezzar's Madness

(The Professor's comments)

The *wise Old Hittite owl* said that before we can talk about <u>Nebuchadnezzar's Restoration</u>, there's more discussion about his madness! King Nebuchadnezzar was not an ordinary man or king! Yes! He was the son of the great, great *king Nabopolassar*. More importantly, Nebuchadnezzar was God's **"choice vessel"** to chastise and baby-sit His *"Chosen people."*

God placed *Daniel*, the *Hebrew Boys* as well as the *Tribes of Judah and Benjamin* in king Nebuchadnezzar's care. In spite of the horrible physical, mental, spiritual, and emotional injustices inflicted upon *Daniel, the Hebrew Boys, and the Southern Kingdom* by *their protector* (the

57

king of Babylon), God *still* allowed king Nebuchadnezzar to witness the *supernatural event* in the fiery furnace from his palace window.

Frankly, God *just* tolerated Nebuchadnezzar's insubordination, but the king's pride, arrogance, and disobedience to God caused his own madness. God did not tell Nebuchadnezzar to make himself a *deity for the people to worship!* God did not tell Nebuchadnezzar to build a *solid* gold image for people to bow down before. And, God did not tell the king to put the Hebrew Boys in the fiery furnace. The king's vanities made him do these things! Obviously, safekeeping people is not hog-tying them and burning them in a fiery furnace! Daniel warned king Nebuchadnezzar to ***"...break off from his sins by righteousness and thine iniquities by shewing mercy to the poor..."*** (Daniel 4:27); but the king took the opposite course. He got lifted up, ***"But when his heart was lifted up, and his mind hardened in pride, he was deposed from his kingly throne..."*** (Daniel 5:20)

Concerning the True Living God and Worship, king Nebuchadnezzar was *"confused, fickle, and dim-witted."* Looking back at **_Nebuchadnezzar's First Forgotten Dream_**, Daniel was the only one to interpret the king's dream and Daniel gave *honor* to God for the interpretation. At that point, the king should have worshipped the **Living God, but** instead, ***"The king fell on his face and worshipped Daniel and commanded that they should offer an oblation and sweet odors unto him."*** (Daniel 2:46) THIS WAS TOTALLY INAPPROPRIATE AND OUT OF CHARACTER!

The *wise Old Hittite owl* said, "I wonder what was going through Daniel's mind when king Nebuchadnezzar ***"... fell on his face and worshipped Daniel and commanded that they should offer an oblation and sweet odors unto him?"*** (Daniel 2:46) We know that Daniel would never condone false worship! Knowing Daniel, there must have been a statement from him to the king. Unfortunately, there is no record between the lines of Daniel 2:46 and Daniel 2:47 what Daniel said to king Nebuchadnezzar. Carefully picking his words, Daniel must have set the king straight about his ridiculous proposal. Still, Daniel purposely omitted his comments to the king from the text (as people sometimes do). Whatever, Daniel told him right! The **_Bible_** states, **_"The king answered unto Daniel, and said, <u>Of a truth it is, that your God is a God of gods, and a Lord of kings, and a revealer of secrets, seeing thou couldest reveal this secret.</u>"_** (Daniel 2:47) But the king really did not mean this from his heart.

(From Madness to Santa Claus)

Moving on, the king was still handing out merit increases and playing Santa Claus, **_"Then the king made Daniel a great man, and gave him many great gifts, and made him ruler over the whole province of Babylon, and chief of the governors over all the wise men of Babylon."_** (Daniel 2:48) Demonstrating his godly wisdom and love for the Hebrews, Daniel took advantage of the king's kindness and accepted the gifts and the position. Moreover, Daniel sought positions for his companions, **_"Then Daniel requested of the king, and he set Shadrach, Meshach, and Abednego, over the affairs of the province of Babylon but Daniel sat in the gate of the king."_** (Daniel 2:48-49)

(Madness to More Madness)

Again, the king reverted to his madness. After the king admitted to Daniel **_"...your God is a God of gods, and a Lord of kings,"_** he *immediately* insulted **Yahweh** by erecting the humongous golden image (12 ½ by 125 feet) for everyone (including the Hebrew captives) to fall down and worship the image! **_Was this a new world religious order?_** Following in the footsteps of Nimrod, king Nebuchadnezzar was forcing all of the residents (of different faiths and backgrounds) in Babylonia to worship the *golden image*! The same devil that compelled Nimrod's false religion was orchestrating Nebuchadnezzar's campaign of *false religion and false worship*. Furthermore, Nebuchadnezzar created a fiasco, fanfare, punishment, and a violent death concerning the dedication of the golden image, *"Then a herald cried aloud, To you it is commanded, O people, nations, and languages, That at what time ye hear the sound of the cornet, flute, harp, sackbut, psaltery, dulcimer, and all kinds of musick, ye fall down and worship the golden image that Nebuchadnezzar the king hath set up. And whoso falleth not down and worshippeth shall the same hour be cast into the midst of a burning fiery furnace."* (Daniel 3:4-6)

The Wolf-man's Metamorphosis

There was so much chatter and excitement that no one paid attention to the latest development. The wolf-man was experiencing another metamorphosis! But no one noticed it!

(Freddie's comments)
Mr. Freddie *(the Babylonian fox)* decided to break up the chatter because he wanted to be Mayor! So, Mr. Freddie said that foxes are supposed to be real smart and that's why the humans use the phrase, "smart as a fox." Like the others, Mr. Freddie was not paying attention to the wolf-man! Instead, Mr. Freddie was angry because too many animals and predators from out-of-town were visiting the Babylonian forest!

Freddie looked up at Kurt *(the Erzurum wolf)* and said, "Yeah Man, you Hittite [25] wolves migrated from Erzurum and Hakkari's snowy mountains to Babylon's forest to invade our territory. *That same evil spirit over Turkey spilled over into Assyria spilled over into Babylon!* You *Erzurum and Hakkari wolves* put a hex, fear, and terror upon every living creature in our Babylonian forest."

(Kurt's comments)
"Oh really!" replied Kurt *(the Erzurum wolf) growling!*

(Freddie's comments)
"Yes, that is the way it is! *replied Freddie (the fox)!"*

---

25   Turkish.

(Mrs. Freddie's comments)

"Hey fellows, hey fellows, hey fellows" yapped Mrs. Freddie *(the fox).* Just a few chapters ago, Kurt *(the Erzurum wolf), you* called *Freddie the fox* your brother. Since then, what happened? Did I miss something? Let's move on with the story. Too many things are happening and we don't need to fight one another. Within the blink of an eye, SUDDENTLY, Mrs. Freddie screamed!"

(The Professor's comments)

Baykus said, "Look the wolf-man changing back into a man again!" We are witnessing HISTORY *(in the making)* and a double miracle! We were the *first* animals to witness the completion of the king's transformation from human to animal, **his seven-year term** in the wild with us, and his transformation from animal **back to** human! *See his feathers are dropping off! His hands and legs are reshaping like a man's. The long hairs of his head and beard look different. His eyes are not sharpened for night vision and his nostrils are shrunken!*

Lycanthropy

(The Professor continues)

The Professor said that Nebuchadnezzar was transformed into a wild animal, given the heart of a beast (rather than a man), and there is a certain name for it, **Lycanthropy**. He said that *Webster's New World Dictionary* gives the following definition for **Lycanthropy:** (1) is a form of mental disorder in which the patient imagines himself to be a wolf; and (2) Folklore the magical power to transform oneself or another into a wolf. In addition, the Professor said that the word, Lycanthrope *means* (1) a person having lycanthropy; and (2) same as werewolf: (A) a person changed into a wolf; (B) one capable of assuming the form of a wolf at will; lycanthrope."

Then the Professor said, "Let me tell you all something, king Nebuchadnezzar did not have: a make-believe mental disorder; nervous breakdown; and he did not just imagine himself to be a wolf-man! God placed a curse on Nebuchadnezzar for seven years! Future generations will not believe this story the king of Babylon was changed into a wolf-man. And, I'll tell you why! People don't believe the story

Constance Lee

about Baby Jesus born to a virgin! In fact, people don't believe in God at all!"

Nebuchadnezzar's Restoration

(Nebuchadnezzar 's comments)

This is what the **_Bible_** states and this is what happened to me, *"And at the end of the days, I Nebuchadnezzar lifted up mine eyes unto heaven, and mine understanding returned unto me, and I blessed the most High, and I praised and honoured him that liveth for ever, who dominion is an everlasting dominion, and his kingdom is from generation to generation: And all the inhabitants of the earth are reputed as nothing: and he doeth according to his will in the army of heaven, and among the inhabitants of the earth: and none stay his hand, or say unto him, What doest thou? At the same time my reason returned unto me; and for the glory of my kingdom, mine honour and brightness returned unto me; and my counselors and my lords sought unto me; and I was established in my kingdom, and excellent majesty was added unto me.* (Daniel 4:34-36)

I acknowledged the God of Heaven and His greatness. I worshipped Him from the depths of my heart. After my appointed time in hell *(seven long years in the wild)*, I slept on grass, dirt, and ate with wild animals! You'd better believe it! I looked up to Heaven and I repented! Faster than a speeding bullet, my understanding, reasoning, the glory of my kingdom, brightness of my reign, my lords and counselors returned to me. I walked back into the Babylon the Great and the people ran out to meet me. They clothed and wrapped me in royal attire! There was much shouting, singing, and dancing. In fact, the Hebrew captives and other foreign residents cheered me as I walked through the *infamous* Ishtar Gate down the main streets of ancient Babylon. Deep in the forest, I use to hear the noise from Babylon's celebrations and festivals. I saw the fireworks! But I did not have the understanding of man and I could not remember what it was all about! I use to watch the Babylonian patrols go by (through the forest), but I was

62

up under the bushes. My animal instincts told me not to snarl or growl at them, or else, they might attack or kill me. I was a wild animal!

Now, I was glad to be home again, but I will never forget the animals and beasts that befriended me in the wild. Many nights, I stood on the palace balcony *crying and praising* the **Lord God** for my deliverance. After I resumed regency, gave me much, much, much more and I never forgot that the **LORD HE IS GOD**, *"Now I Nebuchadnezzar praise and extol and honour the King of heaven, all whose works are truth, and his ways judgment: and those that walk in pride he is able to abase."* (Daniel 4:37)

(Nebuchadnezzar's continued comments)

Next, the king said that I learned my lesson. It took seven long years living in the wild with the beasts of the field. There were times, I had to fight to show my strength and God gave me dominion over the beasts of the field (just like I had ruler ship over men). That's why Daniel said, *"And wheresoever the children of men dwell, the beasts of the field and the fowls of the heaven hath he given into thine hand, and hath made thee ruler over them all."* (Daniel 2:38) Furthermore, Daniel told me, *"The tree that thou sawest, which grew, and was strong, whose height reached unto the heaven, and the sight thereof to all the earth; Whose leaves were fair, and the fruit thereof much, and in it was meat for all; under which the beasts of the field dwelt, and upon whose branches the fowls of the heaven had their habitation; It is thou, O king, that art grown and become strong: for thy greatness is grown, and reacheth unto heaven, and thy dominion to the end of the earth."* (Daniel 4:20-22)

(The Professor's comments)

Professor Baykus *(the old Hittite owl)* said that sometimes the **Lord GOD** has to take people down a notch or two because people get beside themselves! The fall can be tremendous and devastating. Some people lose their jobs, homes, cars, finances, health, love ones, and so on. But there is one thing about the recovery process: GOD IS ABLE! In fact, Abraham *(99 years)* and Sarah *(89 years)* were both old and well stricken in age. And Sarah was past the years of childbearing. But Sarah laughed at the Lord GOD and <u>He heard her laugh!</u> *"And the Lord said* *unto Abraham, Wherefore did Sarah laugh, saying, Shall I of a surety bear a child, which am old? IS ANY THING TOO HARD FOR THE LORD? At the time appointed I will return unto thee, according to the time of life, and Sarah shall have a son."* (Genesis 18:13-14)

Even though God tells us something, we still do not believe His Word! Sarah was the *wife* to the *patriarch*, Abraham (progenitor of the Hebrews and the Arabs). Plus, the world knew that **Yahweh** was in a *covenant relationship* with Abraham and that his seed was blessed! The seeds of the Hebrews and Arabs are greatly multiplied as the sands of the seashore and the stars in the sky. Every one and their mamas knew that **Yahweh** was with "Abraham ***who was rich in cattle, in silver, and in gold...***" (Genesis 13:2) Moreover, Abraham was entertaining divine visitors from Heaven! How much more convincing did Sarah need? How many people get to sit with Jesus and His Angels at their dinner table? Given that opportunity, I'd like to handcuff myself to Jesus' ankles! Sometimes, the blessing is right in front of us, but we refuse to see it! Many times, we throw away the blessing! Then, someone else comes along, picks up the ball *(blessing or opportunity)*, and RUNS TO GLORY WITH IT! Then, we say, "That should have been me..."

Rather than to admit her guilt of unbelief, Sarah lied, "I laughed not for she was afraid." And the Lord said, **"Nay but thou didst laugh."** (Genesis 18:15) Don't be like Sarah! Be honest, surrender to the **Lord GOD**, and ask for His forgiveness. **He is merciful, faithful, and compassionate! He will forgive us and restore us!**

Chapter 11

Watchers and The Holy Ones

<u>(The Professor's comments)</u>

Nebuchadnezzar's narration of his story took a great toll on his vocal chords! For the most part, Nebuchadnezzar had been quoting scriptures, telling the cold-hard facts, and making *"unbelievable"* speeches from an animal's viewpoint. The howling (in the language of the wolves) was slowly diminishing. And, the human voice that was buried deep within his vocal chords was struggling to make a come-back and undergoing an *audible* transformation from animal to man. With each breath, the king's old voice got stronger and stronger!

(Nebuchadnezzar's comments)

Now I am ready to explain the Watchers and Holy Ones,

"I saw in the visions of my head upon my bed, and, behold a watcher *and an* holy one *came down from heaven…"* (Daniel 4:13) *<u>"This matter is by the decree of the</u>* watchers *<u>and the demand by the word of the</u>* holy ones: *to the intent that the living may know that the most High ruleth in the kingdoms of men, and giveth it to whomsoever he will, and setteth up over it the basest of men."* (Daniel 4:17)

(The Professor's comments)

The *old Hittite owl* said, "Please, allow me to define the word *watcher* for you! According to **Webster's NewWord Dictionary**, watcher *means* **"...*an observer; a person authorized to keep watch...*"**

(Nebuchadnezzar's comments)

The king said that he saw a WATCHER (singular) but the WATCHER is not an earthling. Instead, the WATCHER is an angel from heaven who was "...***authorized to keep watch or guard over...***" Also, the king saw a HOLY ONE (not of this world). He said that the HOLY ONE is JESUS (Son of the Living God). Thus, the king admitted they both came down from HEAVEN. So, the HOLY ONE and the WATCHER are "supernatural" Beings from Heaven.

(The Professor's comments)

Furthermore, the Professor said that the Book of Isaiah 1:3-4 gives the identity of the HOLY ONE, "An ox knoweth his owner and the ass his master's crib: ***but Israel doth not know, my people doth not consider. Ah sinful nation, a people laded with iniquity, a seed of evildoers, children that are corrupters: they have forsaken*** THE LORD, ***they have provoked the*** HOLY ONE ***of Israel unto anger, they are gone away backward.***"

"But, I'm not finished," ***said the Professor***, "Allow me to sharpen my whiskers." The *Old Hittite* owl said that Daniel 4:17a states, ***"This matter is by the decree of the*** watchers ***and the demand by the word of the*** holy ones..." The WATCHERS (plural) announce the matter on earth or to selected people or individuals. However, WATCHERS cannot decree anything without being commanded! The HOLY ONES = TRIUNE GOD (plural meaning the Father, Son, and the Holy Ghost – *the Three in One*) are the *only* ONES authorized to give THE *LIVING* WORD! Truly, ***"This matter is by the decree of the watchers, and the demand by the word of the holy ones to the intent that the living may know that the most High ruleth in the kingdom of men, and giveth it to whomsoever he will, and setteth up over it the basest of men."***

(Daniel 4:17)

("The They")

Who are "They?" In general, "They" are the supernatural spirits (Watchers) sent by God to execute judgment in the Earth. This assignment was against king Nebuchadnezzar, ***"And They shall drive thee from men and thy dwelling shall be with the beasts of the field, and They shall make thee to eat grass as oxen, and They shall wet thee with the dew of heaven, and seven times shall pass over thee, till thou know that the most High ruleth in the kingdom of men, and giveth it to whomsoever he will."*** (Daniel 4:32) They (the Watchers) had specific authority to oversee the public and private affairs of king Nebuchadnezzar, "The same hour was the thing fulfilled upon Nebuchadnezzar and he was driven from men, and did eat grass as oxen, and his body was wet with the dew of heaven, til his hairs were grown like eagles' feathers, and his nails like birds' claws." (Daniel 4:33) No earthly being(s) could have stayed in the forest with Nebuchadnezzar: (a) *every* second, *every* minute, and *every* hour for seven lo-o-o-o-o-o-ng years (*without taking shifts*); (b) fought with poisonous snakes, deadly spiders, and ferocious animals; and (c) endure freezing cold temperatures, rains, winter, snow, and blazing hot temperatures. Any normal person or people would leave at sun down.

In other words, the Watchers *possessed* Nebuchadnezzar: took over his mind; made him strip naked; transformed him from human to beast; drove him to the forest; eat grass like the beasts of the field; and grew his nails like birds' claws and his hairs like an eagles' feathers all over his body. Furthermore, king Nebuchadnezzar was compared to a tree stump. The Watchers *(They)* were ***"...commanded to leave the stump of the tree roots; thy kingdom shall be sure unto thee, after that thou shalt have known that the heavens do rule."*** (Daniel 4:26) Without doubt, *only* supernatural spirits *(They)* from God have the authority to execute _decrees_. In particular, "They" preserved Nebuchadnezzar's realm. Moreover, **"They"** *(Watchers)* gave Nebuchadnezzar dominion over all the earth *including the beasts of the forest!* Obviously, the devil did not do this! Afterwards, Daniel told king Belshazzar (Nebuchadnezzar's grandson), ***"O thou king, the most high God gave Nebuchadnezzar thy father a kingdom and majesty, and glory, and honor: <u>And the majesty that he gave him, all people, nations, and languages trembled and feared before him: whom he would he slew; and whom he would he kept alive; and whom he would he set up; and whom he would he put down…"</u>*** (Daniel 5:18-19)

Chapter 12

Jesus' Appearances in the Old & New Testaments

(The Professor's comments)

Baykus said, "In the *Old Testament*, no one knew the *historical* Jesus of the *New Testament* (**i.e., Jesus of Nazareth, the Son of the Living God, and a member of the Triune God**) because (a) the *New Testament* had not been written; (b) in spite of the *Old Testament's* <u>Messianic</u> prophecies and those predicting a <u>*Virgin*</u> would conceive, the prophecies were not fulfilled until the *New Testament*; and (c) the Theophanies were *short term and temporary physical and visible manifestations of God and/or Jesus in variable ways: human form; visions; through nature; the glory of the Lord; the Angel of the Lord; and His name alone which is most precious implies, His Holy Presence. For example, God and/or Jesus (appeared as the Angel of the Lord), and the Holy Spirit (God's Executive Agent) appeared in the Old Testament*: **(1)** ***"And the earth was without form, and void; and darkness was upon the face of the deep. <u>And the Spirit of God moved upon the face of the waters.</u>"*** (Genesis 1:2); **(2)** ***"And <u>the angel of the Lord</u> appeared unto him [Moses] in a flame of fire out of the midst of a bush…I am the God of thy father, the God of Abraham, the God of Isaac, and the God of Jacob."*** (Exodus 3:2, 6); **(3)** ***"And <u>the Lord went before them</u> [children of Israel] by day in a pillar of a cloud, to***

69

lead them the way; and by night in a pillar of fire, to give them light; to go by day and night: He took not away the pillar of the cloud by day, nor the pillar of fire by night, from before the people." (Exodus 13:21-22; 24:16-18); and **(4)** there are many other Theophanies.

(Keci's comments)

Without hesitation, the *old goat* yelled, "Whut! How cum Jesus jest appeered when He ain't born? AND Sides, I jest wants to know ONE thang! Who was in the fire with the Hebrew Boys?"

(The Professor's comments)

"Well now, said Professor Baykus, "The **Lord Jesus** is part of the **Triune God:** The Father, The Son, and The Holy Ghost!" Then the Professor called Keci an ***old hairy goat with a one-track mind***! Then the Professor said that he was not ready to talk about the Hebrew Boys in the Fire just yet! YOU'LL JUST HAVE TO WAIT!

The Unity of God

The *wise old Hittite owl* said, "You need to understand the ***Unity of God***." In Genesis 1:1, the **Triune God** is ONE and they are ALL present and SEPARATE,

"In the beginning God created the heaven and the earth. (Genesis 1:1) and *"In the beginning was the Word, and the Word was with God, and the Word was God. The same was in the beginning with God. All things were made by him; and without him was not anything made that was made."* (John 1:1-3) There are other proofs of the Godhead: *"Let us make man in our image..."* (Genesis 1:24) The Book of Deuteronomy 6:4 states, *"Hear O Israel: the Lord our God is one Lord."* And Romans 1:20 states, *"For the invisible things of him from the creation of the world are clearly seen, being understood by the things that are made, even his eternal power and Godhead...."*

The Triune God's, Flexibility

The Earth underwent drastic stages from *perfection to imperfection*. The Godhead came down from heaven to look at the earth and God (the Father) was distraught! The Earth that was Perfect became Imperfect: Lucifer's flood and sin destroyed the earth, sun, moon, stars refused to shine and the other planets were terribly damaged. ***And the earth was without form, and void; and darkness was upon the face of the deep.***" (Genesis 1:2)

The Triune God split up to perform their separate tasks or functions. By definition, the Triune God consists of THREE PERSONS. Father, Son, and the Holy Spirit. They each have a big job to do! The Triune breakdown is: **The Father**, *the First Person*; **The SON**, *the Second Person*; and **The Holy Spirit**, *the Third Person*. However, they rejoin as ONE BODY! **Moreover, the Triune God (jointly and individually) possesses Omniscience, Omnipresence, and Omnipotence throughout All Eternity and ages to come!**

(1) *GOD CALLS THE PLAYS:* "*And God said, Let there be...*" or "*And God said, Let the...*" (Genesis 1:3, 6, 9, 11, 14, 20, 22, 24, 26) Frankly, God the Father gives the orders and They (Jesus and the Holy Spirit) obey! Apparently, God says, **"Jesus, I need you! Now, do this or that!"** Then, God summons the Holy Spirit (*His Executive Agent*) and sends Him down to Earth! But remember, the Triune God (*jointly and individually*) possesses Omniscience, Omnipresence, and Omnipotence throughout All Eternity and ages to come!

(2) **The Pre-incarnate work of Jesus:** "*And God said let there be light and there was light. And God saw the light, that it was good: and God divided the light from the darkness.*" (Genesis 1:3-4) That light is **Jesus**, God's flashlight to this sinful world. Before God's work on Day Four of Re-Creation, the restoration of the two great lights (the sun and moon), and the lesser lights (the stars), God saw the darkness and chaos over the face of the earth! Apparently, God called Jesus to shine His light on the earth. Naturally, Jesus answered, "Yes, Father." However, Sin (A.K.A. the devil, *the purest form of evil*) was not eradicated or taken out of the earth. **Father GOD had a plan!** Thankfully, Sin was separated from "GOOD" and "GOOD" is synonymous with JESUS. Thus,

there was division placed between good and evil sin as day is to night. JESUS = the Light of the world. ***"In him was life; and the life was the light of men. And the light shines in the darkness, and the darkness, did not comprehend it."*** (John 1:3-4) Furthermore, Jesus possesses all of the attributes of **His Father, GOD**, and yet Jesus came to do the Will of **His Father, GOD**;

(3) God called on the Holy Spirit (His Executive Agent) to do His job! "And the Spirit of God moved upon the face of the waters." (Genesis 1:2) These were the waters of Lucifer's Flood (*the Chaotic Earth Age*) that destroyed the entire Earth: life (above and below the earth); fowls of the air; fish in the sea; and every creeping thing. There is no time frame or date for this period but it happened before the Age of Re-creation of the Earth. (Genesis 1:3-2:25)

In the Old Testament, Prophet Jeremiah stated, ***"I beheld the earth, and lo, it was without form, and void; and the heavens, and they had no light. I beheld the mountains, and lo, they trembled, and all the hills moved lightly. I beheld, and lo, there was no man, and all the birds of the heavens were fled. I beheld, and lo, the fruitful place was a wilderness, and all the cities thereof were broken down at the presence of the Lord, and by his fierce anger."*** (Jeremiah 4:23-26)

In the New Testament, God told the Holy Spirit, **"Go ye therefore, and teach all nations baptizing them in the name of the Father, and of the Son, and of the Holy Ghost." (Matthew 28:19) "Now there are diversities of gifts, but the same Spirit. And there are differences of administrations, but the same Lord. And there are diversities of operations, but it is the same God which worketh all in all."** (I Corinthians 12:4-6)

Old Testament Theophanies

(The Professor continues)

Jesus was there from the Beginning of Time and Creation. However, the incarnate Jesus made appearances to certain people in the ***Old Testament***! Professor Baykus said that others (besides Daniel and the Hebrew Boys) saw the

Lord GOD. Lets look at a few Old Testament witnesses who saw, talked with, or ate with the **Lord GOD**: Adam & Eve; Cain; Enoch; Noah; Abraham, Isaac, and Jacob; Job; Moses, Joshua, Aaron, Nadab, Abihu and seventy elders who attended a banquet with God on Mt. Sinai (Exodus 24:9-11); Balaam & his donkey; Gideon; Manoah and his wife (Samson's mother); Samuel; Elijah; David; Amos; Ezekiel; Isaiah; and others.

God Personally Created Adam & Eve

(The Age of Innocence)

What a wonderful time to be born in <u>The Age of Innocence</u>! [26] Adam and Eve were created without flaws and without sin! They were so perfect that they did not know they were naked! Back then, it was not a crime or sin to be naked in public! There was no law and there was no public! During the Age of Innocence, there was no sin. How about that! ***"And they were both naked, the man and his wife, and were not ashamed."*** (Genesis 2:25)

(Adam's Creation)

The **Lord GOD** *physically* came down to Earth and said, ***"Let us make man in our image, after our likeness..."*** (Genesis 1:24) God used **Earth's powder** *(the original and purest form of dirt)* to make man. God did not concoct bits and pieces of frogs, lizards, gizzards, blueberries, and mustard seeds to make Man. Oh, scientists would love to market God's exclusive recipe for the creation of man. However, we only know one of the ingredients God used to make man, the **Earth's powder** which back then was made from purest and organic mud, *full of nutrients.*

During Adam's creation, the **Earth's powder** was not contaminated as the dirt is today! So far, we have never seen dirt like the original **Earth's powder** used to make Adam, ***"And God said, Let us make man in our image, after our likeness...So God created man in his own image, in***

---

26   The Age of Innocence: Genesis 2:15-3:21. The length of this Age is unknown.

the image of God created he him…" (Genesis 1:26-27) *"And the Lord formed man of the dust of the ground, and breathed* [the Hebrew word is "naphach" which means to breathe out, puff, blow, inflate] *into his nostrils the breath of life; and man became a living soul."* (Genesis 2:7)

(Adam had God Given Intelligence)

Yet, **God** personally gave Adam *godly* knowledge, wisdom, and understanding and **God brought every animal to Adam**. Although Adam never attended college, "Adam gave names to all the cattle, fowls of the air, and to every beasts…" (Genesis 2:20a) **To this day, the animals and fowls of the air have the same names!**

(Eve's Creation)

(Question: Why did Adam need a companion?)

After Adam worked all day, he was lonely! What's more, Adam understood the concepts of male, female, reproduction, multiply and replenish the earth. For certain, the male and female animals mated in Adam's presence, and (in time) they produced offspring. Genesis 2:20b states, "…but for Adam there was not found an help meet for him."

Thus, God created a Lifetime partner for Adam. By the way, it was a female not a male! Like Adam's creation, the **earth's powder** was used, and again, **God** *(the Great Surgeon of Surgeons)* was present when He put Adam to sleep to create Woman. *In fact, Adam purred like a little kitty-cat during the first surgery,* *"And the Lord God caused a deep sleep to fall upon Adam and he slept: and he took one of his ribs, and closed up the flesh instead thereof. And the rib, which the Lord God had taken from man, made he a woman, and brought her unto the man."* (Genesis 2:21-22)

Phenomenally, when Adam awoke, he had God-given knowledge, wisdom, and understanding of the events which transpired during his surgery. There are *only* three explanations for Adam's statement, *"This is now bone of my bones and flesh of my flesh: she shall be called*

Woman, because she was taken out of Man." (Genesis 2:23): **(1)** Per chance, God stored a computer chip in Adam's brain;

(2) Maybe, Adam's membranes sensed the loss of connective tissues and a missing *rib* bone; and **(3)** God gave Adam innate or instinctive knowledge about *the Woman's creation.* Without doubt, number three is the best answer. Although Adam was in a *medical coma* (during the operation), God gave Adam a prophetic gift. After Adam awoke, he spoke prophetically, "Therefore shall a man leave his father and his mother, and shall cleave unto his wife: and they shall be one flesh." (Genesis 2:23-24; Hebrews 13:14; I Timothy 2:13) How did Adam know this? During the Age of Innocence, there were only two people on Planet Earth! ***God created Adam out of the powder of the Earth and in His own image!*** But, Adam spoke about a man (leaving his Father and Mother) and cleaving unto his wife. Adam did not have a Father or Mother. ***God gave Adam this knowledge!***

(The Professor's comments continued)

Professor Baykus said that the next statement is so controversial! Obviously, the **Lord GOD** created the *Woman* to be *Man's* companion. The **Lord GOD** did not create another *"Man"* to be Adam's companion. Instead, God said, "You shall not lie with a male as with a woman. It is an abomination." (Leviticus 18:22)

(Eve as Companion and Helper)

God validated Adam and Eve's relationship. When the **Lord GOD** took Eve from Adam's rib, He put her at his side. He did not make them Siamese twins. The **Lord GOD** created Woman in the image of Adam, but He made her a separate and complete human being with her own *unique body* (arms, legs, eyes, fingers, nose, mouth, female parts, heart, soul, mind, and so on). After her creation, the **Lord GOD** *Himself* took the Woman by the hand to Adam who said, "*bone of my bones and flesh of my flesh: she shall be called Woman, because she was taken out of Man...*" (Genesis 2:18, 21-24)

(God commanded Adam & Eve)

So, God created a *WIFE* and *COMPANION* for *ADAM* and He told them, **"Be fruitful, multiply, replenish the earth, subdue it, and have dominion over** *the fish of the sea, fowl of the air, and over every living thing that moveth upon the earth. And God said, Behold, I have given you every herb bearing seed, which is upon the face of all the earth, and every tree, in the which is the fruit of a tree yielding seed; to you it shall be for meat."* (Genesis 1:28-29)

Jesus Appeared to Abram

The Professor said that we know that certain (O.T.) people communed with God in the person of Jesus who appeared in the Theophany, as the Angel of the Lord. One of those stories is about Abram the Hebrew! The first mention of *Abram the Hebrew* [27] appears in Genesis 14:13-14. Abram & Company (his family and servants born in his service) prepared to deliver Lot (his nephew), his family and possessions. And so, Abram & Company fought four notorious Mesopotamian eastern kings (Amraphel,* Arioch, Chedorlaomer, and Tidal [28]) in the Valley of Siddim (full of slime pits) to deliver Lot and all of his possessions.

(Abraham Worships with Melchizedek)

After the victory of Abram & his confederates, [29] Melchizedek (Theophany of **Jesus the Christ**) the kingly-priest of Salem " *ancient Jerusalem*" brought bread and wine __to__ Abram. Without doubt, the Lord was pleased with Abram's victory over the eastern kings; and He was pleased with Abram's comments and refusal to accept a token of appreciation to Bara, the king of Sodom.

---

27   At this point, <u>Abram the Hebrew</u> (first usage of the word *Hebrew* means other side of the Euphrates) name had not been changed to Abraham. (Genesis 14:13)

28   Amraphel * was the king of Shinar: alternate spellings Ammurabi, Ammuraphi-lu, and phonetically pronounced H-ammurabi; A.K.A. Hammurabi, king of Babylon who wrote the infamous *Hammurabi Code of Laws*); Arioch (king of Ellasar); Chedor-laomer (king of Elam); and Tidal (king of nations: barbarians and Kurds).

29   Abram the Hebrew & his confederates included: Abram's trained servants (about 318 souls born in his house) and Aner, Eshcol, and Mamre (descendants of Ca-naan, son of Ham, son of Noah).

What's more, Melchizedek (the Lord) had one purpose for his visit with Abram: **fellowship and worship**. The kingly-priest said, "Blessed be Abram of the most high God, possessor of heaven and earth. And blessed be the most high God which hath delivered thine enemies into thy hand." (Genesis 14:19-20) And Abram gave Melchizedek one-tenth of his tithes (first mention of paying tithes) of all his conquests.

(God Enlarged the Abrahamic Covenant)

Although the **Lord GOD** visited and ate with Abraham [30] (and spoke prophetically concerning many things including Sarah, Abraham's wife), Abraham did not know God by His name, **"JEHOVAH."** The *Bible* states, *"And when Abram was ninety years old and nine, the Lord appeared to Abram, and said unto him,* I am the Almighty God; *walk before me, and be thou perfect..."* (Genesis 17:1)

The **Lord GOD** was with Abram and enlarged the Abrahamic Covenant, *"And I will make thee exceeding fruitful, and I will make nations of thee, and kings shall come out of thee. And I will establish my covenant between me and thee and thy seed after thee in their generations for an everlasting covenant, to be a God unto thee, and to thy seed after thee. And I will give unto thee, and to thy seed after thee, the land wherein thou art a stranger, all the land of Canaan, for an everlasting possession; and I will be their God."* (Genesis 17:6-8)

(God Appeared to Abraham in Mamre)

Abraham had *three* divine visitors in the plains of Mamre. One day, *"...Abraham sat in the tent door in the heat of the day...And he lift up his eyes and looked, and lo, three men stood by him: and when he saw them he ran to meet them from the tent door, and bowed himself toward the ground..."* (Genesis 18:1-2) By his own admission, we know that Abraham saw the **Lord GOD**, "And said, My Lord, if now I have found favor in thy sight pass not away, I pray thee, from thy servant..." (Genesis 18:3) Next, the Lord (and His angels) ate with him, *"And he*

---

30   God covenanted with Abraham, Isaac, and Jacob.

[Abraham] took butter, milk, and the calf which he had dressed, and set it before them; and he stood by them under the tree, and they did eat." (Genesis 18:8)

Jesus Appeared to Moses

In contrast to the Theophanies *(God's appearances)* with the patriarchs (Abraham, Isaac, and Jacob), the **Lord GOD** revealed His name (JEHOVAH) only to Moses, *"And* God spake unto Moses, and said unto him, I am the Lord. And I appeared unto Abraham, unto Isaac, and unto Jacob, by the name of God Almighty 31 but by my name Jehovah was I not known to them. *I have established my covenant with them, to give them the land of Canaan, the land of their pilgrimage, where in they were strangers. And I have also heard the groaning of the children of Israel, whom the Egyptians keep in bondage; and I have remembered my covenant."* (Exodus 6:2-5)

(Wilderness Journey)

Let's examine (more closely) the children of Israel's *day and night* travel in the wilderness! The children of Israel and all the strangers *(non-Israelites)* were under the same **Protective Covering**: Cloud of Covering (by day) and Pillar of Fire (by night). Who was covering them? Jesus, the Angel of the Lord! Thus, the *Cloud of Covering* **did not** just spot-cover the Israelites and **expose** the poor strangers to the ultra violet rays of the burning sun during the day! Likewise, the *Pillar of Fire* **did not** just **shine-a-light** on the Israelites and **expose** the non-Israelites to the freezing temperatures at night!

However, there was one exception! The **Protective Coverings** (cloud by day and the pillar of fire by night) did not cover the bad-boys, the Egyptians! *"And the angel of God which went before the camp of Israel, removed and went behind them; and the pillar of the cloud went from before their face, and stood behind them: And it came between the camp of the Egyptians and the camp of Israel; and it was a cloud and darkness to them, but it gave light by night to these: so that the one came not near the other all the night."*

---

31   The name of God Almighty is *El Shaddai*, which means the All Sufficient One.

(Exodus 14:19-20)

Isaiah's Vision, The Glory of God

In the Old Testament, Prophet Isaiah was one of the most infamous viewers to see the glory of the Lord, ***"In the year that king Uzziah died, I saw also the Lord sitting upon a throne, high and lifted up, and his train filled the temple.** Above it stood the seraphims: each one had six wings; with twain he covered his face, and with twain he covered his feet, and with twain he did fly. And one cried unto another Holy, holy, holy, is the Lord of hosts: the whole earth is full of his glory…the posts of the door moved at the voice of him that cried, and the house was filled with smoke.*** (Isaiah 6:1-4)

THE NEW TESTAMENT

JESUS, The Incarnation

The Incarnation of Jesus in the New Testament is real! Old Testament prophecies regarding the Birth of Jesus were fulfilled in the New Testament such as ***"the seed of the woman would bruise the head of the serpent…"*** (Genesis 3:13) and ***"…a virgin shall conceive and bear a son…"*** (Isaiah 7:14)

Secondly, the New Testament reveals the Incarnation of Jesus Christ! Apostle John said, (A) ***"And the Word [LOGOS] was made flesh, and dwelt among us, and we beheld his glory, the glory as of the only begotten of the Father, full of grace and truth."*** (John 1:14); (B) ***"I John bare witness of him and cried, saying, This was he of whom I spake, He that cometh after me is preferred before me: for he was before me."*** (John 1:15) God sent John the Baptist, ***"And I knew him not: but he that sent me to baptize with water, the same said unto me, Upon***

Constance Lee

whom thou shalt see the Spirit descending, and remaining on him, the same is he which baptized with the Holy Ghost. And I saw, and bare record that this is the Son of God." (John 1:33-34); (C) The Holy Spirit bare record as recorded by God's messenger, "And John bare record, saying, I saw the Spirit descending from heaven like a dove, and it abode upon him." (John 1:32); and (D) Apostle Paul wrote concerning the free gift, "But the gift of God is eternal through Jesus Christ our Lord." (Romans 6:23b)

God's Worldwide Web

Communication presents no problem for God! GOD has as His own Universal Worldwide Web and messengers:

(1) The Annunciation: God's messenger (a holy angel) was sent from Heaven to Earth, "And in the sixth month the angel Gabriel was sent from God unto a city of Galilee, named Nazareth, to a virgin espoused to a man whose name was Joseph of the house of David; and the virgin's name was Mary. And the angel came in unto her, and said, Hail, thou that are highly favoured, the Lord is with thee: blessed art thou among women...And the angel said unto her, Fear not, Mary for thou hast found favor with God. And, behold, thou shalt conceive in thy womb, and bring forth a son, and shalt call his name Jesus. He shall be great, and shall be called the Son of the Highest: and the Lord God shall give unto him the throne of his father David: And he shall reign over the house of Jacob for ever; and of his kingdom there shall be no end." (Luke 1:26-33);

(2A) Heavenly Stars: Three Eastern Magi traveled long distances to Jerusalem spreading the news and asking questions "Where is he that is born King of the Jews? For we have seen His Star in the east and are come to worship him..." (Matthew 2:2) In fact, Balaam (a strayed prophet in the Old Testament) stated, "...there shall come a Star out of Jacob and a Sceptre shall rise out of Israel, and shall smite the corners

80

of Moab, and destroy all the children of Sheth...Out of Jacob shall come he that shall have dominion..." (Numbers 24:17, 19);

(2B) <u>The Bright Morning & Evening Star</u>: Jesus our LORD is the bright morning and evening star. In fact, Jesus said, *"I Jesus have sent mine angels to testify unto you these things in the churches. I am the root of David, and the bright and morning star."* (Revelation 24:16) Second Peter 1:19 states, *"We have also a more sure word of prophecy whereunto ye do well that ye take heed, as unto a light that shineth in a dark place, until the day dawn, and the day star arise in your hearts..."*

According to the free <u>Wikipedia</u>, *"Venus (the second planet from the Sun) is the brightest natural object in the night sky (after the Moon) that reaches its maximum brightness shortly before sunrise or shortly after sunset for which reason it has been known as the Morning Star and/or Evening Star."* According to Roman mythology, Venus is the goddess of love and beauty. In Greek mythology, Aphrodite is the goddess of love and beauty. However, the world has its ways of perverting the truth. Since Venus is the second planet from the Sun, the world sees her as "goddess of love and beauty" rather than accepting the Word of God that states **JESUS IS LOVE!**

Regardless the phases of the moon, **Jesus' Star** vividly speaks to the Earth as it glows from the Heavens. In the evening, **His Star** shines the brightest in the sky! From the eastern sky (just before dawn), the *Bright and Morning Star* faithfully heralds in the Sun each morning without fail. In fact, it glows brighter and brighter as the Sun's light approaches. Rightfully so, **Jesus** (as the *Bright and Morning Star*) lets us know that He is coming back again for a church (without spot or wrinkle) and even the dead will know it!

On that great **<u>Day of the Lord</u>**, the sun, moon, stars, and the constellations will refuse to shine and time will stand still. (Isaiah 13:6-

16) However, the only light shining will be ***Jesus the Son of the Living God!*** Does this remind you of the Earth's first day of Re-creation? On day four of Re-creation, the solar lights (*sun, moon, and stars*) were restored. However, on day one of Re-creation, God said, ***"Let there be light [JESUS] and there was light…And God saw the light that it was good…"*** (Genesis 1:3-4) The Gospel of John 1:1-5 states, ***"In the beginning…All things were made by him and without him was not any thing made…In him was life and the life was the light of men… and the light shineth in darkness and the darkness comprehended it not."***

Moreover, Apostle Paul tells us not to be sorrowful or ignorant, ***"For if we believe that Jesus died and rose again, even so them also which sleep in Jesus will God bring with him. For this we say unto you by the word of the Lord, that we which are alive and remain unto the coming of the Lord shall not prevent them which are asleep. For the Lord himself shall descend from heaven with a shout, with the voice of the archangel and with the trump of God: and the dead in Christ shall rise first. Then we which are alive and remain shall be caught up together with them in the clouds, to meet the Lord in the air: and so shall we ever be with the Lord. Wherefore comfort one another with these words."*** (I Thessalonians 4:14-18)

To day, **Jesus** is interceding for His people to **GOD the Father** and He shines a flashlight upon the Earth to keep watch over His creation. Regardless to the dark vapors, universe dust, clouds, rain and whatever else is going on in space, Jesus still shines upon the Earth. In spite of sickness, heart ache, pain, suffering, loss of a job and/or home, children or whatever, one can see the Evening Star or rise up at dawn to see the Bright and Morning Star only to know that the Lord is watching over the Earth! Make no mistake; Lucifer is not the Morning Star (he was the son of the Morning Star). The Bible states, ***"How art thou fallen from heaven, <u>O Lucifer, son of the morning</u> How art thou cut down to the ground which didst weaken the nations!"*** (Isaiah 14:12)

In Revelation 2:18-29, the Lord speaks about the **"Morning Star"** and other things to the angel of the church of Thyatira, *"I know thy works, and charity, and service, and faith, and thy patience, and thy works: and the last to be more than the first. Notwithstanding I have a few things against thee, because thou suffered that woman Jezebel, which calleth herself a prophetess, to teach and to seduce my servants to commit fornication, and to eat things sacrificed unto idols. And I gave her space to repent of her fornication; and she repented not... And he that overcometh and keepeth my works unto the end, to him will I give power over the nations: And he shall rule them with a rod of iron; as the vessels of a potter shall they be broken to shivers: even as I received of my Father. And I will give him the morning star. He that hath an ear let him hear what the spirit saith unto the churches."*

In other words, God will give the Bright and Morning Star, JESUS (the root and the offspring of David; the lily of the valley; the rose of Sharon) to **ALL** who overcome sin. (See Revelation 22:16) What does this mean? Frankly, we shall be like **Jesus** as *"Flesh and blood cannot inherit the kingdom of God neither doth corruption inherit incorruption."* (I Corinthians 15:50) Furthermore, Apostle Paul states in First Corinthians 15:51-57, *"Behold, I shew you a mystery: We shall not all sleep, but we shall all be changed. In a moment, in a twinkling of an eye, at the last trump; for the trumpet shall sound, and the dead shall be raised incorruptible, and we shall be changed. For this corruptible must put on incorruption and this mortal must put on immortality...then shall be brought to pass the saying that is written, Death is swallowed up in victory. O death, where is thy sting? O grave, where is thy victory. The sting of death is sin; and the strength of sin is the law. But thanks be to God which giveth us the victory through our Lord Jesus Christ."*

(3) <u>Other Angels</u>: Holy Angels made appearances to mortal men, *"And there were in the same country shepherds abiding in the field,*

keeping watch over their flock by night. And, lo, the angel of the Lord came upon them, and the glory of the Lord shone round about them: and they were sore afraid. And the angel said unto them, Fear not: for, behold, I bring you good tidings of great joy, which shall be to all people. For unto you is born this day in the city of David, a Savior, which is Christ the Lord. And this shall be a sign unto you: Ye shall find the babe wrapped in swaddling clothes, lying in a manner." (Luke 2:8-12);

(4) <u>Multitude of Angels</u>: *"And suddenly there was with the angel a multitude of the heavenly host praising God and saying, Glory to God in the highest, and on earth peace, good will toward men."* (Luke 2:13-14);

(5) <u>Celestial Communication</u>: According to the ***Bible***, there is a twenty-four (24) hour (ongoing) communication and radio waves (called lines) between the celestials: sun, moon, stars, earth, planets, the galaxies, and the extended universe. King David confirms the 24 hour communication theory between the celestials: ***<u>The heavens declare the glory of God; and the firmament sheweth his handiwork…Day unto day uttereth speech, and night unto night, sheweth knowledge…There is no speech nor language where their voice is not heard. Their line [RADIO WAVES] is gone out through all the earth and their words to the end of the world.</u>*** *In them hath he [God] set a tabernacle for the sun which is as a bridegroom coming out of his chamber, and rejoiceth as a strong man to run a race…His going forth is from the end of the heaven, and his circuit unto the ends of it and there is nothing hid from the heat thereof."* (Psalms 19:1-6);

(6) <u>Morning Stars (SUNS)</u>: The Book of Job (one of the oldest Books in the Bible) states that the SUNS *(morning stars in outer space that are much, much larger and similar to the Sun of the Earth's Solar System)* were SINGING while the foundations of the earth were being fastened,

" *...the morning stars sang together...when he* [God] *fastened the foundations of the earth and laid the corner stone.*"
 (Job 38:7);

(7) <u>Prophets</u>: "***God who at sundry times and in divers manners spake in time past unto the fathers by the prophets.***" (Hebrews 1:1-3);

(8) <u>Jesus</u>: "[GOD]...***Hath in these last days spoken unto us by his Son, whom he hath appointed heir of all things, by whom also he made the worlds.*** *Who being the brightness of his glory, and the express image of his person, and upholding all things by the word of his power when he had by himself purged our sins, sat down on the right hand of the Majesty on high.*" (Hebrews 1:1-3)

(9) <u>Jesus is the Living Water</u>: In the Gospel of John Chapter 4, Jesus left Judea purposefully to interview a Samaritan woman, to offer eternal living water, and to teach the truth. After arriving in the city of Sychar at Jacob's Well (about twelve noon), Jesus was thirsty and He asked a Samaritan woman for a drink of water. Her name is unknown, but Jesus' request was unusual because the Jews had no dealings with the Samaritans. This conversation perplexed the woman! Then, Jesus told her, "*If thou knewest the gift of God, and who it is that saith to thee, Give me to drink, thou would have asked of him, and he would have given thee living water.*" (John 4:10) Again, the woman was baffled because Jesus had no vessel to draw water with and the well was deep. Then the woman asked "*Art thou greater than our father Jacob which gave us the well and drank thereof himself, and his children, and his cattle?*" (John 4:12) So Jesus answered and said, "*Whosoever drinketh of this water shall thirst again, <u>But who whosoever drinketh of the water that I shall give him shall never thirst; but the water that I shall give him shall be in him a well of water springing up into everlasting life.</u>*" (John 4:13-14)

(10) <u>Jesus is the Bread of Life</u>: Jesus said that mankind cannot live on bread alone, ***"I am the bread of life. Your fathers did eat manna in the wilderness and are dead. This is the bread which cometh down from heaven that a man may eat thereof and not die. I am the living bread which came down from heaven: if any man eat of this bread, he shall live for ever: <u>and the bread that I will give is my flesh, which I will give for the life of the world.</u>"*** (John 6:48-51)   However, many people (back then and today) cannot understand Jesus' statement *"…my flesh is bread which is life."*   The Bible says, ***"The Jews therefore strove among themselves saying, How can this man give us his flesh to eat?"*** (John 6:52)   The bread represents the Body of Jesus Christ and the wine represents His blood shared on Calvary and before the foundation of the world.   To date, people cannot understand the concept, "Three Persons in One."

(11) <u>The Great Commission, Diversities of Gifts, and the Holy Spirit</u>: At this point, something must be said about the assignment for all believers in the New Testament.   Jesus gave the Great Commission and Diversities of Gifts, ***"Go ye therefore, and teach all nations baptizing them in the name of the Father, and of the Son, and of the Holy Ghost."*** (Matthew 28:19)   ***"Now there are diversities of gifts, but the same Spirit. And there are differences of administrations, but the same Lord. And there are diversities of operations, but it is the same God which worketh all in all."***   (I Corinthians 12:4-7)

However, the greatest spiritual gift of all is <u>LOVE</u>,   ***"Though I speak with the tongues of men and of angels and have not charity, I am become as sounding brass or a tinkling cymbal. And though I have the gift of prophecy and understand all mysteries, and all knowledge; and though I have all faith, so that I could remove mountains, and have not charity, I am nothing. And though I bestow all my goods to feed the poor, and though I give my body to be burned, and have not charity, it profiteth me nothing…And now abideth, faith, hope,*** *charity, these three; but the greatest of these is charity.*" (I Corinthians 13:1-3, 13)

The HOLY SPIRIT (God's Executive Agent) moves and stirs upon certain individuals (Jews and Gentiles alike) in various ways *i.e., names, symbols (such as fire, wind, and oil), seals, and anointing.* Luke 11:13 states, *"If ye then, being evil, know how to give good gifts unto your children: how much more shall your heavenly Father give the Holy Spirit to them that ask Him?"* Like *Salvation*, the *"Holy Spirit"* is a FREE GIFT from God; because it is not something one can purchase! The Bible states, the believer is sealed, *"In whom ye also trusted after that ye heard the word of truth, the gospel of your salvation: in whom also after that ye believed, ye were sealed with that Holy Spirit of promise."* (Ephesians 1:13) Just as the church has been purchased with the *Blood of the Lamb* (before the foundation of the world), the church has been *"...sealed with that Holy Spirit of promise..."* from before the foundation of the world. In fact, it was purchased and sealed at the same time!

The life forces of the Holy Spirit (characteristics and promises) are ascribed *by measure* to all born-again believers. *"But unto every one of us is given grace according to the measure of the gift of Christ."* (Ephesians 4:7) Keep in mind that *"...there are diversities of gifts, but the same Spirit. And there are differences of administrations, but the same Lord. And there are diversities of operations, but it is the same God which worketh all in all."* (I Corinthians 12:4-7) Furthermore Ephesians 4:4-6 states, *"There is one body, and one Spirit, even as ye are called in one hope of your calling; One Lord, one faith, one baptism, One God, and Father of all who is above all, and through all, and in you all."* As Jesus ascended up on high, He issued from his own mouth the Hand Ministry (also known as the Fivefold Ministry), *"He gave some apostles, some prophets, some evangelists, some pastors, and some teachers: For the perfecting of the saints, for the work of the ministry, for the edifying of the body of Christ: Till we all come in*

the unity of the faith, and of the knowledge of the Son of God, unto a perfect man, unto the measure of the stature of the fullness of Christ." (Ephesians 4:8-13)

Just as the Father and Son have different names, the Holy Spirit is recognized by other names such as: the *Spirit of Grace* (Hebrews 10:29); the *Spirit of Burning* (Isaiah 4:4); the *Spirit of God* (Genesis 1:2); the *spirit of Truth* (John 14:17; 16:13); the *Spirit of Life* (Romans 8:2); the *Spirit of Adoption* (Romans 8:15); the *Comforter* (John 14:16); the *Spirit of Christ* (I Corinthians 3:16; Romans 8:9); the *Spirit of Promise* (Ephesians 1:13); the *Spirit of Glory* (I Peter 4:14); the *Spirit of Wisdom and Revelation* (Ephesians 1:17); the *Spirit of Wisdom, Knowledge, and Revelation* (Isaiah 11:2; 61:1-2); and there are others.

In the New Testament, the "Holy Spirit" is a "Promise" to all believers. Jesus refers to the *Holy Spirit* as a *Divine Person*, ***"And I will pray the Father, and he shall give you another Comforter, that he may abide with you for ever. Even the spirit of truth; whom the world cannot receive because it seeth him not neither knoweth him: but ye know him; for he dwelleth with you, and shall be in you. I will not leave you comfortless…"*** (John 14:16-18) Therefore, the *Holy Spirit* is called along side of every born-again believer as an Advocate (Greek mean = parakletos) to plead the cause of another – like a lawyer. ***"But when the Comforter is come, whom I well send unto you from the Father, even the Spirit of truth, which proceedeth from the Father, he shall testify of me."*** (John 15:26) Jesus said, ***"Nevertheless, I tell you that the truth: It is expedient for you that I go away: for if I go not away, the comforter will not come unto you; but if I depart, I will send him unto you."*** (John 16:7)

Chapter 13

The Hebrew Boys & The Old Testament

The Hebrew Boys & the Old Testament

The Hebrew Boys were well acquainted with Hebrew law, The Torah (in the Greek it is called the Pentateuch – the first five Books of the **Bible** written by Moses), other Old Testament books, the patriarchs, the prophets, miraculous stories, the wonderful story of a little shepherd boy who became the king of Israel, and a wealth of history about the Hebrew Nation!

More so, they knew stories about *The True Living* God of Israel who:

(A)   ***"In the beginning created the heavens and the earth."*** (Genesis 1:1);

(B)   ***"…said Let us make man in our image after our likeness…"*** (Genesis 1:26) ***"And the Lord God formed man [the first Adam] of the dust of the ground, breathed into his nostrils the breath of life, and man became a living soul."*** (Genesis 2:7);

(C)   ***"…planted a garden eastward in Eden and there he put the man whom he had formed…to dress it and to keep it…"*** (Genesis 2:8, 15);

(D)   ***"…commanded the man, saying, of every tree of the garden thou***

89

mayest freely eat but of the tree of the knowledge of good and evil, thou shalt not eat of it…" (Genesis 2:16-17);

(E)   *"…said* It is not good that the man should be alone; *I will make him an help meet for him…*And the Lord God caused a deep sleep to fall upon Adam and he slept and he took one of his ribs and closed up the flesh instead thereof; And the rib which the Lord God had taken from man, made he a woman, and brought her unto the man. *And Adam said, This is now bone of my bones, and flesh of my flesh: she shall be called Woman, because she was taken out of Man…"* (Genesis 2:18, 21-24);

(F)   *"…said to them [Adam and Eve]* be fruitful, multiply, replenish, and subdue the earth it…" (Genesis 1:28);

(G)   looked down on the wickedness of mankind "and it repented the Lord that he had made man on the earth and it grieved him at his heart…" (Genesis 6:6);

(H)   and saw that "…the earth was corrupt and filled with violence… for all flesh had corrupted his way upon the earth…" (Genesis 6:11);

(I)   by grace selected Noah *"…a just man and perfect in his generations and Noah walked with God…"* (Genesis 6:9) *"And Noah was five hundred years old and begat Shem, Ham, and Japheth."* (Genesis 5:32);

(J)   *"…said unto Noah* [regarding Noah's Deluge]*,* The end of all flesh is come before me…behold, I will destroy them with the earth….*Make thee an ark of gopher wood; rooms shalt thou make in the ark, and shalt pitch it within and without with pitch.….And, behold I (even I) do bring a flood of waters upon the earth to destroy all flesh wherein is the breath of life from under heaven and every thing that is in the earth shall die…But with thee will I establish my covenant [Noahic Covenant]; and thou shalt come into the ark, thou and thy sons (Shem, Ham, and Japheth), thy wife, and thy sons' wives with thee. And of every living thing of all flesh, two of every sort shalt thou bring into the ark, to keep them alive with thee; they shall be male and female…Thus did Noah according to* *all that God commanded him, so did he.*" (Genesis 6:13-22) "*And Noah was six hundred (600) years old when the flood of waters was upon the earth.*" (Genesis 7:6);

(K)　"...said unto Noah and to his sons with him, behold, I establish my covenant with you and with your seed after you; and with every living creature that is with you, of the fowl, of the cattle, and of every beast, of the earth; from all that go out of the ark to every beast of the earth...for perpetual generations...*I do set my bow [The Colorful Rainbow] in the cloud, and it shall be for a token of a covenant between me and the earth...and I will remember my covenant...and the waters shall no more become a flood to destroy all flesh. And the bow shall be in the cloud and I will look upon it that I may remember the everlasting covenant between God and every living creature of all flesh that is upon the earth...*" (Genesis 9:8-17);

(L)　"*...came down to see the city and the tower which the children of men builded [in the land of Shinar]. And the Lord said, Behold the people is one and they have all one language; and this they begin to do and now nothing will be restrained from them, which they have imagined to do.* Go to, let us down, and there confound their language that they may not understand one another's speech. *So the Lord scattered them abroad from thence upon the face of all the earth and they left off to build the city. Therefore is the name of it called Babel; because the Lord did there confound the language of all the earth; and from hence did the Lord scatter them abroad upon the face of all the earth...*" (Genesis 11:5-9);

(M)　"*...said unto Abram* [Abrahamic Covenant], Get thee out of thy country, and from thy kindred, and from thy father's house, unto a land that I will shew thee. *And I will make of thee a great nation, and I will bless thee, and make thy name great and thou shalt be a blessing. And I will bless them that bless thee, and curse him that curseth thee: and in thee shall all families of the earth be blessed.*" (Genesis12:1-3) "*And*

Abram departed, as the Lord had spoken unto him; and Lot went with him: and Abram was seventy and five years old [75] when he departed out of Haran. And Abram took Sarai his wife, and Lot his brother's son, and all their substance that they had gathered, and the souls that they had gotten in Haran; and they went forth to go into the land of Canaan; and into the land of Canaan they came. And Abram passed through the land unto the place of Sichem, unto the plain of Moreh. And the Canaanite was then in the land. And the Lord appeared unto Abram, and said, Unto thy seed will I give this land: and there builded he an altar unto the Lord, who appeared unto him. And he removed from thence unto a mountain on the east of Bethel, and pitched his tent, having Bethel on the west; and Hai on the east: and there he builded an altar unto the Lord, and called upon the name of the Lord. And Abram journeyed, going on still toward the south." (Genesis 12:4-9);

(N)   "*...appeared to Abram who was ninety years old and nine [99], the Lord appeared to Abram, and said unto him, I am the Almighty God; walk before me, and be thou perfect. And I will make my covenant between me and thee, and will multiply thee exceedingly. And Abram fell on his face and God talk with him, saying, As for me, behold my covenant is with thee, and thou shalt be a father of many nations.* Neither shall thy name any more be called Abram, but thy name shall be Abraham; for a father of many nations have I made thee." (Genesis 17:1-5);

(O)   enlarged the Abrahamic Covenant, and said, "*And I will make thee [Abraham] exceeding fruitful, and I will make nations of thee, and kings shall come out of thee. And I will give unto thee and to thy seed* [referring to Isaac and Jacob] *after* thee *in their generations for an everlasting covenant to be a God unto thee and to thy seed after thee. And I will give unto thee and to thy seed after thee* The land where in thou art a stranger, all the land of Canaan for an everlasting possession; ***and I will be their God.*** " (Genesis 17:6-8);

(P) *"...sent me [Joseph] before you [the children of Jacob, Joseph's brethren]* to preserve you a posterity in the earth and to save your lives by a great deliverance...*it was not you that sent me hither, but God: and made me a father to Pharaoh and lord of all his house, and a ruler throughout all the land of Egypt..."* (Genesis 45:7-8);

(Q) *"...appeared unto Abraham in the plains of Mamre as he sat in the tent door in the heat of the day; And he lift up his eyes and looked, and, lo three men [God and two angels] stood by him; and when he saw them, he ran to meet them from the tent door, and bowed himself toward the ground."* (Genesis 18:1-2);

(R) *"...and said Shall I hide from Abraham that thing which I do. Seeing that Abraham shall surely become a great and mighty nation, and all the nations of the earth shall be blessed in him?* For I know him, *that he will command his children and his household after him, and they shall keep the way of the Lord, to do justice and judgment; that the Lord may bring upon Abraham that which he hath spoken of him. And the Lord said, Because the cry of Sodom and Gomorrah is great, and because their sin is very grievous; I will go down now and see whether they have done altogether according to the cry of it, which is come unto me; and if not, I will know. And the men turned their faces from thence, and went toward Sodom abut Abraham stood yet before the Lord."* (Genesis 18:17-22);

(S) *"...said if I find in Sodom fifty righteous within the city, then I will spare all the place for their sakes......And Abraham answered and said, Behold now, I have taken upon me to speak unto the Lord, which am but dust and ashes...Peradventure there shall lack five of the fifty righteous: wilt thou destroy all the city for lack of five? And he [God] said, If I find there forty and five, I will hot destroy it...And he [Abraham] spoke unto him yet again, and said, Peradventure there shall be forty found there....Peradventure there shall be thirty... Peradventure there shall be twenty... And Abraham said Oh let not the Lord be angry and I will speak yet but this once more... Peradventure then shall be found there ten...* And the Lord said, I will not destroy it for ten's sake. And the Lord went his way..." (Genesis 18:26, 32-33);

93

(T) *"...said unto Abram,* know of a surety that thy seed shall be a stranger in a land [Egypt] that is not theirs, and shall serve them; and they shall afflict them four hundred years (400). *And also that nation, whom they shall serve, will I judge and afterward shall they come out with great substance."* (Genesis 15:13);

(U) *"...I am the Lord thy God which have brought thee out of the land of Egypt out of the house of bondage. Ten Commandments: (1)* Thou shalt have no other gods before me; *(2)* Thou shalt not make unto thee any graven image or any likeness of anything that is in heaven above, or that is in the earth beneath, or that is in the water under the earth. *Thou shalt not bow down thyself to them, nor serve them; for I the Lord thy God am a jealous God, visiting the iniquity of the fathers upon the children unto the third and fourth generation of them that hate me; And shewing mercy unto thousands of them that love me, and keep my commandments; (3)* Thou shalt not take the name of the Lord thy God in vain *for the Lord will not hold him guiltless that taketh his name in vain; (4)* Remember the Sabbath day, to keep it holy. *Six days shalt thou labor and do all thy work: but the seventh day is the Sabbath of the Lord thy God; in it thou shalt not do any work, thou, nor thy son, nor thy daughter, thy manservant, nor thy maidservant, nor thy cattle, nor thy stranger that is within thy gates: For in six days the Lord made heaven and earth, the sea, and all that in them is, and rested the seventh day: wherefore the Lord blessed the Sabbath day, and hallowed it; (5)* Honor thy father and thy mother that thy days may be long upon the land which the Lord thy God giveth thee; *(6)* Thou shalt not kill; *(7)* Thou shalt not commit adultery; *(8)* Thou shalt not steal; *(9)* Thou shalt not bear false witness against thy neighbor; *(10)* Thou shalt not covet thy neighbor's house, thou shalt not covet thy neighbor's wife, nor his manservant, nor his maidservant, nor his ox, nor his ass, nor anything that is thy neighbor's. *And all the people saw the thunderings and the* lightnings, and the noise of the trumpet, and the mountain smoking: and when the people saw it, they removed, and stood afar off. And they said unto Moses, Speak thou with us, and we will hear: but let not God speak with us, lest we die. And Moses said unto the people, Fear not for God is come to prove you, and that his fear may be before your faces, that ye sin not. And the people stood afar off, and Moses drew near unto the thick darkness where God was. And the Lord said unto Moses, Thus thou shalt say unto the children of Israel, Ye have seen that I have talked with you from heaven. Ye shall not make with me gods of silver, neither shall ye make unto you gods of gold. An altar of earth thou shalt make unto me, and shalt sacrifice thereon thy burnt offerings, and thy peace offerings, thy sheep, and thine oxen: in all places where I record my name, I will come unto thee, and I will bless thee. And if thou wilt make me an altar of stone, thou shalt not build it of hewn stone: for if thou lift up thy tool upon it, thou hast polluted it. Neither shalt thou go up by steps unto mine altar, that thy nakedness be not discovered thereon." (Genesis 20:1-26);

(V) "...spake unto Joshua the son of Nun, Moses' minister, saying, Moses my servant is dead; now therefore arise, go over this Jordan, thou, and all this people, unto the land which I do give to them, even to the children of Israel. Every place that the sole of your foot shall tread upon, that have I given unto you, as I said unto Moses. From the wilderness and this Lebanon even unto the great river, the river Euphrates, all the land of the Hittites, and unto the great sea toward the going down of the sun, shall be your coast. There shall not any man be able to stand before thee all the days of thy life; as I was with Moses, so I will be with thee: I will not fail thee, nor forsake thee. Be strong and of a good courage: for unto this people shalt thou divide for an inheritance the land, which I sware unto their fathers to give them." (Joshua 1:1-5);

(W)   *"… said unto Joshua, This day will I begin to magnify thee in the sight of all Israel, that they may know that, as I was with Moses, so I will be with thee. And thou shalt command the priests that bear the ark of the covenant, saying, When ye are come to the brink of the water of Jordan, ye shall stand still in Jordan. And Joshua said unto the children of Israel, <u>Come hither and hear the words of the Lord your God. And Joshua said, Hereby ye shall know that the living God is among you, and that he will without fail drive out from before you the Canaanites, and the Hittites, and the Hivites, and the Perizzites, and the Girgashites, and the Amorites, and the Jebusites</u>…"* (Joshua 3:7-10);

(Joshua 3:14-17)
"And it came to pass, when the people removed from their tents, to pass over Jordan, and the priests bearing the ark of the covenant before the people; And as they that bare the ark were come unto Jordan and the feet of the priests that bare the ark were dipped in the brim of the water (for Jordan overfloweth all his banks all the time of harvest)…that the waters which came down from above stood and rose upon an heap very far from the city Adam [20 miles north of Jericho], *that is beside Zaretan: and those that came down toward the sea of the plain, even the salt sea, failed, and were cut off: and the people passed over right against Jericho. And the priest that bare the ark of the covenant of the Lord stood firm on dry ground in the midst of Jordan, and all the Israelites passed over on dry ground, until all the people were passed clean over Jordan;"*

(Joshua 4:1-10)
"And it came to pass when all the people were clean passed over Jordan, that the Lord spake unto Joshua saying, Take you twelve men out of the people, out of every tribe a man, And command ye them, saying, Take you hence out of the midst of Jordan, out of the place where the priests' feet stood firm, twelve stones, and ye shall carry

them over with you, and leave them in the lodging place, where ye shall lodge this night. Then Joshua called the twelve men, whom he had prepared of the children of Israel, out of every tribe a man... That this may be a sign among you that when your children ask their fathers in time to come, saying, What mean ye by these stones? Then ye shall answer them, That the waters of Jordan were cut off before the ark of the covenant of the Lord; when it passed over Jordan, the waters of Jordan were cut off: and these stones shall be for a memorial unto the children of Israel for ever. And the children of Israel did so as Joshua commanded, and took up twelve stones out of the midst of Jordan, as the Lord spake unto Joshua, according to the number of the tribes of the children of Israel and carried them over with them unto the place where they lodged, and laid them down there. And Joshua set up twelve stones in the midst of Jordan, tin the place where the feet of the priests which bare the ark of the covenant stood: and they are they unto this day. For the priest which bare the ark stood in the midst of Jordan, until every thing was finished that the Lord commanded Joshua to speak unto the people, according to all that Moses commanded Joshua: and the people hasted and passed over;"

(Joshua 4:14)

"On that day the Lord magnified Joshua in the sight of all Israel, and they feared him, as they feared Moses, all the days of his life; "

(Joshua 4:21-24)

"And he [Joshua] *spake unto the children of Israel, saying, When your children shall ask their fathers in time to come, saying What mean these stones? Then ye shall let your children know, saying, Israel came over this Jordan on dry land. For the Lord your God dried up the waters of Jordan from before you, until ye were passed over, as the Lord your God did to the Red Sea, which he dried up from before us, until we were gone over. That all the people of the earth might know the hand of the Lord, that it is mighty that ye might fear the Lord your God for ever;"*

(X)   "… dried up the waters of Jordan from before the children of Israel, until we were passed over, that their heart melted, neither was there spirit in them any more, because of the children of Israel. " (Joshua 5:1);   and

(Y)   "*…was straitly shut up* [Jericho] *because of the children of Israel: none went out, and none came in.* **And the Lord** *said* **unto Joshua, See, I have given into thine hand Jericho, and the king thereof, and the mighty men of valor. And ye shall compass the city, all ye men of war, and go round about the city once. Thus shalt thou do six days. And seven priests shall bear before the ark seven trumpets of rams' horns: and the seventh day ye shall compass the city seven times, and the priests shall blow with the trumpets. And it shall come to pass that when they make a long blast with the ram's horn, and when ye hear the sound of the trumpet, all the people shall shout with a great shout; and the wall of the city shall fall down flat, and the people shall ascend up every man straight before him."** (Joshua 6:1-5)

Finally, the Hebrew Boys knew about the darkest period of Israel's history (the Book of Judges) and the era of the kings of Israel and Judah, especially the story of the little shepherd boy (David) who was anointed the *king of Israel* (in place of king Saul). Also, the Hebrew Boys were contemporary with some of the major and minor prophets: Daniel, Jeremiah, and Ezekiel *(major prophets before the exile)*; and Haggai, Zechariah, and Malachi *(minor prophets after the exile).*

Although the Hebrew Boys never had a close encounter with Jesus, they believed in **Yahweh!** However, they never expected to personally meet the **Second Person of the GODHEAD!**

Chapter 14

The Son of God in the Fire

Basically, king Nebuchadnezzar said that he saw **THREE** men put into the fiery furnace but **FOUR** men were walking in the midst of the fire, no harm was done unto them, and that the fourth man looked like the SON OF GOD! *How prophetic and what a revelation*!

(Kurt's comments)

Kurt, *the Erzurum wolf,* said, "Just like Keci *(the old goat)*, I can't stand the suspense and I want to know one thing! Who was walking around with the Hebrew Boys in the fiery furnace?"

(Keci's comments)

"THAT'S RIGHT!" said, Keci *(the old goat)* "*Ah been asking the same thang* who was in the fire with the Hebrew Boys?"

(The Professor's comments)

Baykus said, "I was not there but I can tell you there is only one person who can perform miraculous things and His name is Jesus, "In the beginning was the Word, and the Word was with God, and the Word was God...And the WORD [JESUS] was made flesh, and dwelt among us and WE BEHOLD HIS GLORY, the glory as of the only begotten of the Father, full of grace and truth." (John 1:1, 14)

Then, the Professor said that the best one *present* to talk about the events *outside of the fiery furnace* is king Nebuchadnezzar! Although, the king was *transformed* into a Babylonian *werewolf*, he was still the king of Babylon because no body sat on his throne for seven years during his absence. All of Babylon took pity and respected the king's office!

Babylon's Fiery Furnace

The king said, "I'll tell you how this whole thing started and I will give you some information about Babylon's fiery furnace. Also, I can only tell you what I saw from a distance and what I have learned since the incident, but I will ask *the Professor* for his help concerning the **_Bible_**. The Babylonians kept a continual (year round) man-made *fiery furnace*. It was used for many purposes such as destroying unwanted things, burning deceased animals, dead bodies, and many times (as punishment) we threw lawbreakers and condemned criminals alive into the fiery furnace.

Types of Fires

Nebuchadnezzar said that fire can destroy, purify, or save but it depends on the type of fire: (a) man-made fires are used (in controlled environments) for burning, cooking, heating, and for weapons; (b) nature's fires are ignited by natural forces like the blazing sun and/or from within the earth as volcanic fires (i.e., flowing lava, hurling rocks, spewing matter into the atmosphere), gases and fumes (sipping through various cracks in the earth from eruptions, earthquakes, and violent tremors); (c) fire-balls from outer-space; and (d) God's fire, the most deadliest *(invincible, unquenchable, indestructible, unconquerable, impregnable, supreme, visible, invisible, and the Fire of fires).*

Nebuchadnezzar's Court Report

The Chaldean babble,

(The Chaldean Accusers)

"Wherefore at that time certain Chaldeans came near and accused the Jews. They spake and said to the king Nebuchadnezzar, O king, live for ever. Thou, O king, hast made a decree, that every many that shall hear the sound of the cornet, flute, harp, sackbut, psaltery, and dulcimer, and all kinds of musick, shall fall down and worship the golden image: and whoso falleth not down and worshippeth, that he should be cast into the midst of a burning fiery furnace.

There are certain Jews whom thou hast set over the affairs of the province of Babylon, Shadrach, Meshach, and Abednego; these men, O king, have not regarded thee: they serve not thy gods, nor worship the golden image which thou hast set up." (Daniel 3:8-12)

(The Hebrew Boys' Inquisition)

The Hebrew Boys had no trial or jury. Instead they went straight from the king's inquisition and slam-dunk verdict to the fire!

"Then Nebuchadnezzar in his rage and fury commanded to bring Shadrach, Meshach, and Abednego. Then they brought these men before the king. Nebuchadnezzar spake and said unto them, Is it true O Shadrach, Meshach, and Abednego, do not ye serve my gods, nor worship the golden image which I have set up? (Daniel 3:13-14)

(Fated Punishment)

King Nebuchadnezzar said that Shadrach, Meshach, and Abednego would not serve or worship Babylon's gods and they refused to bow-down before the newer golden image. Because of their refusal to worship the golden image, the king became fanatical and hopping mad. As king, he was willing to give the Hebrew Boys another chance.

"Now if ye be ready that at what time ye hear the sound of the cornet, flute, harp, a sackbut, psaltery, and dulcimer, and all kinds of musick, ye fall down and worship the image which I have made; well: but if ye worship not, ye shall be cast the same hour into the midst of a burning fiery furnace and who is that God that shall deliver you out of my hands?" (Daniel 3:15)

(Nebuchadnezzar's Full Blown Conceit)
(The Professor's comments)

Baykus saw how angry king Nebuchadnezzar was getting because the king started howling (like *a wolf*) between sentences! Thus, the Professor said, "That part of your animal life is over, *your majesty!* Allow me to speak for you. What's more, I must tell the truth and the truth will hurt. Please forgive me O great king and don't throw me into the fiery furnace!"

Baykus said that the king walked like other Gentiles *"...in the vanity of their mind...Having the understanding darkened, being alienated from the life of God through the ignorance that is in them, because of the blindness of their heart...Who being past feeling have given themselves over unto lasciviousness, to work all uncleanness with greediness..."* (Ephesians 4:17-19)

So, Baykus said that Nebuchadnezzar was *"besides himself"* (as usual) and believed himself more powerful than God. He said that the king was so short-tempered that he would kill people on sight for failing to do their jobs! In addition, Baykus said that the king was fickle and two-faced! Right after the king exalted and rewarded Daniel and the Hebrew Boys, the king *"...answered unto Daniel, and said, your* God is a God of gods, *and a* Lord of kings*..."* (Daniel 2:47) Then, Nebuchadnezzar erected a golden image (12 ½ by 125 feet) for everyone to worship! In fact, the Professor said that it the king made himself look like a fool! Furthermore, it was ludicrous for the king to assume the Hebrews would bow down to worship a false god! And, at the inquisition, king Nebuchadnezzar asked the Hebrew Boys, *"...do not ye serve my gods, nor worship the golden image which I have set up?* (Daniel 3:14) Humbly, the Hebrew Boys answered the king that they can only worship **The God of the Hebrews** not false gods. NEXT, the king insulted the Hebrew God buy asking the Hebrew Boys, *"...and who is that God that shall deliver you out of my hands?"* (Daniel 3:15) So, Baykus said that God's wrath was heated to the 100th degree of the Babylonian furnace and that's when God decided he would do a new thing to Nebuchadnezzar! It's coming...it's coming!

Professor Baykus said that it appeared the king was boiling-hot with the Hebrew Boys, because they would not serve Babylon's gods. Frankly, the Hebrew Boys did not completely surrender to the king's authority because: (a) they were *made* captives; (b) they were *made* orphans; (c) their birth names were changed; (d) they were permanently maimed; (e) they were forced to live with heathens; (f) they were always stressed and tempted to eat and drink foods they disliked; (g) they begged for ten (10) days to prove their diets were healthier than the king's meat; and (h) they were constantly harassed to worship idols and to provoke the **Living God, but they refused to bow down to idols.**

Basically, king Nebuchadnezzar wasn't mad because the Hebrew Boys wouldn't serve the golden image that was just another "fad." The king was angry because the Hebrew Boys refused to completely obey him and he was the great Nebuchadnezzar! Regarding the gods of Babylon, the Babylonians were getting tired of *Bel, Marduk* and *other gods and goddesses.* So they created a new god *(the golden image)* of fashionable interest, fanfare, and vainglory. Baykus smiled and said that the object was probably man-made in China! In short, the king's dignity was insulted because he was the greatest and most powerful king on earth. In his opinion, three *measly* little Hebrew eunuchs refused to bow down to *his majesty (the king of Babylon the Great)* and it bothered him! This was unacceptable! Moreover, the king and his wise men, chancellors, governors, viceroys, generals, captains, mighty men, nobles, and the citizens of Babylon felt inferior to the Hebrews, the Hebrew Boys, Daniel, and the One True, **Living God**. Certainly, there were some real issues going on!

The Hebrew Boys' Confidence in God

(The Professor's comments)

Professor Baykus said, "Listen to Shadrach, Meshach, and Abednego's polite answer to the king,"

*"O Nebuchadnezzar, we are not careful to answer thee in this matter. If it be so, our God whom we serve is able to deliver us from the burning fiery furnace, and he will deliver us out of thine hand, O king. **But if not, be it known unto thee, O king, that we will not serve thy gods, nor worship the golden image which thou hast set up."*** (Daniel 3:17-18)

The Hebrew Boys' Punishment

(The Professor's comments)

Baykus said the following,

The king's facial expression could have knocked the warts off a frog!

Immediately, king Nebuchadnezzar ordered the *mightiest men* from his army to arrest the three frail young Hebrew Boys who didn't even possess a slingshot. They were innocent *"book-worms, scholars, and eunuchs not trained in the art-of-war."* In fact, Shadrach, Meshach, and Abednego received no compassion or mercy. Instead, they were tossed into the fiery furnace. The behavior of Babylon's *mightiest warriors was totally out of character.*

"Then was Nebuchadnezzar full of fury and the form of his visage was changed against Shadrach, Meshach, and Abednego; therefore he

spake and commanded that they should heat the furnace one seven times more than it was wont to be heated.

<u>***And he commanded the most mighty men that were in his army to bind Shadrach, Meshach, and Abednego and to cast them into the burning fiery furnace.***</u>

Then these men were bound in their coats, their hosen, and their hats, and their other garments, and were cast into the midst of the burning fiery furnace." (Daniel 3:19-21); and

(The king's plan backfired)
"At the king's command, the furnace was made seven times hotter than its regular heat and the flames slew the men who threw in the Hebrew Boys. Miraculously, Shadrach, Meshach, and Abednego fell down bound and untouched into the midst of the fiery pit. Therefore because the king's commandment was urgent, and the furnace exceeding hot, the flame of the fire slew those men that took up Shadrach, Meshach, and Abednego. And these three men, Shadrach, Meshach, and Abednego, fell down bound into the midst of the burning fiery furnace.

Then Nebuchadnezzar the king was astonished, and rose up in haste, and spake, and said unto his counselors, Did not we cast three men bound into the midst of the fire? They answered and said unto the king, True, O king.

He [Nebuchadnezzar] answered and said, Lo I see four men loose, walking in the midst of the fire, and they have no hurt; and the form of the fourth is like the Son of God." (Daniel 3:22-25)

(The Professor's comments)
Baykus said that now I can get down to the nitty-gritty! The Hebrew Boys (as any human being) had every right to be afraid, *but they had great hope!* The **_Bible_** states, *"... for He hath said, I will never leave thee, nor forsake thee...* The Lord is my helper, and I will not fear what man shall do unto me....."* (Hebrews 13:5-6)

Getting Ready, Prior to the Fire

(The Professor's comments)

Professor Baykus said that the Hebrew Boys performed two special functions before going into the fire and they got ready the night before the fire! Also, the same God that was (past tense) with the Hebrew Boys is still here (present tense) and will be (future tense) throughout all Eternity!!!

☻Firstly, they put off the *"...former conversation of the old man which is corrupt according to the deceitful lusts."* (Ephesians 4:22)

☺Secondly, *"And* put on the new man which after God is created in righteousness and true holiness. *Wherefore putting away lying, speak every man truth with his neighbor: for we are members one of another. Be ye angry and sin not: let not the sun go down upon your wrath: Neither give place to the devil. Let him that stole steal no more but rather let him labor, working with his hands the thing which is good, that he may have to give to him that needeth. Let no corrupt communication proceed out of your mouth, but that which is good to the use of edifying, that it may minister grace unto the hearers. And grieve not the Holy Spirit of God, whereby ye are sealed unto the day of redemption. Let all bitterness, and wrath, and anger, and clamor, and evil speaking, be put away from you with all malice. And be ye kind one to another, tenderhearted, forgiving one another, even as God for Christ's sake hath forgiven you."* (Ephesians 4:23-32)

Cloaked with Special Armor

(The Professor's comments)

The Hebrew Boys were not just clothed with *just* ordinary garments ☺ They had on the very best protective covering, JESUS!

(The Whole Armor)

"Wherefore take unto you the whole armor of God that ye may be able to withstand in the evil day, and having done all, to stand.

Stand therefore, <u>having your loins girt about with truth</u>, and having <u>the breastplate of righteousness;</u>

And <u>your feet shod with the preparation of the gospel of peace;</u> Above all, taking <u>the shield of faith</u>, wherewith ye shall be able to quench all the fiery darts of the wicked.

And take <u>the helmet of salvation, and the sword of the Spirit</u>, which is the word of God." (Ephesians 6:11-17)

The Nebuchadnezzar's Affirmation

(Nebuchadnezzar's comments)

Nebuchadnezzar said, "Yes, I saw (with mine own eyes) the HOLY ONE walking around in the fiery furnace with the three Hebrew Boys. And without Him, they were doomed! I still get excited thinking about it! Truly, the HOLY ONE is JESUS (KING of Kings and LORD of Lords). Too bad, I did not have a camcorder or a cell phone to record the event. I would have taken pictures for the whole world to see them all alive and well!"

Continuing on, the king said that there was something *phenomenal* going on in the fiery furnace. Mr. Immortality Himself was in the Fiery Furnace, **Jesus!**

The king said, "I ordered the Babylonian furnace to be heated seven times hotter and no one on earth could withstand that much heat (even if they wore a space suit)." He said that the mighty men that threw Shadrach, Meshach, and Abednego into the fire were instantly slain by the intensive heat. (Daniel 3:22)

Constance Lee

"Up until now," said king Nebuchadnezzar, "I thought it was the heat of the Babylonian fire that killed these mighty warriors!" But the Babylonian fire did not kill the Hebrew Boys!!! Instead, the Hebrew Boys fell down bound and unharmed into the midst of the burning fiery furnace. Suddenly, the Three Boys were up walking around and unbound as free men (not burned victims or ghosts) with the HOLY ONE! So I determined that the HOLY ONE saved one group and destroyed the other!"

"Moreover," said king Nebuchadnezzar, "I determined that The HOLY ONE was ALREADY THERE in the Babylonian furnace! Now, I know it was the fire of the HOLY ONE that brought judgment upon my men. I know that the HOLY ONE's Purified Fire extinguished the **SIN** *in the Babylonian fire in the furnace.* Therefore, all of the Babylonian fire was swallowed up in *death* by the HOLY ONE's Fire. In other words, the Purified Fire of the Holy One *overpowered and ravished* the earthly fire that burned in the fiery furnace. Furthermore, the HOLY ONE has "All Power" in His Hands! In fact, I have a news statement for CNN! **"Jesus robbed death, hell, and the grave by protecting the Hebrew Boys within His Own immortality!"**

The Refiner's Fire

One of the attributes of the HOLY FIRE is THE REFINER'S FIRE, *"But who may abide the day of his coming? And who shall stand when he appeareth? For he is like a refiner's fire and like fullers' soap* [BOTH ARE METAPHORICAL REFERENCES TO PURIFICATION FROM SIN]. *And he shall sit as a refiner and purifier of silver: and he shall purify the sons of Levi and purge them as gold and silver that they may offer unto the Lord an offering in righteousness."* (Malachi 3:2-3) The HOLY ONE purged the Hebrew Boys from sin! JESUS is The Refiner and His HOLY FIRE is the "FIRE OF FIRES."

108

The **_Bible_** states, **_"But who may abide the day of his coming?"_** (Malachi 3:2) God will purge the earth of all sin. For this reason, God is preparing the LAKE OF FIRE (HELL'S FIRE) as divine justice to all sinners from every tribe of the earth throughout all ages. **Revelation 19:20 states**, (a) **_"And the beast was taken, and with him the false prophet that wrought miracles before him, with which he deceived them that had received the mark of the beast, and them that worshipped his image. These both were cast alive into a lake of fire burning with brimstone;"_** and (b) After one thousand years, **Revelation 20:10 states**, **_"... the devil that deceived them was cast into the lake of fire and brimstone, where the beast and the false prophet are and shall be tormented day and night for ever and ever."_**

Immortality in the Fires of God

There's only one conclusion to make. The king said that there is **_"Immortality in the Fires of God."_** Just like the Hebrew Boys were *immortalized* in the Babylonian fiery furnace, the Lake of Fire (in the Book of Revelation) will eternally burn and immortalize the devil, the false prophet, the beast, and sinners from all tribes, nations, ages, and dispensations.

TAKE HEED THIS WARNING! Avoid the Lake of Fire & Brimstone. Repent as soon as possible, **_"And if thy foot offend thee, cut it off: it is better for thee to enter halt into life [Heaven], than having two feet to be cast into hell, into the fire that never shall be quenched:_** Where the worm dieth not, and the fire is not quenched...For every one shall be salted with fire, and every sacrifice shall be salted with salt." (Mark 9:44, 46, 48)

The Watchers

King Nebuchadnezzar said, "Remember, I saw the Watcher and the HOLY ONE in my vision, **_"I saw in the visions of my head upon my bed, and, behold a_** watcher **_and an_** holy one **_came down from heaven..."_** (Daniel 4:13) The king said that the Watcher was an angel who came down to spy on the affairs of men! The Angel (Watcher) reported to the HOLY ONE as a newspaper reporter gives information to his editor. Then, the HOLY ONE decided that He (personally) would intervene! In His anger, the HOLY ONE said, "Excuse me to the Watcher, I need to jump into this, Myself!" And, He did! In fact, the Watcher watched the HOLY ONE descend into the fiery furnace without opening the furnace's door. Again, like I said, "The HOLY ONE was waiting to rescue [32] the Hebrew Boys on the other side of the closed door. When the mighty men opened the door to the furnace, the anger and Divine justice of the Holy One gave them a blast they will never forget!"

Remember, *"The eyes of the Lord are in every place beholding the good and the evil!"* (Proverbs 15:3) In other words, Daniel said, ___This matter is by **the decree** [announcement] *of the* Watchers **and the demand** [command] *by* **the Word** [declaration] *of the* Holy Ones___*: to the intent that the living may know that the most High ruleth in the kingdoms of men, and giveth it to whomsoever he will, and setteth up over it the basest of men."* (Daniel 4:17)

(The Professor's comments)

The Professor said that king David wrote a beautiful song regarding purification,"

(Psalm 51:7-19)

"Purge me with hyssop and I shall be clean: wash me and I shall be whiter than snow. Make me to hear joy and gladness; that the bones which thou hast broken may rejoice. Hide thy face from my sins, and blot out my iniquities. Create in me a clean heart, O God;

---

32 Note from the author. Don't worry! The Lord will rescue you! Just call on Him and stand firm on His Word. He will come through every time. The enemy is constantly setting traps for you and closing doors. The devil may be at your house, in your kids, in your spouse, in your boyfriend or girlfriend, mother, father, brother, sister, cousin, boss, supervisor, or somebody! He may be at your local bank, mortgage company, gym, school, or social club! The devil is the prince of the air. And like the air, he is everywhere! However, First John 4:4 reads, **"...GREATER IS HE [LORD JESUS] THAT IS IN YOU THAN HE THAT IS IN THE WORLD!"**

and renew a right spirit within me. Cast me not away from thy presence; and take not thy holy spirit from me. Restore unto me the joy of thy salvation; and uphold me with thy free spirit. Then will I teach transgressors thy ways; and sinners shall be converted unto thee. Deliver me from bloodguiltiness [33] *O God, thou God of my salvation: and my tongue shall sing aloud of thy righteousness. O Lord, open thou my lips; and my mouth shall shew forth thy praise. For thou desirest not sacrifice; else would I give it: thou delightest not in burnt offerings. The sacrifices of God are a broken spirit, O God, thou wilt not despise. Do good in thy good pleasure unto Zion: build thou the walls of Jerusalem. Then shalt thou be pleased with the sacrifices of righteousness, with burnt offering and whole burnt offering: then shall they offer bullocks upon thine altar."*

The Professor said there are more Scriptures regarding "purification" such as Proverbs 25:20; and Jeremiah 2:22; 4:14 which gives Israel and Judah metaphorical references of cleansing "sin" by washing with *fuller's* soap or niter. According to Webster's NewWorld Dictionary, the definition of niter (and its alternate spelling is *nitre*) is *(1) "a strong, alkaline solution obtained by leaching wood ashes;" (2) any strongly alkaline substance, usually sodium or potassium hydroxide. Lye is used in cleaning and making soap."*

God's Other Fires

(The Professor's comments)

As stated earlier, the **Bible** states there is an on-going fire in Hades. The Word of God warns us not to go there! *"And if thine eye offend*

---

33   King David's crime of passion and premeditated murder sent *Uriah the Hittite (Bathsheba's first husband)* out to die in battle with the Ammonites. Uriah was one of the king's *Mighty Men (hand picked warriors)*. David wrote a letter to his nephew, Joab (Commander-in-Chief) and sent the letter by Uriah's own hand, *"Set ye Uriah in the forefront of the hottest battle and retire ye from him, that he may be smitten, and die."* (II Samuel 11:15) This was heartless of king David! After Uriah's death, David married Bathsheba to hide their *sin of adultery* and the *pregnancy*. However, **Yahweh** dealt with them!

thee, pluck it out: it is better for thee to enter into the kingdom of God with one eye, than having two eyes to be cast into hell fire: Where their worm dieth not, and the fire is not quenched. For every one shall be salted with fire, and every sacrifice shall be salted with salt.” (Mark 9:47-49)

(Hell Fires of Sodom, Gomorrah & Cities of the Plain)

There was another huge fire that wiped out several cities in the Old Testament. One day, the **Lord GOD** confided in a friend about His intentions for certain sinful cities, *“And the Lord said, Shall I hide from Abraham that thing which I do? Seeing that Abraham shall surely become a great and mighty nation, and all the nations of the earth shall be blessed in him?”* (Genesis 18:17-18)

Because of the cities' horrible wickedness, the **Lord GOD** was on His way to destroy Sodom, Gomorrah, and the cities of the plain. With no luck, Abraham interceded on behalf of the wicked for the Lord to spare the cities but there weren't enough righteous souls (not even ten) living in the city to spare it from destruction. *“And he said, Oh let not the Lord be angry, and I will speak yet but this once: Peradventure ten shall be found there. And he said, I will not destroy it for ten's sake.”* (Genesis 18:32)

“And Abraham gat up early in the morning to the place where he stood before the Lord: And he looked toward Sodom and Gomorrah, and toward all the land of the plain, and beheld, and lo, the smoke of the country went up as the smoke of a furnace. And it came to pass, when God destroyed the cities of the plan, that God remembered Abraham, and sent Lot out of the midst of the overthrow, when he overthrew the cities in the which Lot dwelt.” (Genesis 19:27-29)

(Fires sent upon Two Priests)

"*And Nadab and Abihu* [the oldest] *two sons of Aaron, took either of them his censer, and put fire therein, and put incense thereon, and offered strange fire before the Lord, which he commanded them not. And there went out fire from the Lord, and devoured them, and they died before the Lord. Then Moses said unto Aaron, This is it that the Lord spake, saying, I will be sanctified in them that come nigh me, and before all the people I will be glorified. And Aaron held his peace.*" (Leviticus 10:1-3)

(Fire Warnings Given to Eleazar & Ithamar)

"*And Moses said unto Aaron, and unto Eleazar and unto Ithamar, his sons, Uncover not your heads, neither rend your clothes; lest ye die, and lest wrath come upon all the people: but let your brethren, the whole house of Israel bewail the burning which the Lord hath kindled. And ye shall not go out from the door of the tabernacle of the congregation, lest ye die: for the anoint oil of the Lord is upon you. And they did according to the word of Moses.*" (Leviticus 10:6-7)

(Fire Warnings, Against Graven Images)

"*Take heed unto yourselves, lest ye forget the covenant of the Lord your God, which he made with you, and make you a graven image, or the likeness of any thing, which the Lord thy God hath forbidden thee. For the Lord thy God is a consuming fire, even a jealous God.*" (Deuteronomy 4:23-24)

(Elijah Calls Down Fire From Heaven

"*And Elijah said unto all the people, Come near unto me. And all the people came near unto him. And he repaired the altar of the Lord that was broken down. And Elijah took twelve stones, according to the number of the tribes of the sons of Jacob, unto whom the word of the Lord came, saying, Israel shall be thy name: And with the stones he built an altar in the name of the Lord: and he made a trench about the altar, as great as would contain two measure of seed. And he put wood in order, and cut the bullock in pieces, and laid him on the wood, and said, Fill four barrels with water, and pour it on the burnt sacrifice, and on the wood. And he said, Do it the second time. And they did it the second time. And he said, Do it the third time. And they did it the third time. And the water ran round about the altar; and he filled the trench also with water.*

And it came to pass at the time of the offering of the evening sacrifice, that Elijah the prophet came near, and said, Lord God of Abraham, Isaac, and of Israel, let it be known this day that thou are God in Israel, and that I am thy servant, and that I have done all these things at thy word. Hear me, O Lord, hear me, that this people may know that thou art the Lord God, and that thou hast turned their heart back again.

<u>*Then the fire of the Lord fell, and consumed the burnt sacrifice, and the wood, and the stones, and the dust, and licked up the water that was in the trench.*</u> *And when all the people saw it, they fell on their faces: and they said, The Lord, he is the God; the Lord, he is the God.*" (I Kings 18:30-39)

(Fire of God burns 7,000 Sheep & Unknown Number of Servants)

"And there was day when his [Job] *sons and his daughters were eating and drinking wine in their eldest brother's house: and there came a messenger unto Job, and said, The oxen were plowing, and the asses feeding beside them: And the Sabeans fell upon them, and took them away; yea, they have slain the servants with the edge of the sword; and I only am escaped alone to tell thee. While he was yet speaking, there came also another, and said,* <u>*The fire of God is fallen*</u>

114

from heaven, and hath burned up the sheep, and the servants, and consumed them; and I only am escaped alone to tell thee..." (Job 1:13-16)

(Psalm of David Regarding Hell Fire)

"*Thine hand shall find out all thine enemies: thy right hand shall find out those that hate thee. Thou shalt make them as a fiery oven in the time of thine anger: the Lord shall swallow them up in his wrath, and the fire shall devour them. Their fruit shalt thou destroy from the earth, and their seed from among the children of men. For they intended evil against thee: they imagined a mischievous device, which they are not able to perform.*" (Psalm 21:8-11)

(Power in the Lord's Voice)

"*The voice of the Lord is upon the waters: the God of glory thundereth: the Lord is upon many waters. The voice of the Lord is powerful; the voice of the Lord is full of majesty. The voice of the Lord breaketh the cedars; yea, the Lord breaketh the cedars of Lebanon. He maketh them also to skip like a calf; Lebanon and Sirion like a young unicorn. **The voice of the Lord divideth the flames of fire.** The voice of the Lord shaketh the wilderness; the Lord shaketh the wilderness of Kadesh. The voice of the Lord maketh the hinds to calve, and discovereth the forests: and in his temple doth every one speak of his glory. The Lord sitteth upon the flood; yea, the Lord sitteth King for ever. The Lord will give strength unto his people with peace.*" (Psalm 29:3-11)

(A Fire Goeth Before God)

"*The Lord reigneth; let the earth rejoice; let the multitude of isles be glad thereof. Clouds and darkness are round about him; righteousness and judgment are the habitation of his throne A fire goeth before him, and burneth up his enemies round about. His lightnings enlightened the world: the earth saw, and trembled. The hills melted like wax at the presence of the Lord, at the presence of the Lord of the whole earth. The heaven declare his righteousness, and all the people see his glory."* (Psalm 97:1-6)

Chapter 15

The Hebrew Boys' Encounter With Jesus

Jesus "THE WORD" as FIRE

God said, "Is not my WORD like as a FIRE... *and* like a hammer that breaketh the rock in pieces?" (Jeremiah 23:29) And, the Gospel of John tells us, "In the beginning was the WORD, *and the* WORD *was with* GOD *and the* WORD *was* GOD. *The same was in the beginning with God. All things were made by him; and without him was not anything made that was made. In him was life; and the life was the light of men. And the light shineth in darkness; and the darkness comprehended it not...*And the WORD was made FLESH, and dwelt among us, *(and we beheld his glory, the glory as of the only begotten of the Father) full of grace and truth.*" (John 1:1-5, 14)

The Messianic Psalm 23

David faced *many attempted assassinations* on his life by: (1) king Saul and his men; and (2) and with warring nations (Philistines, Amalekites, Assyrians, Syrians, giants like *Goliath of Gath* and his *giant* brothers, and other *Rephaims*, giants). Regardless, king David trusted in the Lord. With all that in mind, David still found the time to "sing" and to compose songs. In this one particular song, David calls the **Lord**, Jehovah Roi (My Shepherd) as follows,

"The Lord is my shepherd; I shall not want. He maketh me to lie down in green pastures: he leadeth me beside the still waters. He restoreth my soul: he leadeth me in the paths of righteousness for his name's sake. Yea, though I walk through the valley of the shadow of death, I will fear no evil for thou art with me; thy rod and thy staff they comfort me. *Thou preparest a table before me in the presence of mine enemies: thou anointest my head with oil; my cup runneth over. Surely goodness and mercy shall follow me all the days of my life: and I will dwell in the house of the Lord for ever."*

Jesus in the Fiery Furnace

As stated earlier, this same **JESUS *(The Son of the Living God)*** was in the fiery furnace with the Three Hebrew Boys (engulfed in the midst of *fiery death)* and **JESUS** comforted them. Because, they took God at His WORD, their *extraordinary* faith protected them. We are assured of this because of Psalm 23:4, "Yea, though I walk through the valley of the shadow of death, I will fear no evil for thou art with me; thy rod and thy staff they comfort me..." Definitely, we know the Hebrew Boys had *plenty* light, comfort, and protection in the face of death!

The Hebrew Boys' Testimony Inside the Fiery Furnace

The time had come for The Hebrew Boys to speak up about the **Divine Deity** with them inside of the fiery furnace, "And the WORD was made FLESH, and dwelt among us... " (John 1:14)

(Shadrach's Testimony)

Shadrach said that they prayed all night for **Yahweh's** deliverance. Somehow, they believed that **Yahweh will make a way of escape but they did not how. The night before execution, they could not eat, drink, or sleep in anticipation of the pending punishment.** Early the next morning (before the sun arose), several fearful *mighty men* from the army came into their prison cell. These men bound them head to toe with ropes allowing them just enough slack to walk upright. As they arrived to the fiery furnace they saw the furnace keepers shoving more and more coals into the fiery furnace!

When the *mighty men* opened the furnace doors, there was a bright blinding flash of light *(like an atomic explosion)*. Shadrach said that he looked back at the *mighty men* and they were incinerated (within the blink of an eye) into a *simmering* pile of black ashes (at the opening of the furnace's door). He could not believe his eyes! These powerful warriors were fully dressed for battle with their helmets, swords, breastplates, and shields. They were melted down like tissue paper *as nothing* just like that! *How could this be?*

Quickly, Shadrach turned his head looking forward *(wondering why he and the other Hebrew Boys were not burned to ashes and there was no smell of fire on their clothes)* and he saw **"...seven golden candlesticks and in the midst of the seven candlesticks, one like unto the Son of Man..."** (Revelation 1:12-13) Without a doubt, there was Jesus, **Son of the Living God,** smiling at them. Shadrach said that *suddenly* they were standing with Jesus in the middle of the fiery furnace untouched by the fire! Jesus welcomed them into His bosom and told them that He was remarkably proud of their *unwavering* faith!

Jesus went on saying that in spite of the enormous pressure from king Nebuchadnezzar, the lying accusers, dishonest counsel members, and the entire wicked kingdom of Babylon, Jesus said that he was mighty proud of the Hebrew Boys. With all confidence, Jesus said, *"Where are your accusers?"* Then, Shadrach said that he looked back for the *smoking* pile of black ashes, but the furnace door was closed!

Shadrach said that Jesus' *"…great voice was as of a trumpet."* (Revelation 1:10) As they walked with the Divine One, Jesus said, *"I am Alpha and Omega, the beginning and the ending…which is, and which was, and which is to come, the Almighty.* (Revelation 1:8) Shadrach said that the Divine One kept repeating Himself, *"I am Alpha and Omega, the first and the last…"* (Revelation 1:11, 17-18) Strategically, the Divine One emphasized this point several times because He wanted them to know that there is none other like Him. Most certainly, there are no in-betweens. Shadrach said that he answered, "Yea, Lord."

Then, Shadrach said, *"…the Son of man was clothed with a garment down to the foot and girt about the paps with a golden girdle. His head and his hairs were white like wool, as white as snow; and his eyes were as a flame of fire. His feet were like unto fine brass, <u>as if they burned in a furnace</u> and his voice as the sound of many waters. And he had in his right hand seven stars. Out of his mouth went a sharp two-edged sword and his countenance was as the sun shineth in his strength."* (Revelation 1:12-15)

Shadrach said the shock of seeing all this took away his breath and spirit out of his body. However, his body (including the other Hebrew Boys) was glowing as if he was transformed from the *corruptible into the incorruptible!* He said they were rejoicing as if they'd lost their minds – they were invincible! Literally, this defied the laws of nature, physics, chemistry, and all the other sciences known to mankind. It was unbelievable, fantastic, out of this world!

Shadrach said, "As I looked down, the Divine One had seven stars in His right hand. I thought it was the most wonderful thing I've ever seen." He said that the stars were small, glowing, floating, and circling each other in the hand of the Divine One who said, "The mystery of the seven stars which thou sawest in my right hand, and the seven golden candlesticks [are as follows], The seven stars are the seven angels [messengers or pastors] of the seven churches and the seven candlesticks which thou sawest are the seven churches [Ephesus, Smyrna, Pergamos, Thyatira, Sardis, Philadelphia, Laodicea]." (Revelation 1:20)

Furthermore, the Divine One said, *"How then shall they call on him in whom they have not believed? And how shall they believe in him of whom they have not heard? And how shall they hear without a preacher?"* (Romans 10:14)

Moving on, the Divine One said, *"I know your works, your labor, your patience and that you cannot bear those who are evil. And you have tested those who say they are apostles and are not, and have found them liars. And you have persevered and have patience, and have labored for My name's sake and have not become weary…He who has an ear, let him hear what the Spirit says to the churches. <u>To him who overcomes I will give to eat from the tree of life which is in the midst of the Paradise of God</u>.*" (Revelation 2:1-3, 7)

(Meshach's Testimony)

Secondly, Meshach thought he passed from life to death and was part of the *spirit* world. However, he was still surrounded by the most unusual fire that burned people at will, and he was certain (being a devout Hebrew) that he was not in Hades with the lost souls. On the other hand, he was not in Paradise because he did not see his natural Father, Mother, Abraham or Lazarus or even the Great Divide! If this was Paradise, where was the Great Divide?

Yet there was complete comfort, perfection, and joy for Meshach (including the other Hebrew Boys) in the midst of the fiery furnace. Why? Meshach could not believe the fire didn't burn his flesh or clothes. For sure, his clothes *were not* fireproof! Like Shadrach and Abednego, Meshach saw the *simmering pile of ashes of the mighty men* (before the furnace door closed). The smoldering remains of the mighty men (killed in their military garbs) mesmerized Meshach who was a scholar not a warrior! These soldiers were just obeying the king's orders but God's wrath prevailed against them! So, following man's orders *don't make it right*! Yet, the same fire did not destroy the Hebrew Boys. Instead, they survived and they walked, danced the *hully-gully*, *skipped-to-my-Lou*, and leaped for joy with **JESUS** *in the middle of the furnace*!

The Divine One said, *"I am the First and the Last, who was dead, and came to life. I know your works, tribulation, and poverty (but you are rich); and I know the blasphemy of those who say they are Jews and are not,* [including that heathen king Nebuchadnezzar and those wicked Babylonians] *but are the synagogue of Satan. Do not fear any of those things you suffer. Indeed, the devil is...testing you...be faithful unto death, and I will give you the crown of life. He who has an ear, let him hear what the Spirit says to the churches. He who overcomes shall not be hurt by the second death."* (Revelation 2:8-11)

With tears of joy in his eyes, Meshach said that he marveled at the fact the Divine One came down to save them. This made Meshach feel very honored! More so, the Divine One understood their sufferings: deaths of their parents, loss of wealth and inheritance rights, and deportation as *"princes"* of Jerusalem to *"captives"* to *"poor eunuchs"* in Babylon. The first trauma (loosing their parents) was devastating. Meshach and the other Hebrew Boys learned to live in poverty without material goods. However, the last trauma was extremely difficult being made eunuchs in a heathen land and *never being able to produce off springs*. In this respect, the Hebrew Boys were robbed of the possibilities of marriage and relationships between husbands and wives.

(Abednego's Testimony)

Thirdly, Abednego said, *"These things said the <u>Son of God</u> (who has eyes like a flame of fire, and His feet like fine brass): I know your works, love, service, faith, and your patience, and as for your works, the last are more than the first....I am He who searches the minds and hearts. And I will give to each one of you according to your works... Hold fast what you have till I come...And he who overcomes and keeps My works until the end, to him I will give power over the nations...*

122

And I will give him the morning star...He who has an ear, let him hear what the Spirit says to the churches..." (Revelation 2:18-29)

Abednego said that **JESUS** had seven stars in His right hand which are the Seven Spirits of God: *(1) Love=God; (2) wisdom; (3) understanding; (4) counsel; (5) might; (6) knowledge; and (7) fear or reverence for God.* (Isaiah 11:2)   Then, the Son of God said, *"You have a few names ... who have not defiled their garments; and they shall walk with Me in white, for they are worthy...He who overcomes shall be clothed in white garments, and I will not blot out his name from the Book of Life; but I will confess his name before My Father and before His Angels. He who has an ear, let him hear what the Spirit says to the churches."* (Revelation 3:1-2, 4-6)

What's more, He who is holy, He who is true, He who has the key of David, and He who opens and no one shuts, and shuts and no one opens said, *" I know your works. Ye I have set before you an open door, and no one can shut it; for you have a little strength, have kept My word, and have not denied My name. Indeed I will make those of the synagogue of Satan, who say they are Jews and are not, but lie... indeed I will make them come and worship before your feet, and to know that I have loved you. Because you have kept My command to persevere, I also will keep you from the hour of trial which shall come upon the whole world to test those who dwell on the earth...Hold fast what you have that no one may take your crown...He who overcomes, I will make him a pillar in the temple of My God, and he shall go out no more."* (Revelation 3:7-12)

In addition, Abednego said that the Divine One said something about putting Tattoos on certain people! *"I will write on him the name of My God and the name of the city of My God, the New Jerusalem, which comes down out of heaven from My God. And I will write on him My new name. He who has an ear, let him hear what the Spirit says to the churches."* (Revelation 3:13)

Finally, Abednego said that the Divine One *(also called himself: the Amen, the Faithful, and True Witness)* made the following statement, ***"I Know your works...I counsel you to buy from Me gold refined in the fire that you may be rich and white garments that you may be clothed...Behold I stand at the door and knock. If anyone hears My voice and opens the door, I will come in to him and dine with him, and he with Me. To him who overcomes I will grant to sit with me on My throne, as I also overcame and sat down with My Father on His throne. He who has an ear, let him hear what the Spirit says to the churches."*** (Revelation 3:14-15a, 18, 20-22)

God's Light in the Fiery Furnace

Because the Hebrew Boys were in **"The *LIGHT*" (and that Light is the Son of God)**, they had *fellowship* not only with one another but also with Jesus Christ **(The *LIGHT)*** in the midst of the fiery furnace *in the very presence and shadow of death*. Furthermore, they were sinless! In fact, the Hebrew Boys were dripping in the Blood of the Lamb already ***"...slain from the foundation of the world."*** (Revelation 13:8) The **Bible** states, ***"But if we walk in the light, as he is in the light, we have fellowship one with another,*** and the blood of Jesus Christ, his Son cleanseth us from all sin." (I John 1:7)

Having all power, Jesus' "sanctification, purity, and fire" *consumed* (ate up) the blazing Babylonian fire *(its sinful nature, robbed death, hell, and the grave)* and gave the Three Hebrew Boys "immortality" in **The Light or Pre-Incarnate, JESUS. After JESUS left the fiery furnace, the Hebrew Boys stepped back into mortality (out-of-immortality) and the Babylonian fire returned to its sinful nature! Without the presence of the Lord there is sin!**

Immortality in the Light

According to Apostle Paul, **God** (synonymous is light) has authority for ever over EVERYTHING in heaven and earth including: those who are sick, lame, shut-in, lonely-in-heart, dying, deaf, dumb, blind, without speech, the dead. Also, He has control over the elements, the galaxies, the universe, and over a myriad of things.

"Which in his time shall shew, who is the blessed and only Potentate, the King of kings, and Lord of lords; Who only hath immortality, dwelling in the light *which no man can approach unto; whom no man hath seen, nor can see: to whom be honour and power everlasting."* (I Timothy 6:15-16)

Light Sprung in the Shadow of Death

However, we are focusing on the two phrases: *"shadow of death"* and *"light is sprung up."* According to Matthew 4:16, *"The people which sat in darkness saw great light: and to them which sat in the region and shadow of death light is sprung up."* Of course, this passage speaks of Jesus' visit to Capernaum [34] (by the Sea of Galilee) that bordered the **tribes of Zebulun** [35] *(means = dwelling, habitation)*, Jacob's tenth son and and **Naphtali** [36] *(means = my wrestling)*, Jacob's sixth son.

The Hebrew Boys stood face to face with the *"shadow of death,"* and at the same time, they stood face to face with *"the light which sprung up within the fiery furnace."* Unlike the people of Capernaum (in the Book of Matthew 4:16) who sat in the *shadow of death* and did not

---

34   Capernaum is not mentioned in the Old Testament. In the New Testament, Capernaum was a large city with a Jewish Synagogue (built and put their by Rome's government to collect taxes), and the headquarters for Jesus' ministry.
35   Leah was the Mother of Zebulun.
36   Bilhah (Rachel's maid) was the Mother of Naphtali.

understand meaning of the *great light,* **the Hebrew Boys understood the meaning of** shadow of death **and *the*** great light. Also, they were aware of the presence of God!

The Shekinah Glory of God

The word Shekinah means ***"that which dwells"*** and is used to speak of **the presence of God (Yahweh)**. In His presence there is love, joy, peace, goodness, happiness, life, and so forth. In human language, the Shekinah Glory is incomprehensible! Because God is Divine and His Glory is infinite, the human mind *cannot* understand the things of God. Only the *Spirit of God* which dwells in believers can understand the things of God!

(Moses and the Glory of God)

Moses saw just a little of the glory of God. The only difference is that Moses asked to see God's glory but was only allowed to see the back parts of God.

"And he [Moses] said, I beseech thee, shew me thy glory. And he [God] said, I will make all my goodness pass before thee, and I will proclaim the name for the Lord before thee; and will be gracious to whom I will be gracious, and will shew mercy on whom I will shew mercy. And he said, thou canst not see my face: for there shall no man see me, and live. And the Lord said, Behold there is a place by me, and thou shalt stand upon a rock:

"And it shall come to pass, while my glory passeth by, that I will put thee in a clift of the rock, and will cover thee with my hand while I pass by:

And I will take away mine hand, and thou shalt see my back parts: but my face shall not be seen." (Exodus 33: 11-23)

(Nebuchadnezzar Saw the "Glory of God")

Unlike Moses who asked to see the *"Glory of God,"* king Nebuchadnezzar did not ask to see the *"Glory,"* but God allowed the king to witness a spectacular event! Because Nebuchadnezzar was the choice vessel to correct and to save God's chosen people, God permitted the king (from his palace window) to see part of His Glory in the fiery furnace. However, Nebuchadnezzar did not fully understand the Glory of God, he just said, *"I see four men loose, walking in the midst of the fire, and they have no hurt;* and the form of the fourth is like the Son of God."* (Daniel 3:25)

Where were the Other Hebrew Captives?

For some unknown reason, there were only THREE HEBREW BOYS spotted at the ceremony (of the golden image) who refused to bow down and worship. What happened to the rest of the captives about twelve thousand or more, including Daniel?

This is an anomaly because everyone in Babylon was summoned to the dedication service including the captives (the Hebrew Nation). However, there is no explanation why Daniel or the Hebrew captives were not spotted (if present at the ceremony) and arrested. Surely, king Nebuchadnezzar could not burn all twelve thousands (or more) of Hebrew captives in the fiery furnace!

Certainly, Daniel would never bow down to the golden image. There is only one excuse for Daniel's absence. Maybe Daniel was indoors taking care of official business. But this does not account or excuse the rest of the Hebrew Nation's absence from the dedication. Lets assume the Hebrew

127

captives were present! In fear of the consequences, perhaps, they bowed down to the *golden image*. This does not mean that they worshipped the golden image (in their hearts), but they made the appearance of paying homage to it! However, the **_Bible_** does not explain why three little eunuchs out of thousands of people were arrested.

God Uses Whom He Wills

True, God used king Nebuchadnezzar *(a heathen)* to inflict judgment on Jerusalem. At God's command, the children of Israel were captives in Babylon and their princes were made eunuchs in the palace of the king. This fact remains unchanged regardless to the circumstances! What's more, God had further plans for the king (one of the most *infamous* kings in Biblical History) and The Great City of Babylon (one of the Seven Wonders of the World).

The **Lord GOD** can use whom so ever He wills (including *heathens, degenerates, and righteous people* to carry-out **His Will**)! In the *Old Testament*, read the story of Balaam. (Numbers 22:21-20) God used Balaam (a false prophet) and his donkey to carry out His Word. The donkey *saw the Angel of the Lord,* opened his mouth, and spoke in *the human tongue* warning Balaam of the impending danger. In the *New Testament*, Apostle Peter talks about Balaam's sin, ***"Having eyes full of adultery that cannot cease from sin; beguiling unstable souls…Which have forsaken the right way and are gone astray following the way of Balaam the son of Bosor, who loved the wages of unrighteousness…But was rebuked for his iniquity: the dumb ass speaking with man's voice forbad the madness of the prophet…These are wells without water, clouds that are carried with a tempest*** [FALSE PROPHETS AND TEACHERS FULL OF EMPTINESS AND SIN]…"** (II Peter 2:14-17)

Like Balaam *(a false prophet),* the people of Babylon and other eastern religions worshiped false gods and rebelled against the True Living GOD. In Balaam's earlier years, he was a true prophet. But, in his latter years,

Balaam was backslidden, estranged from God, and was killed by Moses in a battle. Unlike Balaam, king Nebuchadnezzar will make *an-about-face* at the latter end of his life! A terrible and breath taking event will force Nebuchadnezzar to admit there is only One True Living GOD!

Unwavering Faith & The Hebrew Boys

Without question, the Hebrew Boys had *extraordinary* faith! According to their upbringing and age, these boys were exceptional! If a worldwide search could be conducted throughout the ages, there are very few cases (with the exception of Noah, Daniel in the lion's den, and the first century Christian martyrs murdered in the Roman arena) who exhibited remarkable faith as "The Hebrew Boys."

Their "unwavering faith" is an example for all people of the earth to take notice and imitate! Hebrews 10:23 states, ***"Let us hold fast the profession of our faith without wavering for he is faithful that promised."*** And, Hebrews 11:6 states, "But without faith, it is impossible to please him: for he that cometh to God must believe that he is, and that he is a rewarder of them that diligently seek him."

Faith saved the Hebrew Boys! Before Hananiah, Mishael, and Azariah (the original names of the Three Hebrew Boys) were cast into the fire, their homework was done! **In fact, JEHOVAH saved them before they got into the fiery furnace!** Why? Before the foundation of the world, their names were already recorded in the Lamb's Book of Life. What an awesome fact for all believers! The Lord Jesus was compassionately waiting for them inside the fire. However, the night before the fiery experience, the Hebrew Boys: (a) prayed all night to **Yahweh**; (b) kept solid testimonies about **Yahweh**; (c) reaffirmed their faith in **Yahweh**; and (d) were willing to perish for their beliefs in **Yahweh!**

As stated so many times, the king's mighty men were burned-up at the entrance door to the fiery furnace but the Hebrew Boys were saved! JEHOVAH greeted both parties at the entrance door to the fiery furnace. However, these *so-called* mighty men were defenseless against The Lord's fire. Besides, JEHOVAH'S FIRE engulfed and overpowered the flames of the Babylonian *sinful* fire; so the Babylonian fire no longer existed inside the fiery furnace!

Jehovah's Revenge

The **_Bible_** states, "And whosoever shall offend one of these little ones that believe in me, it is better for him that a millstone were hanged about his neck, and he were cast into the sea." (Mark 9:42)

Also, the **_Bible_** says, **_"The Lord thy God is a consuming fire..."_** (Deuteronomy 4:24) Furthermore, Moses said, "Understand therefore this day, that the Lord thy God is he which goeth over before thee; as a consuming fire he shall destroy them, and he shall bring them down before thy face: so shalt thou drive them out, and destroy them quickly, as the Lord hath said unto thee." (Deuteronomy 9:3)

Trials by Fire

Don't forget, the Babylonian's fiery furnace was heated seven (7) times hotter; yet, its heat was no match for JEHOVAH'S FIRE. Coincidentally, the Bible speaks of the number seven (7) and fire, "The words of the Lord are pure words: as silver tried in a furnace of earth, purified seven times." (Psalm 12:6) In this sense, the silver is purified of all dross, scum, and worthless matter.

Apostle Peter states that the believers faith is perfected by fire, **_"Wherein ye greatly rejoice, though now for a season, if need be, ye are in heaviness through manifold temptations:_** That the trial of your faith being much more precious than of gold that perish, though it be tried with fire, ***might be found unto praise and honor and glory at the appearing of Jesus Christ.*** " (I Peter 1:7)

James, the servant of God and of the Lord Jesus Christ, states, "Blessed is the man that endureth temptation: for when he is tried, he shall receive the crown of life, which the Lord hath promised to them that love him." (James 1:12)

In the Book of Revelation, Apostle John talks about faith, "I counsel thee to buy of me gold tried in the fire, that thou mayest be rich; ***and white raiment, that thou mayest be clothed, and that the shame of thy nakedness do not appear; and anoint thine eyes with eyesalve, that thou mayest see.*** " (Revelation 3:18)

The Whole World is Guilty of Sin

In the New Testament, Apostle Paul states that the entire world is guilty before God, ***"For the wrath of God is revealed from heaven against all ungodliness and unrighteousness of men, who hold the truth in unrighteousness. Because that which may be known of God is manifest in them; for God hath shewed it unto them. For the invisible things of him from the creation of the world are clearly seen, being understood by the things that are made, even his eternal power and Godhead; so that they are without excuse. Because that, when they knew God, they glorified him not as God, neither were thankful; but became vain in their imaginations, and their foolish heart was darkened.*** Professing themselves to be wise, they became fools, and changed the glory of the uncorruptible God into an image made like to corruptible man, and to birds, and fourfooted beasts, and creeping things. ***Wherefore God also gave them up to uncleanness through the lusts of their own hearts, to dishonor their own bodies between themselves.*** " (Romans 1:19-24)

Constance Lee

(The Professor's comments)

Baykus said that cruelty is the mother of all beasts! There is no mercy in the animal kingdom or among men who were made in the image of God. This hardhearted and hateful world owes its failures to sin! Basically, it's the same old story!

God loves every inch of His *Creation* from heaven *"...his throne..."* (Isaiah 66:1) to earth because *"...it is his footstool..."* (Isaiah 66:1) ***"And, God created man in his own image, in the image of God created he him; male and female created he them. And God blessed them [Adam and Eve], and God said unto them,*** Be fruitful, and multiply, and replenish the earth, and subdue it: ***and have dominion over the fish of the sea, and over every living thing that moveth upon the earth. And God said, Behold, I have given you every herb bearing seed, which is upon the face of all the earth, and every tree, in the which is the fruit of a tree yielding seed; to you it shall be for meat. And to every beast of the earth, and to every fowl of the air, and to every thing that creepeth upon the earth, wherein there is life, I have I have given every green herb for meat: and it was so. And God saw everything that he had made, and, behold, it was very good. And the evening and the morning were the sixth day."*** (Genesis 1:27-31)

Sin Is the Blame

Baykus said, "Adam and Eve could not follow God's instructions!" They failed to obey God's commandment, ***"Of every tree of the garden thou mayest freely eat;*** But of the tree of the knowledge of good and evil, thou shalt not eat of it: ***for in the day that thou eatest thereof thou shalt surely die."*** (Genesis 2:15-17) Adam and Eve ate the "forbidden fruit" and they experienced a *spiritual separation from God!* In that sense of the word *"spiritual death not physical death,"* God expelled Adam and Eve from the Garden of Eden.

God's Plan of Redemption

Because the first Adam failed, all mankind slipped into sin! Baykus said that people want to do right but they cannot fight against the principalities of darkness and spiritual wickedness. But don't worry! For a while, the situation looked hopeless, but God called on the second Adam to step into the picture! God had a plan of redemption for mankind, JESUS, **The Lamb of God.**

Chapter 16

Isaiah's Prophecies of Judah

So, God devised ways to speak to His people! "God who at sundry times and in divers manners spake in time past unto the fathers by the prophets." (Hebrews 1:1)

The Prophet Isaiah

Isaiah *(means = the Lord is salvation)* was the son of Amoz and born into a prominent, respectable family in Jerusalem. As an upper class citizen, Isaiah had first hand information concerning the injustices of government, political, foreign, economic, class struggles, and cultural policies, and issues in Jerusalem. Although, Isaiah was aware of the "sin" in the city, he was not authorized to address these issues or preach to the people. Being born into a highly regarded family did not make Isaiah a qualified candidate for **Yahweh's** work! In fact, none of the other attributes such as *good looks, money, talent, or education* qualified Isaiah (or anyone) to serve the Lord who selects, calls, commissions, anoints, and empowers at will! In fact, Apostle Peter said, ***"Of a truth I perceive that God is no respecter of persons."*** (Acts 10:34) However, Isaiah was a willing candidate! Moreover, Peter said, ***"How God anointed Jesus of Nazareth with the Holy Ghost and with power: who went about doing good, and healing all that were oppressed of the devil; for God was with him."*** (Acts 10:38)

Isaiah admitted that he was unworthy, *"Woe is me for I am undone because I am a man of unclean lips, and I dwell in the midst of a people of unclean lips: for mine eyes have seen the King, the Lord of hosts."* (Isaiah 6:5) But, God fixed that problem! Isaiah states, *"Then flew one of the seraphims unto me having a live coal in his hand which he had taken with the tongs from off the altar: And he laid it upon my mouth, and said, Lo, this hath touched thy lips; and thine iniquity is taken away, and they sin purged."* (Isaiah 6:6-7)

Isaiah's Call & Commission

One day, Isaiah was in the Holies of Holy (Solomon's Temple, *Jerusalem*) and he saw a vision of the Lord! "In the year that king Uzziah died I [Isaiah] saw also the Lord sitting upon a throne, high and lifted up, and his train filled the temple. Above it stood the seraphims: each one had six wings; with twain he covered his face, and with twain he covered his feet and with twain he did fly. And one cried unto another and said, Holy, holy, holy, is the Lord of hosts: the whole earth is full of his glory. And the posts of the door moved at the voice of him that cried, and the house was filled with smoke." (Isaiah 6:1-4)

(The Dialog)

The Question: So, **Yahweh** said, *"Whom shall I send, and who will go for us?"* (Isaiah 6:8)

The Answer: "Then said I [Isaiah], Here am I; send me." (Isaiah 6:8)

The Commission: *"And he* **[Yahweh]** *said, Go and tell this people, Hear ye indeed but understand not; and see ye indeed but perceive not. Make the heart of this people fat, and make their ears heavy, and shut their eyes; lest they see with their eyes, and hear with their*

Constance Lee

ears, and understand with their heart, and convert, and be healed." (Isaiah 6:9-10)

The Question: *"Then said I [Isaiah] , Lord how long?* (Isaiah 6:11)

The Answer: "And *He [Yahweh] answered* Until the cities be wasted without inhabitant, and the houses without man, and the land be utterly desolate. **And the Lord have removed men far away, and there be a great forsaking in the midst of the land."** (Isaiah 6:11-12)

Regarding spiritual revelations for Jerusalem, God advertised for a prophet and put out an S.O.S. for the right candidate! As stated earlier, Jerusalem was filled with iniquity and God wanted to warn His people and give them a chance to repent or else! As always, God allows people the choice to do *"right or wrong."* As usual, **Yahweh** was looking for a spokesperson.

God called, commissioned, prepared, anointed, and empowered Isaiah for the position of prophet. Isaiah (who lived and prophesied about 792 to 722 B.C.) means "Yahweh saves or the Lord is salvation." Without doubt, Isaiah knew *exactly* what he was doing when he said, "...send me." (Isaiah 6:8)

Coincidentally, the *Book of Isaiah* has as many chapters as the Books of the Bible, sixty-six (66) in total. Like the Bible, the *Book of Isaiah* is divided into two parts: (1) The first thirty-nine (39) chapters talks about judgment and punishment (because of sin, apostasy, and idolatry) for Jews *(including their captivity)* and Gentiles alike; and (2) The remaining twenty-seven (27) chapters talks about redemption for the Jews and Gentiles, the Millennium, and the *New Heaven and Earth* which shall remain for ever. There is just one uncertainty! It is not known if Isaiah could *see* his horrible execution – *he was cut in two pieces.*

Isaiah's ministry spanned through the following kings of Judah,

136

king Uzziah (just before his death about 791-740 B.C.);
king Jotham (about 750-736 B.C.);
king Ahaz (about 736-716 B.C.); and
king Hezekiah (about 716-687 B.C.)

Isaiah's Notice to the Celestial and Terrestrial

Prophet Isaiah said, "Hear, O heavens, and give ear, O earth: for the Lord hath spoken, I have nourished and brought up children, and they have rebelled against me. The ox knoweth his owner and the ass his master's crib but Israel doth not know, my people doth not consider. A sinful nation, a people laden with iniquity, a seed of evildoers, children that are corrupters: they have forsaken the Lord, they have provoked the Holy One of Israel unto anger, they are gone away backward." (Isaiah 1:2-4)

Isaiah's Family, Chosen

Isaiah testified that his family was chosen by **Yahweh**, *"Behold, I and the children whom the Lord hath given me are for signs and for wonders in Israel from the Lord of Hosts, which dwelleth in mount Zion."* (Isaiah 8:18)

When God selects a person to speak or minister on His behalf, God may use that person's entire family (or selective members of the person's family) as instruments of instruction, type, or revelation as a podium for His WORD. Remember, God is Omnipotent (all powerful), Omnipresent (always present), and Omniscient (all knowing)!

The Isaiah's (Mr. and Mrs.) had two sons and both of their names were *prophetically* used in God's messages to His people. In this regard, their sons were used as forecasts to the Nation of Israel and they were critical to Isaiah's ministry. Mrs. Isaiah carried Isaiah's seeds in her womb and without her there were no children! Moreover, Mrs. Isaiah was not an ordinary woman: she was a prophetess and a holy woman of God. Yet, there is no mention of her name but what an honor to be the wife of one of the greatest men of God and recognized in the **_Bible_** as a *prophetess and holy woman.*

(A) The first son was named Shear-jashub that means = a remnant shall return.

Before the child was weaned from his Mother's milk or had the intelligence *to accept good and reject evil* (Isaiah 7:15), God warned Judah: not to worry about the king of Syria and the king of Israel *(Northern Tribe)*; **not to trust in Assyria or else God's wrath would come upon them**; mercifully, a small group would be saved in Judah; the intruding kings would be meet justice; God told Ahaz to ask for a sign; then, God gave the *miraculous* sign yet to come.

(God's Word)
    "*And it came to pass in the days of Ahaz the son of Jotham, the son of Uzziah, king of Judah, that Rezin the king of Syria, and Pekah the son of Remaliah, king of Israel, went up toward Jerusalem to war against it, but could not prevail against it. And it was told the house of David, saying,* Syria is confederate with Ephraim [the ten tribes of the Northern Kingdom]. **And his heart was moved, and the heart of his people, as the trees of the wood are moved with the wind.**" (Isaiah 7:1-2)

(Isaiah 7:3-17)
    "***The Lord said unto Isaiah, Go forth now to meet*** *Ahaz [king of the Northern Tribe of Israel]* **and** Shear-jashub thy son, ***at the end of the conduit of the upper pool in the highway of the fuller's field;*** And say unto him, Take heed, and be quiet: fear not neither be fainthearted for the two tails of these smoking firebrands, ***for the fierce anger of Rezin with Syria, and of the son of Remaliah.***

Because Syria [king Rezin], Ephraim [king Pekah of Israel]³⁷ and the son of Remaliah, have taken evil counsel against thee, saying, Let us go up against Judah, and vex it, and let us make a breach therein for us, and set a king in the midst of it, even the son of Tabeal. Thus saith the Lord God, It shall not stand, neither shall to come to pass.

For the head of Syria is Damascus, and the head of Damascus is Rezin; and within threescore and five years shall Ephraim be broken, that it be not a people. And the head of Ephraim is Samaria, and the head of Samaria is Remaliah's son. If ye will not believe, surely ye shall not be established.

Moreover the Lord spake again unto Ahaz, saying Ask thee a sign of the Lord thy God; ask it either in the depth, or in the height above. *But Ahaz said, I will not ask, neither will I tempt the Lord. And he said, Hear ye now. O house of David; is it a small thing for you to weary men, but will ye weary my God also?* Therefore the Lord himself shall give you a sign; Behold, a virgin shall conceive and bear a son, and shall call his name Immanuel [God With Us].

Butter and honey shall he [Shear-jashub] *eat, that he may know to refuse the evil, and choose the good, the land that thou abhorrest shall be forsaken of both her kings. The Lord shall bring upon thee, and upon thy people, and upon thy father's house, days that have not come, from the day that Ephraim departed from Judah; even the king of Assyria."*

---

37   Pekah was the son of Remaliah and an army officer (with the backing of the Syrians) murdered the king of Israel, Pekahiah (the son of king Menahem). *"Pekah... a captain of his* [Pekahiah] *conspired against him, and smote him in Samaria, in the palace of the king's house, with Argob and Arieb, and with him fifty men of the Gileadites: and he killed him, and reigned in his room."* (II Kings 15:25)

(The Professor's comments)

Right away, Baykus pulled out his Bible and said, "Let me tell you about the *infamous and wicked* king Ahaz,

(II Chronicles 28:1-9)

"Ahaz was twenty years old when he began to reign, and he reigned sixteen years in Jerusalem: but he did not that which was right in the sight of the Lord, like David his father: For he walked in the ways of the kings of Israel, and made also molten images for Baalim.

Moreover he burnt incense in the valley of the son of Hinnom, and burnt his children in the fire, after the abominations of the heathen whom the Lord had cast out before the children of Israel. He sacrificed also and burnt incense in the high places, and on the hills, and under every green tree. Wherefore the Lord his God delivered him into the hand of the king of Syria; and they smote him, and carried away a great multitude of them captives, and brought them to Damascus. And he was also delivered into the hand of the king of Israel, who smote him with a great slaughter. For Pekah [king of Israel] *the son of Remaliah slew in Judah a hundred and twenty thousand (120,000) in one day, which were all valiant men, because they had forsaken the Lord God of their fathers.*

And Zichri, a mighty man of Ephraim, slew Maaseiah, son to king Ahaz, and Azrikam the governor of the house, and Elkanah that was next to the king. And the children of Israel carried away captive of their brethren two hundred thousand (200,000), women, sons, and daughters, and took also away much spoil to Samaria."

(Prophet Oded's Warnings)

(II Chronicles 28:10)

"But a prophet of the Lord was there, whose name was ODED: *and he went out before the host that came to Samaria, and said unto them, behold,*

BECAUSE THE LORD GOD OF YOUR FATHERS WAS WROTH WITH JUDAH, HE HATH DELIVERED THEM INTO YOUR HAND, AND YE HAVE SLAIN THEM IN A RAGE THAT REACHETH UP UNTO HEAVEN."

"And now ye purpose to keep under the children of Judah and Jerusalem for bondmen and bondwomen unto you: but are there not with you, even with you sins against the Lord your God?"

"NOW **HEAR ME** *THEREFORE, AND DELIVER THE CAPTIVES AGAIN, WHICH YE HAVE TAKEN CAPTIVE OF YOUR BRETHREN:* **FOR THE FIERCE WRATH OF THE LORD IS UPON YOU."**

(Ephraim's Leaders Respond)

(II Chronicles 28:12-15)

"Then certain of the heads of the children of Ephraim, Azariah, the son of Johanan, Berechiah the son of Meshillemoth, and Jehizkiah the son of Shallum, and Amasa the son of Hadlai, stood up against them that came from the war, And said unto them, Ye shall not bring in the captives hither: for whereas we have offended against the Lord already, ye intend to add more to our sins and to our trespass: for our trespass is great, and there is fierce wrath against Israel. So the armed men left the captives and the spoil before the princes and all the congregation. And the men which were expressed by name rose up, and took the captives, and with the spoil clothed all that were naked among them, and arrayed them, and shod them, and gave them to eat and to drink, and anointed them, and carried all the feeble of them upon asses, and brought them to Jericho, the city of palm trees, to their brethren: then they returned to Samaria."

(King Ahaz Requests Assyria's Help)

(II Chronicles 28:16-19)

"At that time did king Ahaz send unto the kings of Assyria to help him. For the Lord brought Judah low because of Ahaz king of Israel; for he made Judah naked, and transgressed sore against the Lord. For again the Edomites had come and smitten Judah, and carried away captives. The Philistines also had invaded the cities of the low country, and of the south of Judah, and had taken Beth-shemesh, and Ajalon, and Gederoth, and Shocho with the villages thereof, and Timnah with the villages, Gimzo also and the villages thereof: and they dwelt there."

(Assyria Backstabs King Ahaz)

(II Chronicles 28:20-21)

"And Tilgath-pilneser king of Assyria came unto him, and distressed him, but strengthened him not."

For Ahaz took away a portion out of the house of the Lord, and out of the house of the king, and of the house of the king, and of the princes, and gave it unto the king of Assyria: but he helped him not."

(The Professor's comments)

The *wise old Hittite owl* said, "It gets worse,"

(Yahweh Stripped Judah)

(II Chronicles 28:19)

"For the Lord brought Judah low because of Ahaz king of Israel: for he made Judah naked, and transgressed sore against the Lord."

(II Chronicles 28:22-25)

<u>*"And in the time of his [Ahaz] distress did he trespass yet more*</u>

against the Lord: this is that king Ahaz. For he sacrificed unto the gods of Damascus, which smote him: and he said, Because the gods of the kings of Syria help them, therefore will I sacrifice to them that they may help me. But they were the ruin of him, and of all Israel.

And Ahaz gathered together the vessels of the house of God, and cut in pieces the vessels of the house of God, and shut up the doors of the house of the Lord, and he made him altars in every corner of Jerusalem. And in every several city of Judah he made high places to burn incense unto other gods, and provoked to anger the Lord God of his fathers."

(The Death of king Ahaz)
(II Chronicles 28:26-27)

"Now the rest of his acts and of all his ways, first and last, behold, they are written in the Book of the Kings of Judah and Israel.

And Ahaz slept with his fathers, and they buried him in the city, even in Jerusalem: but they brought him to into the sepulchers of the kings of Israel: and Hezekiah his son reigned in his stead."

(B) The Isaiah's second son was named Maher-shalal-hash-baz [38] = quick to the plunder and swift to the spoil.

This name was given to Isaiah before the child's birth and it seems to be a five-step process:

(1)   *The Command.* *"Moreover, the Lord said unto me, Take thee*

---

38   The name and birth of this *unborn baby*, **Maher-shalal-hash-baz**, was given one of the *longest name* (totaling eighteen letters) in the **Bible**. It's a wonder if the child ever pronounced his own name! The other longest name is Jonath-elem-rechokim (totaling eighteen letters) means = a dove on distant Oaks and it is found in the Book of Psalms 56.

a great roll, and write in it with a man's pen concerning Maher-shalal-hash-baz." (Isaiah 8:1);

(2) <u>*Matter of Record*</u>. **"And I took unto me faithful witnesses to record, Uriah, the priest, and Zechariah the son of Jeberechiah."** (Isaiah 8:2);

(3) <u>*The Seeding Process*</u>. **"And I went unto the prophetess; and she conceived, and bare a son. Then said the Lord to me, Call his name Maher-shalal-hash-baz."** (Isaiah 8:3);

(4) <u>*The Prophecy*</u>. **"For before the child shall have knowledge to cry, My father, and my mother, the riches of Damascus and the spoil of Samaria shall be taken away before the king of Assyria."** (Isaiah 8:4); and

(5) <u>*Another Prophecy*</u>. **"The Lord spake also unto me again, saying, Foreasmuch as this people refuseth the waters of Shiloah that go softly, and rejoice in Rezin and Remaliah's son** [Pekah]*; **Now therefore, behold, the Lord bringeth up upon them the waters of the river, strong and many, even the king of Assyria, and all his glory: all his channels, and go over all his banks: And he shall pass through Judah; he shall overflow and go over, he shall reach even to the neck; and the stretching out of his wings shall fill the breath of thy land, O Immanuel."** (Isaiah 8:5-8)

God's Song to His Beloved

(Isaiah 5:1-7)

"Now will I sing to my well-beloved a song of my beloved touching his vineyard. My well-beloved hath a vineyard in a very fruitful hill: And he fenced it and gathered out the stones thereof, and planted it with the choicest vine, and built a tower in the midst of it, and also made a winepress therein: and he looked that it should bring for the grapes, and it brought forth wild grapes.

And now, O inhabitants of Jerusalem, and men of Judah, judge, I pray you, betwixt me and my vineyard. What could have been done more to my vineyard, that I have not done in it? Wherefore, when I looked that it should bring forth grapes, brought it forth wild grapes.

And now go to; I will tell you what I will do to my vineyard: I will take away the hedge thereof, and it shall be eaten up; and break down the wall thereof, and it shall be trodden down: And I will lay it waste: it shall not be printed, nor digged; but there shall come up briers and thorns: I will also command the clouds that they rain no rain upon it.

For the vineyard of the Lord of hosts is the house of Israel, and the men of Judah his pleasant plant: and he looked for judgment, but behold oppression; for righteousness, but behold a cry."

Woes to Jerusalem

(1)   *"Woe unto them that join house to house that lay field to field, till there be no place, that they may be placed alone in the midst of the earth!"* (Isaiah 5:8);

(2)   *"Woe unto them that rise up early in the morning, that they may follow strong drink; that continue until night, till wine inflame them!"* (Isaiah 5:11);

(3)   *"Woe unto them that draw iniquity with cords of vanity, and sin as it were with a cart rope: That say, Let him make speed, and hasten his work, that we may see it: and let the counsel of the Holy One of Israel draw nigh and come that we may know it!"* (Isaiah 5:18-19);

(4)   ***"Woe unto them that call evil good, and good evil that put darkness for light, and light for darkness; that put bitter for sweet, and sweet for bitter!"*** (Isaiah 5:20);

(5)   ***"Woe unto them that are wise in their own eyes, and prudent in their own sight!"*** (Isaiah 5:21); and

(6)   ***"Woe unto them that are might to drink wine, and men of strength to mingle strong drink: Which justify the wicked for reward, and take away the righteousness of the righteous from him!"*** (Isaiah 5:22-23)

Isaiah's Visions

Isaiah did not withhold his tongue. God spoke to Isaiah through visions. Unfortunately, the children of Israel did not listen to the warnings. Instead, they continued to mimic the heathen nations, serve false gods, and provoke God.

(1)   ***"The vision of Isaiah the son of Amoz which he saw concerning Judah and Jerusalem..."*** (Isaiah 1:1);

(2)   ***"A grievous vision is declared unto me; the treacherous dealer dealeth treacherously, and the spoiler spoileth. Go up, O Elam: besiege, O Media; all the sighing thereof have I made to cease."*** (Isaiah 21:1);

(3)   ***"The burden of the valley of vision. What aileth thee now, that thou art wholly gone up to the housetops? Thou that art full of stirs, a tumultuous city, a joyous city: thy slain men are not slain with the sword, nor dead in battle. All thy rulers are fled together, they are bound by the archers: all that are found in thee are bound together, which have fled from far."*** (Isaiah 22:1);

(4)   ***"For it is a day of trouble and of treading down, and of***

perplexity by the Lord God of hosts in the valley of vision, breaking down the walls, and of crying to the mountains."* (Isaiah 22:5);

(5) *"But they also have erred through wine, and through strong drink are out of the way; the priest and the prophet have erred through strong drink, they are swallowed up of wine, they are out of the way through strong drink; they err in vision, they stumble in judgment."* (Isaiah 28:7);

(6) *"And the multitude of all the nations that fight against Ariel, even all that fight against her and her munition, and that distress her, shall be as a dream of a night vision. It shall even be as when an hungry man dreameth, and, behold, he eateth; but he awaketh, and his soul is empty: or as when a thirsty man dreameth, and, behold, he drinketh; but he awaketh, and behold, he is faint, and his soul hath appetite: so shall the multitude of all the nations be, that fight against Mount Zion."* (Isaiah 29:7); and

(7) *"And the vision of all is become unto you as the words of a book that is sealed, which men deliver to one that is learned, saying, read this, I pray thee: and he saith, I cannot; for it is sealed."* (Isaiah 29:11)

God's Appeals to His People

Isaiah 1:16-18:

☺ Wash yourself,
☺ Be clean;
☺ Put away the evil of your doings from before mine eyes;
☺ Cease to do evil;
☺ Learn to do well;

☺ Seek judgment;

☺ Relieve the oppressed;

☺ Judge the fatherless;

☺ Plead for the widow; and

☺ Come now and let us reason together, saith the Lord: though your sins be as scarlet, they shall be as white as snow; though they be red like crimson, they shall be as wool.

Pending Judgment on Jerusalem

Isaiah said, "***Wherefore hear the word of the Lord, ye scornful men, that rule this people which is in Jerusalem. Because ye have said, We have made a covenant with death and with hell are we at agreement; when the overflowing scourge shall pass through, it shall not come unto us: for we have made lies our refuge, and under falsehood have we hid ourselves. Therefore thus saith the Lord God, Behold I lay in Zion for a foundation a stone, a tried stone, a precious corner stone, a sure foundation: he that believeth shall not make haste. Judgment also will I lay to the line, and righteousness to the plummet: and the hail shall sweep away the refuge of lies and the waters shall overflow the hiding place. And your covenant with death shall be disannulled and your agreement with hell shall not stand; when the overflowing scourge shall pass through, then, ye shall be trodden down. From the time that it goeth forth it shall take you: for morning by morning shall it pass over, by day and by night: and it shall be a vexation only to understand the report. For the bed is shorter than that a man can stretch himself on it: and the covering narrower than that he can wrap himself in it. For the Lord shall rise up as in mount Perazim, he shall be wroth as in the valley of Gibeon, that he may do his work, his strange work; and bring to pass his act, his strange act. Now therefore be ye not mockers, lest your bands be made strong: for I have heard*** *from the Lord God of hosts a consumption, even determined upon the whole earth."* (Isaiah 28:14-22)

Isaiah's Prophecy to King Hezekiah of Judah

The story begins with king Hezekiah who was terminally *"...sick unto death."* (Isaiah 38:1) One day, Isaiah *(the prophet)* told Hezekiah, *"Set thine house in order for thou shalt die and not live."* (Isaiah 38:2)

After a long period of suffering, king Hezekiah couldn't stand the pain, so he turned his face to the wall and prayed to God! With a penitent heart and a short prayer of less than thirty-one words, king Hezekiah said, *"Remember now O Lord, I beseech thee, how I have walked before thee in truth and with a perfect heart, and have done that which is good in thy sight. And Hezekiah wept sore."*
(Isaiah 38:1-3)

(1)　　IMMEDIATELY, God's answer to king Hezekiah,

(Isaiah 38:4-8)
"Then came the word of the Lord to Isaiah, saying, Go, and say to Hezekiah, Thus saith the Lord, the God of David thy father, I have heard thy prayer I have seen thy tears: behold, I will add unto thy days fifteen years. <u>And I will deliver thee and this city out of the hand of the king of Assyria and I will defend this city.</u> And this shall be a sign unto thee from the Lord, that the Lord will do this thing that he hath spoken; Behold, I will bring again the shadow of the degrees which is gone down in the sundial of Ahaz, ten degrees backward. So the sun returned ten degrees, by which degrees it was gone down."

(2)   THE SAME STORY REPEATED, God's answer to king Hezekiah,

(II Kings 20:1-5)

"In those days was Hezekiah sick unto death. And the prophet Isaiah, the son of Amoz came to him, and said unto him, Thus saith the Lord, Set thine house in order; for thou shalt die, and not live.

Then he turned his face to the wall, and prayed unto the Lord, saying, I beseech thee, O Lord, remember now how I have walked before thee in truth and with a perfect heart, and have done that which is good in thy sight. And Hezekiah wept sore.

And it came to pass, afore Isaiah was gone out into the middle court, that the word of the Lord came to him, saying, Turn again, and tell Hezekiah the captain of my people, Thus saith the Lord, the God of David thy father, I have heard thy prayer, I have seen thy tears: behold, I will heal thee: on the third day thou shalt go up unto the house of the Lord. And I will add unto thy days fifteen years; and I will deliver thee and this city out of the hand of the king of Assyria; and I will defend this city for mine own sake, and for my servant David's sake. And Isaiah said, Take a lump of figs. And they took and laid it on the boil, and he recovered."

(3)   Hezekiah's great depression,

(Isaiah 38:10-18)

"I said in the cutting off of my days, I shall go to the gates of the grave. [39]   I am deprived of the residue of my years. I said, I shall

---

[39]   Sheol = the unseen world and place of departed spirits. In the Old Testament, Sheol (a.k.a Hades, Hell] was the under ground world place where all souls (righteous and wicked) went. After Jesus Christ's resurrection (in the New Testament), the righteous souls no longer go into Sheol but rather to Heaven.

not see the Lord, even the Lord, in the land of the living: I shall behold man no more with the inhabitants of the world. Mine age is departed, and is removed from me as a shepherd's tent: I have cut off like a waver my life: he will cut me off with pining sickness: from day even to night wilt thou make an end of me. Like a crane or a swallow, so did I chatter: I did mourn as a dove: mine eyes fail with looking upward: O Lord, I am oppressed; undertake for me.

What shall I say? He hath both spoken unto me, and himself hath done it: I shall go softly all my years in the bitterness of my soul. O Lord, by these things men live and in all these things is the life of my spirit: so wilt thou recover me and make me to live.

Behold, for peace I had great bitterness: but thou hast in love to my soul delivered it from the pit of corruption: for thou has cast all my sins behind thy back.

For the grave cannot praise thee, death cannot celebrate thee; they that go down into the pit cannot hope for thy truth."

(4)　Hezekiah's healing from a natural fruit,

(Isaiah 38:21-22)
*"For Isaiah had said, <u>**Let them take a lump of figs, and lay it for a plaster upon the boil, and he shall recover**</u>. Hezekiah also had said, What is the sign that I shall go up to the house of the Lord? "*

(5)　Hezekiah's song (celebration) of his healing,

(Isaiah 38:19-20)
"The living, the living, he shall praise thee, as I do this day: the father to the

children shall make known thy truth. The Lord was ready to save me: therefore we will sing my songs to the stringed instruments all the days of our life in the house of the Lord ."

Hezekiah's Wonderful Reign in Judah

As a great reformer and king of Judah from about 715-686 B.C., Hezekiah *(the son of the wicked king Ahaz* [40] *who reigned about 735-715 B.C. and the son of Abi, daughter of Zachariah)* was twenty-five years old and a *true believer* in **Yahweh**: *"And he did that which was right in the sight of the Lord, according to all that David his father did."* (II Kings 18:2-3)

The first thing Hezekiah did was to destroy false idols,

(II Kings 18:1-8)
"He removed the high places, and brake the images, and cut down the groves, and brake in pieces the brasen serpent that Moses had made; for unto those days the children of Israel did burn incense to it: *and he called it Nehushtan. He trusted in the Lord God of Israel; so that after him was none like him among all the kings of Judah, nor any that were before him. For he clave* [41] *to the Lord, and departed not from following him, but kept his commandments, which the Lord commanded Moses. And the Lord was with him: and he prospered whithersoever he went forth: and he rebelled against the king of Assyria, and served him not. He smote the Philistines, even unto*

40 *"King Ahaz was twenty years old when he began to reign, and reigned sixteen years in Jerusalem, and did not that which was right in the sight of the Lord his God, like David his father. But he walked in the way of the kings of Israel, yea, and made his son to pass through the fire, according to the abominations of the heathen, whom the Lord cast out from before the children of Israel. And he sacrificed and burnt incense in the high places, and on the hills, and under every green tree."* (II Kings 16:2-4)
41 According to *Webster's New World Dictionary*, the word clave is cleave: (1) to adhere; cling; (2) to be faithful.

Gaza, and the borders thereof, from the tower of the watchmen to the fenced city."

Secondly, Hezekiah did not waste any time repairing the temple,

(II Chronicles 29:3-10)
"He in the first year of his reign, in the first month, opened the doors of the house of the Lord, and repaired them. And he brought in the priests and the Levites, and gathered them together into the east street. And said unto them, Hear me, ye Levites, sanctify now yourselves, and sanctify the house of the Lord God of your fathers, and carry forth the filthiness out of the holy place. For our father [especially his father king Ahaz] have trespassed, and done that which was evil in the eyes of the Lord our God, and have forsaken him, and have turned away their faces from the habitation of the Lord, and turned their backs. Also, they have shut up the doors of the porch, and put out the lamps, and have not burned incense nor offered burnt offerings in the holy place unto the God of Israel. Wherefore the wrath of the Lord was upon Judah and Jerusalem, and he hath delivered them to trouble, to astonishment, and to hissing, as ye see with your eyes...Now it is in mine heart to make a covenant with the Lord God of Israel, that his fierce wrath may turn away from us."

Hezekiah's Folly and Punishment Foretold

Professor Baykus said that after God provided great healing, signs, and wonders to the Judean king, Hezekiah acted inappropriately. During his first reign about 721-710 B.C., Merodach-Baladan, the king of Babylon (A.K.A. Berodach-Baladan in II Kings 20:12) sent spies to *flatter* the king of Judah. Without thinking, king Hezekiah showed them all the treasures in the palace and storehouses. The ***Bible*** says,

(Isaiah 39:1-8)

"At that time, Merodach-Baladan, the son of Baladan, king of Babylon, sent letters and a present to Hezekiah: for he had heard that he had been sick and was recovered.

And Hezekiah was glad of them, and shewed them the house of his precious things, the silver, and the gold, and the spices, and the precious ointment, and all the house of his armor, and all that was found in his treasures: there was nothing in his house, nor in all his dominion, that Hezekiah shewed them not.

Then came Isaiah the prophet unto king Hezekiah and said unto him, What said these men? And from whence came they unto thee? And Hezekiah said, They are come from a country unto me, even from Babylon. Then said he, What have they seen in thine house? And Hezekiah, All that is in mine house have they seen: there is nothing among my treasures that I have not shewed them. Then said Isaiah to Hezekiah, Hear the word of the Lord of hosts: Behold, the days come, that all that is in thine house, and that which thy fathers have laid up in store until this day, shall be carried to Babylon: nothing shall be left, saith the Lord. And of thy sons that shall issue from thee which thou shalt beget, shall they take away; and they shall be eunuchs in the palace of the king of Babylon. Then said Hezekiah to Isaiah, Good is the word of the Lord which thou hast spoken. He said moreover, For there shall be peace and truth in my days."

God's Sign, king Hezekiah's Healing

Two of Earth's most historical days concerning the stoppage of time involve stories [42] in the ***Bible***. One of these miraculous signs concerned king Hezekiah. God turned back time for king Hezekiah,

---

42   Joshua's battle against the five kings of the Amorites and their hosts who en-
camped before Gibeon and made war against it because the Gibeonites made peace

(1) *"And Hezekiah said unto Isaiah, What shall be the sign that the Lord will heal me, and that I shall go up into the house of the Lord the third day?"* (II Kings 20:8);

(2) Prophet Isaiah's answer and question to king Hezekiah, *"And Isaiah said, This sign shalt thou have of the Lord, that the Lord will do the thing that he hath spoken: shall the shadow go forward ten degrees or go back ten degrees?"* (II Kings 20:9);

(3) King Hezekiah answer to Isaiah, *"It is a light thing for the shadow to go down ten degrees: nay but let the shadow return backward ten degrees."* (II Kings 20:10); and

(4) Isaiah's prayer to the Lord GOD, *"And Isaiah cried unto the Lord:* and he brought the shadow ten degrees backward, by which it had gone down in the dial of Ahaz." (II Kings 20:11)

---

with Joshua and the children of Israel. *"And the Lord said unto Joshua, Fear them not: for I have delivered them into thine hand; there shall not a man of them stand before thee. Joshua came to them suddenly, and went up from Gilgal all night. And the Lord discomforted them before Israel, and slew them with a great slaughter at Gibeon, and chased them along the way that goeth up to Bethhoron, and smote them to Azekah, and unto Makkedah. And it came to pass, as they fled from before Israel, and were in the going down to Bethhoron, that the Lord cast down great stones from heaven upon them unto Azekah, and they died: they were more which died with hailstones than they whom the children of Israel slew with the sword. EARTH, SUN, MOON STOOD STILL: Then spake Joshua to the Lord in the day when the Lord delivered up the Amorites before the children of Israel, and he said in the sight of Israel, Sun, stand thou still upon Gibeon; and thou, Moon, in the valley of Ajalon. And the sun stood still, and the moon stayed until the people had avenged themselves upon their enemies. Is not this written in the book of Jasher? So the sun stood still in the midst of heaven, and hasted not to go down about a whole day. And there was no day like that before it or after it, that the Lord hearkened unto the voice of a man: for the Lord fought for Israel."* (Joshua 10:5-14)

155

Babylonian Spies Visit king Hezekiah

Basically, the residents of the whole earth recorded that stoppage of time because "...time was turned backward by which it had gone down." Frankly, this fact was recorded by many ancient cultures during king Hezekiah's day! All of the eastern and Asian countries studied the heavenly solar system and they

knew that something abnormal occurred. Also, they heard about the GOD OF THE CHILDREN OF ISRAEL and HIS MIGHTY WONDERS AND MIRACLES!

One of those cultures visited from Babylon. Merodach-Baladan (king of Babylon about 721-711 B.C.). Like the rest of the world, the Babylonians (enchanters, star gazers, etc.) heard about the dial of Ahaz going backwards by ten degrees. Also, they wanted a reason to spy on Judah!

The True Reason for the Spies' Visit

Unfortunately, Merodach-Baladan was just a *puppet* king for Sennacherib (the king of Assyria) who hated Judah! However, king Merodach-Baladan had an underlining reason for sending the spies to visit king Hezekiah. The Assyrians were constantly at war with the children of Israel and they captured the Northern Tribe of Israel (Judah's sister).

In fact, Sennacherib was working behind the scenes to get a value on Judah's net worth. However, Isaiah's prophecy was coming to light because he foretold that a Babylonian king would conqueror Zion (Judah, the Southern Kingdom of Israel) and take the king's sons captive and make them eunuchs. At the time of Isaiah's prophecy, king Hezekiah did not have a son. [43]

---

43   II Kings 20:20-21; and the prophecy fulfilled in Daniel 1:3-21.

The Prophecy Fulfilled Against King Hezekiah

Then, king Nebuchadnezzar *(the wolf-man)* said that he captured the City of Jerusalem and burned it with fire. At that point, our history collided with Jerusalem's (and their inhabitants) for another seventy years. I ordered their choicest nobles and princes to be brought into my palace for safekeeping, training and education. Although, I am ashamed for my actions, I believe that the God of Heaven willed me,

"[Nebuchadnezzar] ***The king spake unto Ashpenaz the master of his eunuchs that he should bring certain of the children of Israel, and of the king's seed, and of the princes;***

Children in whom was no blemish, but well favored, and skilful in all wisdom, and cunning in knowledge, and understanding science, and such as had ability in them to stand in the king's palace, and whom they might teach the learning and the tongue of the Chaldeans.

And [Nebuchadnezzar] *the king appointed them a daily provision of the king's meat, and of wine which he [the king] drank:* so nourishing them three years, *that at the end thereof they might stand before [me] the king.*"
(Daniel 1:3-7)

Chapter 17

Jeremiah's Prophecies of Judah

(The Professor's comments)

Before we talk about Jeremiah, something must be said about his background. Jeremiah (means = *may Yahweh lift up or the Lord establishes*) was **"...the son of Hilkiah, a priest from Anathoth** [three miles northeast of Jerusalem] **in the land of Benjamin."** (Jeremiah 1:1) Also, Jeremiah was born during the reign of Judah's *most* wicked king, Manasseh (about 696-642 B.C.) Perhaps, this casts a shadow over Jeremiah being dubbed the weeping prophet, **"Oh that my head were waters and mine eyes a fountain of tears that I might weep day and night for the slain of the daughter of my people!"** (Jeremiah 9:1) Jeremiah grew up in controversy from within and without. In fact, his own *priestly brothers and relatives* fought with him, **"For even thy brethren and the house of thy father, even they have dealt treacherously with thee; yea, they have called a multitude after thee: believe them not, though they speak fair words unto thee."** (Jeremiah 12:6) Jeremiah had a lucrative background but he gave up his heritage, **"I have forsaken mine house, I have left mine heritage; I have given the dearly beloved of my soul into the hand of her enemies. Mine heritage is unto me as a lion in the forest; it crieth out against me: therefore have I hated it. Mine heritage is unto me as a speckled bird, the birds round about are against her; come ye, assemble all the beasts of the field, come to devour."** (Jeremiah 12:6-9) Eventually, Jeremiah was arrested and thrown into dungeons! But he did not give up!

Jeremiah, House of Ithamar

(A) Ithamar who was the *fourth* son of Aaron *(First High Priest and brother of Moses)* and Elisheba (wife of Ithamar) (Exodus 6:23);

(B) Ahimelech (the *High Priest* at Nob City) the *infamous and innocent priest* who offered David *(running for his life from king Saul, played a madman to Achish, king of Gath, and hid in the Cave of Adullam);* hallowed *(holy, consecrated)* bread and *rightfully* the sword of Goliath the Philistine, killed by the *boyish*, David. (I Samuel 21:15) Also, Ahimelech was the *great-grandson* of Eli [44] *(a descendant of Ithamar)* whose male descendants were cursed with a short-life span (because Eli did not remove his wicked sons from their priestly office);

(C) Abiathar (Ahimelech's son) who escaped the bloody massacre at the City of Nob that was initiated by king Saul's command to Doeg the Edomite to slay all *eighty-five* priests wearing "linen ephods" and king Saul's order to destroy every resident including the animals at Nob. (I Samuel 22:18-19). Furthermore, Abiathar was made High Priest by king David (who also made Zadok, *a joint High Priest*, of the line of the Levites). But king Solomon banished Abiathar (during the latter end of David's reign for betraying the king and aiding Adonijah (who appointed himself king before the death of his father, king David). Also, Solomon

---

44   Eli was the last of the judges in Israel, the High Priest in Shiloh, father to two wicked, priestly sons (Hophni and Phinehas), and care giver, mentor to little Samuel who at the age of five (after weaning) his mother, Hannah, placed him in the care of Eli. And Eli died tragically falling backwards (breaking his neck) after hearing about the deaths of both his sons, and the capture of the Ark of God by the Philistines. (I Samuel 4:12-18) Prior to Eli's death, Samuel's first prophecy was the destruction to Eli's wicked house, *"And the Lord said to Samuel, Behold, I will do a thing in Israel, at which both the ears of every one that heareth shall tingle. For I have told him that I will judge his house for ever for the iniquity which he knoweth: because his sons made themselves vile, and he restrained them not."* (I Samuel 3:11-20)

appointed Zadok the High Priest for his allegiance to king David; and

(D)   Hilkiah, the High Priest (believed to be Jeremiah's father) found the lost *"Book of the Law"* in Jerusalem. He gave the book to Shapan (the scribe) to read and commanded him to give it to king Josiah. (II Kings 22:8-10) Also, Hilkiah is credited with Judah's reforms under king Josiah and the elimination of Baal worship. (II Kings 23:4)

Jeremiah's Call and Commission

Moreover, Jeremiah was priest and prophet. [45] Like the Prophet Isaiah, Jeremiah was extremely vocal during the lives of several kings and Jeremiah witnessed the captivity of Judah by the Babylonians. Jeremiah was called to be a prophet during the thirteenth year of Josiah's reign.

(A)   *king Josiah* (reigned about 640-608 B.C.);
(B)   *king Jehoahaz* (A.K.A. *Shallum;* reigned about 608 B.C.);
(C)   *king Jehoiakim* (reigned about 608-597 B.C.);
(D)   *king Jehoiachin* (*A.K.A. Jeconiah and Coniah*; reigned about 597 B.C.);* and
(E)   *king Zedekiah* (the last Judean king) reigned about 597-586 B.C.) [46]

Unlike Prophet Isaiah (who was about twenty-five years old when called), the **Lord GOD** called, sanctified, and ordained Jeremiah before he was born, *"Then the word of the Lord came unto me, saying, Before I formed thee in the belly I knew thee; and before thou came forth out of the womb, I sanctified thee, and I ordained thee a prophet unto the nations."* (Jeremiah 1:4-5) This statement proves that souls are immortal and they exist in Heaven in the well of

---

45   In the Old Testament Scripture, there was a total of four prophets/priests: *Jeremiah* (Jeremiah 1:1); *Nathan* (I Kings. 4:5); *Ezekiel* (Ezekiel 1:3); and *Zechariah* (Zechariah 1:1).
46   Fall of Jerusalem about 586 B.C.

souls. **Moreover, the Lord GOD knows every soul by name just as He knows, calls, and numbers every star by name (Psalm 147:4), and the Lord GOD summons every soul at will to place them on Earth according to His plans for every Age and Dispensation right down to the very second!**

The **_Bible_** states, *"**Great is our Lord, and of great power: his understanding is infinite.**"* (Psalm 147:4) Amos 5:8 states, *"**Seek him that maketh the seven stars and Orion, [47] and turneth the shadow of death into the morning, and maketh the day dark with night: that calleth for the waters of the sea, and poureth them out upon the face of the earth: The Lord is his name.**"* Job 9:6-10 described God's might as, *"**Which removeth the mountains...Which shaketh the earth out of her place and the pillars thereof tremble...Which commandeth the sun, and it riseth not; and sealeth up the stars...Which alone spreadeth out the heavens and treadeth upon the waves of the sea...Which maketh Arcturus, [48] Orion, and Pleiades,[49] and the chambers of the south... Which doeth great things past finding out; yea, and wonders without number.**"*

But, Jeremiah did not want the job, "Then said I, Ah, Lord God! Behold, I cannot speak: for I am a child." (Jeremiah 1:4-5) No one knows Jeremiah's exact age when God called him. However, it is believed Jeremiah was between twelve to twenty-five years of age, "But the Lord

---

47   **Orion** is *The Giant or The Hunter* (Greek mythology) is a famous constellation located on the celestial equator and seen throughout the world. It includes prominent stars known as the Belt of Orion and in the middle of it is the Orion Nebula.

48   **Arcturus** is believed the brightest star (an orange giant) in the constellation Bootes. Arcturus is older and enormously larger than the Earth's Sun. In size comparison, Arcturus is like an elephant to an ant (our Sun). In Greek Mythology, Arcturus forms the left foot of the Bear (in the constellation of Bootes).

49   **Pleiades** (A.K.A. Seven Sisters, *the sailing ones,* in Greek Mythology) is a cluster of hot blue and shimmering stars in the constellation of Taurus. However, there are numerous stars in the Pleiades but nine of them are brighter and hotter than the others. Therefore, these nine are given more significance. It is believed that two of the nine are the father and mother and the remaining are their seven daughters! Also, there is a reflecting nebula from the blue light of the stars and its beautiful to look upon.

said unto me, Say not, I am a child: for thou shalt go to all that I shall send thee, and whatsoever I command thee thou shalt speak. Be not afraid of their faces: for I am with thee to deliver thee, saith the Lord." (Jeremiah 1:7-8)

Jeremiah experienced a miraculous act of purging! Similar to Prophet Isaiah (who God ordered a ***"...seraphim to place a live coal which he had taken with the tongs from off the altar and laid it upon Isaiah's mouth, and said, Lo, this hath touched thy lips; and thine iniquity is taken away, and they sin purged."*** (Isaiah 6:6-7) Unlike, Prophet Isaiah, a much Higher Force touched Jeremiah's mouth, "Then the Lord put forth his hand and touched my mouth. And the Lord said unto me, Behold I have put my words in thy mouth. See, I have this day set thee over the nations and over the kingdoms, to root out, and to pull down, and to destroy, and to throw down, to build, and to plant." (Jeremiah 1:7-10)

(Jeremiah 2:2-11)

"Go and cry in the ears of Jerusalem, saying, Thus saith the Lord: I remember thee, the kindness of thy youth, the love of thine espousals when thou wentest after me in the wilderness in a land that was not sown. Israel was holiness unto the Lord, and the firstfruits of his increase: all that devour him shall offend; evil shall come upon them saith the Lord.

Hear ye the word of the Lord, O house of Jacob and all the families of the house of Israel:

Thus saith the Lord, what iniquity have your fathers found in me that they are gone far from me, and have walked after vanity, and are become vain? ***Neither said they, Where is the Lord that brought us up out of the land of Egypt, that led us through the wilderness, through a land of deserts and of pits through a land of drought, and of the shadow of death, through a land that no man passed through, and where no*** *man dwelt? And I brought you into a plentiful country, to eat the fruit thereof; but when ye entered ye defiled my land, and made mine heritage an abomination.* The priests said not, Where is the Lord? *And they that handle the law knew me not: the pastors also transgressed against me, and the prophets prophesied by Baal, and walked after things that do not profit. Wherefore I will yet plead with you...with your children's children will I plead...* Hath a nation changed their gods, which are yet no gods? *But my people have changed their glory for that which doth not profit.*

Be astonished, O ye heavens, at this, and be horribly afraid, be ye very desolate saith the Lord.

For my people have committed two evils: they have forsaken me the fountain of living waters, and hewed them out cisterns, broken cisterns, that can hold no water."

God, Married to His People

"Turn, O backsliding children, saith the Lord: for **I am married unto you**...In those days the house of Judah shall walk with the house of Israel, *and they shall come together out of the land of the north to the land that I have given for an inheritance unto your fathers....* **Thou shalt call me, My father**; *and shalt not turn away from me. Surely as a wife treacherously departeth from her husband, so have ye dealt treacherously with me, O house of Israel, saith the Lord."* (Jeremiah 3:14, 18-20)

Jeremiah, Forbidden to Marry

Unlike the Prophet Isaiah (who had a family), the **Lord GOD** told Jeremiah,

163

"Thou shalt not take thee a wife, neither shall thou have sons or daughters in this place. *For thus saith the Lord concerning the sons and concerning the daughters that are born in this place, and concerning their mothers that bare them, and concerning their fathers that begat them in this land: they shall die of grievous deaths; they shall not be lamented; neither shall they be buried; but they shall be as dung upon the face of the earth; and they shall be consumed by the sword, and by famine; and their carcases shall be meat for the fowls of heaven, and for the beasts of the earth. For thus saith the Lord, Enter not into the house of mourning, neither go to lament no bemoan them: for I have taken away my peace from this people, saith the Lord, even lovingkindness and mercies. Both great and small shall die In this land: they shall not be buried, neither shall men lament for them, nor cut themselves, nor make themselves bald for them: Neither shall men themselves for them in mourning, to comfort them for the dead; neither shall men give them the cup of consolation to drink for their father or their mother. Thou shalt not also go into the house of feasting, to sit with them to eat and to drink. For thus saith the Lord of hosts, the God of Israel; behold, I will cause to cease out of this place in your eyes, and in your days, the voice of mirth, and the voice of gladness, the voice of the bridegroom, and the voice of the bride."* (Jeremiah 16:1-9)

God's Delight

"Thus saith the Lord, Let not the wise man glory in his wisdom, neither let the mighty man glory in his might, let not the rich man glory in his riches: **<u>But let him that glorieth glory in this, that he understandeth and knoweth me, that I am the Lord which exercise lovingkindness, judgment, and righteousness, in the earth</u>:** *for in these things I delight, saith the Lord."*
(Jeremiah 9:23-24)

God's Mind Made Up!

(Jeremiah 4: 13-14)
"Behold, he [the executioner, Nebuchadnezzar] shall come up as clouds

and his chariots shall be as a whirlwind: his horses are swifter than eagles. Woe unto us! For we are spoiled...Oh Jerusalem, wash thine heart from wickedness, that thou mayest be saved. How long shall thy vain thoughts lodge within thee?

Lo, I will bring a nation upon you from far, O house of Israel, saith the Lord: it is a mighty nation, it is an ancient nation, a nation whose language thou knowest not, neither understandest what they say. Their quiver is as an open sepulcher, they are all mighty men. And they shall eat up thine harvest, and thy bread, which thy sons and thy daughters should eat: they shall eat up thy flocks and thine herds: they shall eat up thy vines and thy fig trees: they shall impoverish thy fenced cities, wherein thou trustest, with the sword. Nevertheless in those days, saith the Lord, I will not make a full end with you. And it shall come to pass, when ye shall say, Wherefore doeth the Lord our God all these things unto us? Then shalt thou answer them, Like as ye have forsaken me, and served strange gods in your land, so shall ye serve strangers in a land that is not yours."

All the Unrighteous, Punished

(Jeremiah 9:25-26)

"Behold, the days come, saith the Lord, that I will punish all them which are circumcised with the uncircumcised; Egypt, Judah, Edom, the children of Ammon, Moab, and all that are in the utmost corners that dwell in the wilderness for all these nations are uncircumcised, and all the house of Israel are uncircumcised to the heart."

The Potter's House

(Jeremiah 18:1-10)

"Then the word which came to Jeremiah from the Lord saying, **Arise, and go down to the potter's house,** *and there I will cause thee to hear my words. Then I went down to the potter's house, and, behold, he wrought a work on the wheels. And the vessel that he made of clay was marred in the hand of the potter: so he made it against another vessel, as seemed good to the potter to make it...*

O House of Israel, cannot I do with you as this potter? *Saith the Lord. Behold, as the clay is in the potter's hand, so are ye in mine hand, O house of Israel. At what instant I shall speak concerning a nation, and concerning a kingdom, to pluck up, and to pull down, and to destroy it; If that nation, against whom I have pronounced, turn from their evil, I will repent of the evil that I thought to do unto them. And at what instant I shall speak concerning a nation and concerning a kingdom, to build and to plant it; If it do evil in my sight, that it obey not my voice, then I will repent of the good, wherewith I said I would benefit them."*

The Valley of Hinnom (Slaughter)

(Jeremiah 19:1-10)

"Thus saith the Lord, Go and get a potter's earthen bottle, and take of the ancients of the people, and of the ancients of the priests; And go forth unto the valley of the son of Hinnom...and proclaim there the words that I shall tell thee, And say,

Hear ye the word of the Lord, O kings of Judah and inhabitants of Jerusalem; Thus saith the Lord of hosts, the God of Israel; behold, I will bring evil upon this place, the which whosoever heareth, his ears shall tingle. **Because they have forsaken me, and have estranged this place, and have burned incense in it unto other gods, whom neither they nor their fathers have known, nor the kings of Judah, and have filled this place with blood of innocents;**

They have built also the high place of Baal, to burn their sons with fire for burnt offerings unto Baal, which I commanded not, nor spake it, neither came it into my mind; Therefore, behold, the days come, saith the Lord, that this place shall no more be called Tophet, nor The valley of the son of Hinnom, but the valley of slaughter. And I will make void the counsel of Judah and Jerusalem in this place; and I will cause them to fall by the sword before their enemies, and by the hands of them that seek their lives…Then shalt thou break the bottle in the sight of the men that go with thee."

THE CALL, Return to God

"For thus saith the Lord to the men of Judah and Jerusalem, Break up your fallow ground, and sow not among thorns…" (Jeremiah 4:3)

SEVEN COMMANDS TO RETURN

1. **Return again unto me…**(Jeremiah 3:1);
2. **Return ye backsliding Israel…**(Jeremiah 3:12)
3. **Return ye backsliding children…**(Jeremiah 3:22)
4. **Return unto me…**(Jeremiah 4:1)
5. **Return every one from his evil way…**(Jeremiah 18:11)
6. **Return unto Me with your whole heart…**(Jeremiah 24:7)
7. **Return now everyone from his evil way and amend your doings…** (Jeremiah 35:15)

Jeremiah's Plea

(Jeremiah 14:19-22)
"Hast thou utterly rejected Judah? Hath thy soul loathed Zion? Why hast thou smitten us, and there is no healing for us? We looked

for peace, and there is no good; and for the time of healing, and behold trouble!

We acknowledge, O Lord, our wickedness, and the iniquity of our fathers for we have sinned against thee. Do not abhor us, for thy name's sake, do not disgrace the throne of thy glory: remember, break not thy covenant with us.

Are there any among the vanities of the Gentiles that can cause rain or call the heavens give showers? Are not thou he, O Lord our God? Therefore we will wait upon thee: for thou hast made all these things."

The Fruitful Place, A Wilderness

(Professor Baykus' comments)

"Did you read about the first destruction of the *original* earth? Listen up! Everybody, this is really important! The **Lord GOD** planned to make the land of Palestine desolate as the destruction of the original earth!" Accordingly, Prophet Jeremiah said, *"I beheld the earth, and, lo, it was without form, and void: and the heavens, and they had no light. I beheld the mountains, and lo, they trembled, and all the hills moved lightly. I beheld, and lo, there was no man, and all the birds of the heavens were fled. I beheld, and lo, the fruitful place was a wilderness, and all the cities thereof were broken down at the presence of the Lord, and by his fierce anger."* (Jeremiah 4: 23-26; Genesis 1:2; Isaiah 14:12-14; II Peter 3:3-8)

The **Lord GOD** said, *"The whole land shall be desolate; yet will I not make a full end. For this shall the earth mourn, and the heavens above be black: because I have spoken it,* I have purposed it, and will not repent, neither will I turn back from it. *The whole city shall flee for the noise of the horsemen and bowmen; they shall go into thickets, and* *climb up upon the rocks: every city shall be forsaken, and not a man dwell therein. And when thou art spoiled, what wilt thou do? Though thou clothest thyself with crimson, thou deckest thee with ornaments of gold, though thou rentest thy face with painting, in vain shalt thou make thyself fair; thy lovers will despise thee, they will seek thy life. For I have heard a voice as of a woman in travail, and the anguish as of her that bringeth forth her first child the voice of the daughter of Zion, that bewaileth herself, that spreadeth her hands, saying, Woe is me now? for my soul is wearied because of murderers."* (Jeremiah 4:27-31)

(Jeremiah 5:1-2, 6-12)

Basically, the inhabitants of Jerusalem were told to, "Run ye to and fro through the streets of Jerusalem, *and see now, and know and seek in the broad places thereof, if ye can find a man, if there be any that executeth judgment, that seeketh the truth; and I will pardon it. And though they say, The Lord liveth; surely they swear falsely...*Wherefore a lion out of the forest shall slay them, and a wolf of the evenings shall spoil them, a leopard shall watch over their cities: everyone one that goeth out thence shall be torn in pieces: because their transgressions are many, and their backslidings are increased.

How shall I pardon thee for this? *Thy children have forsaken me, and sworn by them that are no gods: when I had fed them to the full, they then committed adultery, and assembled themselves by troops in the harlots' houses. They were as fed horses in the morning: everyone neighed after his neighbor's wife. Shall I not visit for these things? Saith the Lord: and shall not my soul be avenged on such a nation as this? Go ye up upon her walls, and destroy; but make not a full end: take away her battlements; for they are not the Lord's. For the house of Israel and the house of Judah have dealt very treacherously against me, saith the Lord. They have belied the Lord and said, It is not he; neither shall evil come upon us; neither shall we see sword nor famine..."*

God's Judgment

(Jeremiah 15:1-6)

"*Then said the Lord unto me,* [Jeremiah] **Though Moses and Samuel stood before me, yet my mind could not be toward this people**: *cast them out of my sight, and let them go forth. And it shall come to pass, if they say unto thee, whither shall we go forth? Then thou shalt tell them, Thus saith the Lord; Such as are for death, to death; and such as are for the sword, to the sword; and such as are for the famine, to the famine; and such as are for the captivity, to the captivity.*

And I will appoint over them four kinds, saith the Lord: the sword to slay, and the dogs to tear, and the fowls of the heaven, and the beasts of the earth, to devour and destroy.

And I will cause them to be removed into all kingdoms of the earth, because of Manasseh, the son of Hezekiah king of Judah, for that which he did in Jerusalem.

For who shall have pity upon thee, O Jerusalem? Or who shall bemoan thee? Or who shall go aside to ask how thou doest?

Thou hast forsaken me, saith the Lord, thou art gone backward: therefore will I stretch out my hand against thee, and destroy thee; I am weary with repenting."

Manasseh

Manasseh *(means = "one who causes forgetfulness")* was the most **wickedest** king of Judah!

Manasseh reigned (about 696-641 B.C.) approximately fifty-five years the longest reign of the kings of Judah. He was a "love child" greatly needed to carry on the family's name as heir to the throne. Because king Hezekiah loved his wife Hephzibah *(means = "my delight is in her")*, Manasseh should have been a good son, but he was nothing like his father (Hezekiah).

The Hezekiah's waited a long time for a son! In fact, Manasseh was born about fifteen years after Isaiah's prophecy to king Hezekiah, *"... thy sons that shall issue from thee, which thou shalt beget, shall they take away; and they shall be eunuchs in the place of the king of Babylon. Then said Hezekiah unto Isaiah, Good is the word of the Lord which thou hast spoken. And he said, Is it not good, if peace and truth be in my days?"* (II Kings 20:18-20) More than likely (in their old age), Manasseh's parents poured out gifts, blessings, and affection on him. From the day of his birth, they probably prepared great banquets for each year of his birthday!

Certainly, Manasseh watched his father (king Hezekiah) tear down the altars of false worshippers, punish, and imprison troublemakers. First handedly, Manasseh witnessed king Hezekiah (one of the greatest reforming kings of Judah) in *action* who was a builder, visionary, revivalist, true, and faithful worshipper of **Yahweh**. Surely, Prince Manasseh received special treatment: (a) sat at the king's side (as often as possible) at breakfast, snack time, dinner, in the throne room, and at Temple Worship; (b) witnessed one of the greatest revivals and reformation in Judah's history; (c) educated by the best teachers; (d) instructed in the ways of the Judean kings; (e) talked *face to face* with great prophets *(like Isaiah)* and priests; and (f) given spiritual lessons by scribes. Without a doubt, there is no excuse for Manasseh's *ill* behavior, sinfulness, and wickedness at such an early age, *twelve*.

(II Kings 21:1-9)

<u>At the age of twelve</u>, Manasseh became king of Judah, "And he did that which was evil in the sight of the Lord, *after the abominations of the heathen, whom the Lord cast out before the children of Israel.* **For <u>he built up again the high places which Hezekiah his father had destroyed; and he reared</u>**

up altars for Baal, and made a grove, as did Ahab king of Israel; and worshipped all the host of heaven [sun, moon, and stars], and served them.

And he built altars in the house of the Lord, *of which the Lord said, In Jerusalem will I put my name.* **And he built altars for all the host of heaven in the two courts of the house of the Lord.**

And he made his son pass through the fire, *and observed times, and used enchantments and dealt with familiar spirits and wizards:* **he wrought much wickedness in the sight of the Lord, to provoke him to anger.**

And he set a graven image of the grove that he had made in the house, of which the Lord said to David, and to Solomon his son, In this house, and in Jerusalem, which I have chosen out of all tribes of Israel, will I put my name for ever: *Neither will I make the feet of Israel move any more out of the land which I gave their fathers; only if they will observe to do according to all that I have commanded them, and according to all the law that my servant Moses commanded them. But they hearkened not: and Manasseh seduced them to do more evil than did the nations whom the Lord destroyed before the children of Israel."*

Punishment against Manasseh

"And the Lord spake by his servants the prophets, saying,

Because Manasseh king of Judah hath done these abominations, and hath done wickedly above all that the Amorites did, which were before him, and hath made Judah also to sin with his idols: Therefore thus saith the Lord God of Israel, Behold, I am bringing such evil upon Jerusalem and Judah, that whosoever heareth of it, both his ears shall tingle.

And I will stretch over Jerusalem the line of Samaria, and the plummet of the house of Ahab: and I will wipe Jerusalem as a man wipeth a dish, wiping it, and turning it upside down. And I will forsake the remnant of mine inheritance, and deliver them into the hand of their enemies; and they shall become a prey and a spoil to all their enemies:

Because they have done that which was evil in my sight, and have provoked me to anger, since the day their fathers came forth out of Egypt, even unto this day. Moreover Manasseh shed innocent blood very much till he had filled Jerusalem from one end to another; beside his sin wherewith he made Judah to sin, in doing that which was evil in the sight of the Lord." (II Kings 21:10-16; also see II Chronicles 33:11-19)

(Manasseh's Burial)

After Manasseh died, he was buried in the garden of his own house and not with the kings of Judah.

The Pen of Iron & the Point of a Diamond

"The sin of Judah is written with a pen of iron and with the point of a diamond: it is graven upon the table of their heart, and upon the horns of your altars..." (Jeremiah 17:1) The people were well aware of their sins. Basically, it was impossible for the people to forget their abominations: the cries of the innocent children (sacrificed in the fires of Molech) could still be heard from the Valley of Hinnom (Jeremiah 17:2); men making and worshiping gods unto themselves (Jeremiah 16:20); and the land was filled with detestable and abominable things (Jeremiah 16:18). God compared their sins as being chiseled with iron upon their stony hearts and with the fine point of a diamond!

<u>Seventy Years Captivity</u>

(Jeremiah 25:8-11)

"Therefore thus saith the Lord of hosts; Because ye have not heard my words, Behold, I will send and take all the families of the north, **and** Nebuchadnezzar the king of Babylon, my servant, *and will bring them against this land, and against the inhabitants thereof, and against all these nations round about, and will utterly destroy them, and make them an astonishment, and an hissing, and perpetual desolations. Moreover I will take from them the voice of mirth, and the voice of gladness, the voice of the bridegroom, and the voice of the bride, the sound of the millstones, and the light of the candle. And this whole land shall be a desolation, and an astonishment; and these nations shall serve the king of Babylon seventy years."*

<u>A Message of HOPE during Captivity</u>

(Jeremiah 29:4-14)

"Thus saith the Lord of hosts, the God of Israel, unto all that are carried away captives, <u>whom I have caused to be carried away from Jerusalem unto Babylon;</u>

Build ye houses, and dwell in them; and plant gardens, and eat the fruit of them; Take ye wives, and beget sons and daughters; and take wives for your sons, and give your daughters to husbands, that they may bear sons and daughters; that ye may be increased there, and not diminished. And seek the peace of the city whither I have caused you to be carried away captives and pray unto the Lord for it: for in the peace thereof shall ye have peace...

For thus saith the Lord, that after seventy years be accomplished at Babylon I will visit you, and perform my good word toward you, in causing you to return to this place.

For I know the thoughts that I think toward you, saith the Lord, thoughts of peace, and not of evil, to give you an expected end. Then shall ye call upon me, and ye shall go and pray unto me, and I will hearken unto you. And ye shall seek me, and fine me, when ye shall search for me with all your heart. And I will be found of you, saith the Lord: and I will turn away your captivity, and I will gather you from all the nations, and from all the places whither I have driven you, saith the Lord; and I will bring you again into the place whence I caused you to be carried away captive. "

False Prophets

"For thus saith the Lord of hosts, the God of Israel; Let not your prophets and your diviners, that be in the midst of you, deceive you, neither hearken to your dreams which ye cause to be dreamed. For they prophesy falsely unto you in my name: I have not sent them, saith the Lord." (Jeremiah 29:8-9)

Punishment on False Prophets

During Judah's captivity in Babylon, there were many false prophets. Specifically, there were a few prophets (some with the same names of important kings): (1) Ahab, the son of Kolaiah (not king Ahab of Israel who was dead for many years); (2) Zedekiah, the son of Maaseiah (not the king of Judah); and (3) Shemaiah the Nehelamite (dreamer) who was the leader of the false prophets.

"Hear ye therefore the word of the Lord, all ye of the captivity, whom I have sent from Jerusalem to Babylon:

Thus saith the Lord of Hosts...of Ahab the son of Kolaiah and Zedekiah the son of Maaseiah, which prophesy a lie unto you in my name; Behold, I will deliver them into the hand of Nebuchadnezzar king of Babylon; and he shall slay them before your eyes:

And of them shall be taken up a curse by all the captivity of Judah which are in Babylon, saying, The Lord make thee like Zedekiah and like Ahab whom the king of Babylon roasted in the fire;

Because they have committed villainy in Israel, and have committed adultery with their neighbors' wives and have spoken lying words in my name, which I have not commanded them; even I know and am a witness, saith the Lord.

Thus shalt thou also speak to Shemaiah the Nehelamite, saying, Thus speaketh the Lord of Hosts...Because thou hast sent letter in thy name unto all the people that are at Jerusalem and to Zephaniah the son of Maaseiah the priest, and to all the priests, saying,

The Lord hath made thee priest in the stead of Jehoiada the priest, that ye should be officers in the house of the Lord...Now therefore why hast thou ot reproved Jeremiah of Anathoth, which maketh himself a prophet to you?

Thus saith the Lord...Because Shemaiah hath prophesied unto you, and I sent him not, and he caused you to trust in a lie: Therefore I will punish Shemaiah the Nehelamite and his seed: he shall not have a man to dwell among this people; neither shall he behold the good that I will do for my people, saith the Lord; because he hath taught rebellion against the Lord." (Jeremiah 29:20-32)

Jeremiah's Lamentations

Throughout the Book of Lamentations, Jeremiah speaks from the depth of his heart. Basically, there are five divisions. Here are a few excerpts:

(The First Poem)

(Lamentations 1:1-10)

"How doth the city sit solitary that was full of people! How is she become a widow! She that was great among the nations and princess among the provinces, how is she become tributary! She weepeth sore in the night, and her tears are on her cheeks: among all her lovers she hath one to comfort her: all her friends have dealt treacherously with her, they are become her enemies. Judah is gone into captivity because of affliction and because of great servitude: she dwelleth among the heathen, she findeth no rest: al her persecutors overtook her between the straits... none come to the solemn feasts: all her gates are desolate: her priests sigh, her virgins are afflicted, and she is in bitterness... Her adversaries are the chief, her enemies prosper; the Lord hath afflicted her for the multitude of her transgressions; her children are gone into captivity before the enemy...And from the daughter of Zion, all her beauty is departed: her princes are become like harts that find no pasture... without strength before the pursuer...Jerusalem hath grievously sinned; therefore she is removed: all that honored her despise her because they have seen her nakedness...her filthiness is in her skirts: she remembereth not her last end; she came down: she had no comforter...The adversary hath spread out his hand upon all her pleasant things: she hath seen the that the heathen entered into her sanctuary...All her people sigh, they seek bread; they have given their pleasant things for meat to relieve the soul..."

(Jeremiah's prayers: Jeremiah 1:11, 22)

"... See, O Lord, and consider; for I am become vile." (Jeremiah

177

1:11)   *"Let all their wickedness come before thee and do unto them as thou hast done unto me for all my transgressions: for my sighs are many and my heart is faint."*

(The Second Poem)

(Lamentations 2:11-22)

"Mine eyes do fail with tears, my bowels are troubled, my liver is poured upon the earth, for the destruction of the daughter of my people; because the children and the sucklings swoon in the streets of the city. They say to their mothers, Where is corn and wine? When they swooned as the wounded in the streets of the city, when their soul was poured out into their mothers' bosom. What thing shall I take to witness for thee? What thing of Jerusalem? What shall I equal to thee, that I am comfort thee O virgin daughter of Zion? For thy breach is great like the sea: who can heal thee? Thy prophets have seen vain and foolish things for thee: and they have not discovered thine iniquity, to turn away thy captivity; but have seen for thee false burdens and causes of banishment. All that pass by clap their hands at thee; they hiss and wag their head at the daughter of Jerusalem, saying, Is this the city that men call The perfection of beauty, The joy of the whole earth? All thine enemies have opened their mouth against thee: they hiss and gnash the teeth: they say, we have swallowed her up: certainly this is the day that we looked for; we have found, we have seen it. The Lord hath done that which he had devised; he hath fulfilled his word that he had commanded in the days of old: he hath thrown down, and hath not pitied: and he hath caused thine enemy to rejoice over thee, he hath set up the horn of thine adversaries."

(Jeremiah's prayer: Lamentations 2:20-22)

"Behold, O Lord, and consider to whom thou hast done this. Shall the women eat their fruit,[50] and children of a span long? Shall the

---

50   The prophet *was not* talking about the women eating fruit from the trees! Instead, Jeremiah was referring to the "children" as the "fruit of the womb" and they were very young children *"...a span long."* These curses and plagues were placed upon Israel

priest and the prophet be slain in the sanctuary of the Lord? The young and the old lie on the ground in the streets: my virgins and my young men are fallen by the sword; thou hast slain them in the day of thine anger; thou hast killed and not pitied. Thou hast called as in a solemn day my terrors round about, so that in the day of the Lord's anger none escaped nor remained: those that I have swaddled and brought up hath mine enemy consumed."

(The Third Poem)

The prophet intermingles his calamities with the nation of Israel. In this way, Jeremiah pivots from the singular pronoun to the plural, then, from the plural back to the singular pronoun. Here is an outline for Jeremiah's Third Poem: Lamentations 3:1-21 (Singular); Lamentations 3:22-23 (Plural); Lamentations 3:24-39 (Singular); Lamentations 3:40-47 (Plural); and Lamentations 3:48-66 (Singular).

(Lamentations 3:1-21; Singular)

"I am the man that hath seen affliction by the rod of his wrath. He hath led me, and brought me into darkness, but not into light. Surely against me is he turned; he turneth his hand against me all the day. My flesh and my skin hath he made old; he hath broken my bones. He hath builded against me, and compassed me with gall and travail. He hath set me in dark places, as they that be dead of old. He hath hedged me about, that I cannot get out: he hath made my chain heavy. Also when I cry and shout, he shutteth out my prayer.

---

for walking contrary to Yahweh's Word, *"And if ye will not for all this hearken unto me, but walk contrary unto me; Then I will walk contrary unto you also in fury... And ye shall eat the flesh of your sons and the flesh of your daughters shall ye eat... And I will make your cities waste and bring your sanctuaries unto desolation..."* (Leviticus 26:27-31) Furthermore, Yahweh said that He would bring the land into desolation and scatter His people among the heathen with the sword, *"Then shall the land enjoy her Sabbaths, as long as it lieth desolate, and ye be in your enemies' land...As long as it lieth desolate it shall rest; because it did not rest in your Sabbaths when ye dwelt upon it."* (Leviticus 26:34-35) For more information read: II Kings 6:28-29; Jeremiah 19:8-9; Leviticus 26; and Deuteronomy 28-53.

He hath enclosed my ways with hewn stone, he hath made my paths crooked. He was unto me as a bear lying in wait, and as lion in secret places. He hath turned aside my ways, and pulled me in pieces: he hath made my desolate. He hath bent his bow, and set me as a mark for the arrow. He hath caused the arrows of his quiver to enter in my reins. I was a derision to all my people; and their song all the day. He hath also broken my teeth with gravel stones, he hath covered me with ashes. And thou hast removed my soul far off from peace: I forgot prosperity. And I said, My strength and my hope is perished from the Lord: Remembering mine affliction and my misery, the wormwood and the gall. My soul hath them still in remembrance, and is humbled in me. This I recall to my mind, therefore have I hope."

(Lamentations 3:22-23; Plural)
"It is of the Lord's mercies that we are not consumed, because his compassions fail not. They are new every morning: great is thy faithfulness."

(Lamentations 3:24-39; Singular)
"The Lord is my portion, saith my soul; therefore will I hope in him. The Lord is good unto them that wait for him, to the soul that seeketh him. It is good that a man should both hope and quietly wait for the salvation of the Lord. It is good for a man that he bear the yoke in his youth. He sitteth alone and keepeth silence, because he hath borne it upon him. He putteth his mouth in the dust; if so be there may be hope. He giveth his cheek to him that smiteth him: he is filled full with reproach. For the Lord will not cast off for ever: But though he cause grief, yet will he have compassion according to the multitude of his mercies. For he doth not afflict willingly nor grieve the children of men. To crush under his feet all the prisoners of the earth, To turn aside the right of a man before the face of the most High, To subvert a man in his cause, the Lord approveth not. Who is he that saith, and it cometh to pass, when the Lord commandeth it not? Out of the mouth of the most High proceedeth not evil and good?

Wherefore doth a living man complain, a man for the punishment of his sins?"

(Lamentations 3:40-47; Plural)

"Let us lift up our heart with our hands unto God in the heavens. We have transgressed and have rebelled: thou hast not pardoned. Thou hast covered with anger, and persecuted us: thou hast slain, thou hast not pitied. Thou hast covered thyself with a cloud, that our prayer should not pass through. Thou hast made us as the offscouring and refuse in the midst of the people. All of our enemies have opened their mouths against us. Fear and a snare is come upon us, desolation and destruction."

(Lamentations 3:48-63; Singular)

"Mine eye runneth down with rivers of water for the destruction of the daughter of my people. Mine eye trickleth down and ceaseth not, without any intermission, Till the Lord look down, and behold form heaven. Mine eye affecteth mine heart because of all the daughters of my city. Mine enemies chased me sore, like a bird, without cause. They have cut off my life in the dungeon, and cast a stone upon me. Waters flowed over mine head; then I said, I am cut of. I called upon thy name, O Lord, out of the low dungeon. Thou has heard my voice: hide not thine ear at my breathing, at my cry. Thou drewest near in the day that I called upon thee: thou sadist, Fear not. O Lord, thou hast pleaded the causes of my soul; thou hast redeemed my life. O Lord, thou hast seen my wrong: judge thou my cause. Thou hast heard their reproach, O Lord, and all their imaginations against me; The lips of those that rose up against me, and their device against me all the day. Behold their sitting down, and their rising up; I am their musick."

(Jeremiah's prayer: Lamentations 3:64-66)

"Render unto them a recompence, O Lord, according to the work of their hands. Give them sorrow of heart, thy curse unto them.

Persecute and destroy them in anger from under the heavens of the Lord."

(The Fourth Poem)

(Lamentations 4:1-11)

"How is the gold become dim! How is the most fine gold changed! The stones of the sanctuary are poured out in the top of every district. The precious sons of Zion, comparable to fine gold, how are they esteemed as earthen pitchers, the work of the hands of the potter! Even the sea monsters draw out the breast, they give suck to their young ones: the daughter of my people is become cruel, like the ostriches in the wilderness. The tongue of the sucking child cleaveth to the roof of his mouth for thirst: the young children ask bread and no man breaketh it unto them. They that did feed delicately are desolate in the streets: they that are brought up in scarlet embrace dunghills. For the punishment of the iniquity of the daughter of my people is greater than the punishment of the sin of Sodom that was overthrown as in a moment and no hands stayed on her. Her Nazarites were purer than snow, they were whiter than milk, they were more ready in body than rubies, their polishing was of sapphire. Their visage is blacker than a coal; they are not known in the streets: their skin cleaveth to their bones; it is withered it is become like a stick. They that be slain with the sword are better than they that be slain with hunger: for these pine away, stricken through for want of the fruits of the field. The hands of the pitiful women have sodden [boiled] *their own children: they were their meat in the destruction of the daughter of my people. The Lord hath accomplished his fury; he hath poured out his fierce anger and kindled a fire in Zion and it hath devoured the foundations thereof. The kings of the earth and all the inhabitants of the world would not have believed that the adversary and the enemy should have entered into the gates of Jerusalem."*

182

(Lamentations 4:21-22)

Jeremiah speaks of the reasons for judgment against Judah, *"The kings of the earth, and all the inhabitants of the world would not have believed that the adversary and the enemy should have entered into the gates of Jerusalem. For the sins of her prophets and the iniquities of her priests that have shed the blood of the just in the midst of her. They have wandered as blind men in the streets, they have polluted themselves with blood so that men could not touch their garments. They cried unto them, Depart ye; it is unclean; depart, depart, touch not: when they fled away and wandered, they said among the heathen, They shall no more sojourn there. The anger of the Lord hath divided them; he will no more regard them: they respected not the persons of the priests, they favored not the elders. As for us, our eyes as yet failed for our vain help: in our watching we have watched for a nation that could not save us. They hunt our steps...for our end is come...Our persecutors are swifter than the eagles of the heaven: they pursued us upon the mountains, they laid wait for us in the wilderness...The breath of our nostrils, the anointed of the Lord, was taken in their pits...Under his shadow we shall live among the heathen..."*

(Lamentations 4:21-22)

In this Lamentation, Jeremiah's message is a prophesy of hope for Israel who was tormented by the Edomites (the descendants of Esau, the twin brother to Jacob). Down through many generations, the Edomites were thorns to Israel. Therefore, the prophet mocks the Edomites, *"Rejoice and be glad [THE PROPHET IS BEING IRONIC. HE IS TELLING EDOM THAT THEIR PAYBACK/CALAMITY IS ON THE WAY], O daughter of Edom, that dwellest in the land of Uz; the cup also shall pass through unto thee: thou shall be drunken and shalt make thyself naked... he will visit thine iniquity, O daughter of Edom; he will discover thy sins."* (Lamentations 4:21, 22b) This prophecy was fulfilled in Jeremiah 49:7-22. King Nebuchadnezzar and his army destroyed Edom.

The second part of the prophecy is futuristic. Lamentations 4:22a predicts restoration to the entire Nation of Israel, ***"The punishment of thine iniquity is accomplished. O daughter of Zion; he will no more carry thee away into captivity…"***

(The Fifth Poem)

(Lamentations 5:1-22)

Jeremiah pleads with the Lord, ***"For this our heart is faint for these things our eyes are dim. Because of the mountain of Zion, which is desolate, the foxes walk upon it. Thou, O Lord, remainest for ever; thy throne from generation to generation. Wherefore dost thou forget us for ever, and forsake us so long time? Turn thou us unto thee, O Lord, and we shall be turned; renew our days as of old. But thou has utterly rejected us; thou art very wroth against us."***

(Jeremiah's prayer: Lamentations 5:1-16)

"Remember, O Lord, what is come upon us: consider and behold our reproach. Our inheritance is turned to strangers, our houses to aliens. We are orphans and fatherless, our mothers are as widows. We have drunken our water for money; our wood is sold unto us. Our necks are under persecution: we labor and have no rest. We have given the hand to the Egyptians and to the Assyrians to be satisfied with bread. Our fathers have sinned and are not; and we have borne their iniquities. Servants have ruled over us: there is none that doth deliver us out of their hand. We gat our bread with the peril of our lives because of the sword of the wilderness. Our skin was black like an oven because of the terrible famine. They ravished the women in Zion and the maids in the cities of Judah. Princes are hanged up by their hands: the faces of elders were not honored. They took the young men to grind and the children fell under the wood. The elders have ceased from the gate, the young men from their musick. The joy of our heart is ceased; our dance is turned into mourning. The crown is fallen from our head: woe unto us that we have sinned.

Jeremiah's Mission: Body, Soul, and Mind

So far, Jeremiah was completely submissive in delivering God's messages to Israel, *"...for thou shalt go to all that I shall send thee and whatsoever I command thee thou shalt speak. Be not afraid of their faces for I am with thee to deliver thee, saith the Lord."* (Jeremiah 1:7-8) The latter illustrates God's commission to Jeremiah and Jeremiah's obedience to the commission.

Moreover, Jeremiah's mission affected his body, soul, and mind. Now, Jeremiah compared his sufferings for Judah to the physical sufferings within his body. Descriptively, Jeremiah states, *"My bowels, my bowels! I am pained at my very heart; my heart maketh noise in me; I cannot hold my peace because thou hast heard, O my soul, the sound of the trumpet, the alarm of war. Destruction upon destruction is cried; for the whole land is spoiled; suddenly are my tents spoiled, and my curtains in a moment. How long shall I see the standard, and hear the sound of the trumpet?"* (Jeremiah 4:19-21)

Also, Jeremiah wanted this burden to be proclaimed to all Judean hearers! Since there was no worldwide internet or radio-broadcasts, Jeremiah chose a *specific* musical instrument in his writings so that when Baruch read scroll to the listeners, an emphasis would be placed on the loudest instrument known to the ancient people at that time. Therefore, Jeremiah picked the *trumpet* (a brass-wind instrument with a blaring tone) to SOUND THE ALARM! Most likely, Baruch stood straight up as if he was a *trumpeter* (putting his hand up to his lips as if he was holding a trumpet) and yelled aloud, "O my soul, the sound of the trumpet, the alarm of war..." (Jeremiah 4:19b)

In other words, the viewers could imagine and visualize the sound of a blasting trumpet, foretelling, and/or announcing the significant news of *imminent destruction*. Moreover, Jeremiah repeatedly said, "... blow the trumpet [AND/OR] sound the trumpet..." through his book. (See Jeremiah 4:5; 4:19b; 4:21; 6:1; 6:17; 42:14) In Jeremiah 51:27, he expanded the alarm (pending destruction) to all nations, ***"Set ye up a standard in the land, blow the trumpet among the nations, prepare the nations..."***

Although Jeremiah was an obedient and humble prophet, he was put in prison. Just because someone is faithful to God, it does not mean that they will not suffer. In fact, Jeremiah did not commit any crimes, he only told the "truth." In spite of the many incarcerations, Jeremiah continued his "writing and prophecies in prison."

Jeremiah in Prison, (Jonathan's Dungeon)

In fear of the Egyptians, the army of Chaldeans backed away from Jerusalem. At that time, Jeremiah was a free man to go and come at will. Being weary of the trouble within Jerusalem, Jeremiah decided to leave the city and travel to the land of Benjamin where he purchased a field from his cousin (Hanameel, *the son of Shallum*).

Unfortunately, Irijah (an army captain) saw Jeremiah leaving and accused him of defecting over to the Chaldeans. Because of Jeremiah's *numerous* warnings for Jerusalem *"to accept captivity under the Babylonians,"* Irijah believed that Jeremiah was a traitor and he brought Jeremiah before the princes who cast Jeremiah ***"...into prison in the house of Jonathan the scribe...Jeremiah was entered into the dungeon and into the cabins, and remained there many days..."*** (Jeremiah 37:11-16)

"Then Zedekiah the king sent, and took him out and the king asked him secretly in his house, ***and said,*** Is there any word from the Lord? ***And Jeremiah said,*** **<u>There is</u>**: *for, said he,* <u>***thou shalt be delivered into the hand of the king of Babylon***</u>." (Jeremiah 37:17) For some reason, king Zedekiah hoped for the **Lord GOD** to change His mind! However, God's decision remained the same as stated in the same chapter, ***"Thus saith the Lord...***And the Chaldeans shall come again, and fight against this city, and take it, and burn it with fire..." (Jeremiah 37:8)

Jeremiah, Transferred to the Prison Court

Out of anger, king Zedekiah *"commanded that they should commit Jeremiah into the court of the prison, and that they should give him daily a piece of bread out of the bakers' street, until all the bread in the city were spent..."* (Jeremiah 37:21) However, Jeremiah continued preaching the Word of the Lord and this made the princes of Judah furious! Thus, they demanded the *death penalty* for Jeremiah, *"...for he weakeneth the hands of the mean of war that remain in this city, and the hands of all the people, in speaking such words unto them: for this man seeketh not the welfare of this people, but the hurt."* (Jeremiah 37:4) Without hesitation, king Zedekiah said, *"Behold, he is in your hand..."* (Jeremiah 37:5)

Jeremiah, Cast into the Miry Dungeon

At this point, the princes of Judah were outraged with Jeremiah, *"They took Jeremiah and cast him into the dungeon of Malchiah the son of Hammelech, that was in the court of the prison: and they let down Jeremiah with cords. And in the dungeon there was no water, but mire: so Jeremiah sunk in the mire."* (Jeremiah 38:6)

Jeremiah, Saved by a (Black) Ethiopian Eunuch

God always provides a way out for His people!

(Jeremiah 38:7-13)

"Now when Ebedmelech the Ethiopian, one of the eunuchs which was in the King's house, heard that they had put Jeremiah in the dungeon; the king then sitting in the gate of Benjamin;

Ebedmelech went forth out of the king's house, and spake to the king, saying, My Lord the king, these men have done evil in all that they have done to Jeremiah the prophet, whom they have cast into the dungeon; and he is like to die for hunger in the place where he is: for there I s no more bread in the city.

Then the king commanded Ebedmelech the Ethiopian, saying, Take from hence thirty men with thee, and take up Jeremiah the prophet out of the dungeon before he die. So Ebedmelech took men with him, and went into the house of the king under the treasury, and took thence old cast clouts and old rotten rags, and let them down by cords into the dungeon to Jeremiah.

And Ebedmelech said unto Jeremiah, Put now these old cast clouts and rotten rags under thine armholes under the cords. And Jeremiah did so. So they drew up Jeremiah with cords, and took him up out of the dungeon: and Jeremiah remained in the court of the prison."

Conditional Mercy Extended

In spite of being placed in the dungeon, Jeremiah did not have a hostile attitude toward king Zedekiah. Instead, Jeremiah spoke words of encouragement to the king,

(Jeremiah 38:17-20)

"Thus saith the Lord, the God of hosts, the God of Israel; If thou wilt assuredly go forth unto the king of Babylon's princes, then thy

soul shall live, and this city shall not be burned with fire; and thou shalt live, and thine house:

But if thou wilt not go forth to the king of Babylon's princes, then shall this city be given into the hand of the Chaldeans, and they shall burn it with fire, and thou shalt not escape out of their hand.

And Zedekiah the king said unto Jeremiah, I am afraid of the Jews that are fallen to the Chaldeans, lest they deliver me into their hand, and they mock me. But Jeremiah said, They shall not deliver thee. Obey, I beseech thee, the voice of the Lord, which I speak unto thee: so it shall be well unto thee and thy soul shall live."

Captivity Fulfilled

As stated in Jeremiah's prophecy, king Zedekiah is kept alive but his sons (along with many nobles of Jerusalem) are killed before his eyes; and the king is blinded!

King Nebuchadnezzar and his army besieged Jerusalem,

(Jeremiah 39:1-7)
"In the ninth year of Zedekiah king of Judah, in the tenth month, came Nebuchadnezzar king of Babylon and all his army against Jerusalem, and they besieged it. And in the eleventh year of Zedekiah, in the fourth month, the ninth day of the month, the city was broken up. And all the princes of the king of Babylon came in, and sat in the middle gate, even Nergalsharezer, Samgarnebo, Sarsechim, Rabsaris, Nergalsharezer, Rabmag, with all the residue of the princes of the king of Babylon.

And it came to pass, that when Zedekiah the king of Judah saw them, and all the men of war, then they fled, and went forth out of the city by night, by the way of the King's garden, by the gate betwixt the two walls: and he went out the way of the plan.

But the Chaldeans' army pursued after them, and overtook Zedekiah in the plains of Jericho: and when they had taken him, they brought him up to <u>Nebuchadnezzar king of Babylon</u> *to Riblah in the land of Hamath, where he gave judgment upon him.*

Then the king of Babylon slew the sons of Zedekiah in Riblah before his eyes: also the king of Babylon slew all the nobles of Judah.

Moreover he put out Zedekiah's eyes, and bound him with chains, to carry him to Babylon.

And the Chaldeans burned the king's house, and the houses of the people, with fire, and brake down the walls of Jerusalem.

Then <u>Nebuzaradan the captain of the guard</u> *carried away captive into Babylon the remnant of the people that remained in the city, and those that fell away, that fell to him with the rest of the people that remained. But* <u>Nebuzaradan the captain of the guard</u> *left of the poor of the people, which had nothing, in the land of Judah, and gave them vineyards and fields at the same time."*

The Right of Kinsman Redemption

The **Lord GOD** loves all of His people. Symbolically, His plan of redemption (to the Tribe of Judah and displayed through the Law of the Kinsman Redemption [51]) was displayed by Jeremiah's dramatic scene

---

51   Moses issued <u>The Right of Kinsman Redemption</u> in Leviticus 25:25-34. Also, the same law is displayed in the story of Naomi, Ruth (the Moabitess) and Boaz. Ruth's husband (Mahlon, son of Naomi & Elimelech) died in the land of Moab. In fact, Elimelech died first; then both of his sons, Mahlon and Chilion). Ruth decided to ac-

(in the prison court) to buy the field of his kinsman. Before Hanameel *(his cousin)* approached Jeremiah, the ***"Word of the Lord came unto Jeremiah."*** (Jeremiah 32:6-8) Thus, Jeremiah did not purchase the field out of greed: (1) in compliance to God's will; and (2) in " *obedience under the right of redemption* and *the right of inheritance as a kinsman."* (Jeremiah 32:9) Remarkably, Jeremiah bought the field for ***"seventeen shekels of silver [17 shekels @ .64 cents = $10.88]."*** (Jeremiah 32:10) Moreover, the purchase of the field was recorded by Baruch (Jeremiah's *personal scribe*); witnessed in the presence of people (Hanameel and the Jews who sat in the court of the prison); and a charge was given to Baruch, ***"Thus saith the Lord of hosts, the God of Israel; Take these evidences, this evidence of the purchase, both which is sealed, and this evidence which is open; and put them in an earthen vessel, that they may continue many days. For thus saith the Lord of hosts, the God of Israel; Houses and fields and vineyards shall be possessed again in this land."*** (Jeremiah 32:11-14)

Final Restoration for Israel

The Prophet Jeremiah knew about God's futuristic plans for His people. Therefore, it is necessary to expand the phrase ***"The punishment of thine iniquity is accomplished. O daughter of Zion..."*** (Lamentations

---

company her mother-in-law (Naomi) from the land of Moab back to Bethlehem-Judah where she worked in the fields of Boaz (a wealthy man who favored Ruth). Through her marriage to Elimelech, Naomi was related to Boaz who claimed the Right of Kinsman Redemption in order to marry Ruth (a widow) ***"...that the name of the dead be not cut off from among his brethren..."*** (Ruth 4:10) ***"And he [Boaz] took ten men of the elders of the city, and said, Sit ye down here. And they sat down. And he said unto the kinsman, Naomi, that is come gain out of the country of Moab, selleth a parcel of land, which was our brother Elimelech's...if thou wilt not redeem it, then tell me...I am after thee..."*** But the first kinsman could not buy the parcel and said, ***"I cannot redeem it for myself lest I mar mine own inheritance: redeem thou my right to thyself..."*** (Ruth 4:2-7) So, Boaz took off his shoe and gave it to the elders as a symbol: "the transfer of the property and all the rights and privileges including marriage to Ruth." (See the Book of Ruth, Chapters 3-4)

4:22a) The latter phrase predicts the end of punishment to the Nation of Israel.

The phrase *"...he will no more carry thee away into captivity..."* (Lamentations 4:22b) is futuristic and twofold regarding the period of time before and after the Second Advent of Christ. For a more comprehensive view, we must look at the Book of Zechariah 14:1-11 (the Battle of Armageddon),

[BEFORE THE SECOND ADVENT OF CHRIST]

"Behold the day of the Lord cometh, and thy spoil shall be divided in the midst of thee. For I will gather all nations against Jerusalem to battle; and the city shall be taken, and the houses rifled, and the women ravished; and half of the city shall go forth into captivity, and the residue of the people shall not be cut off from the city." (Zechariah 14:3-1-2)

[AFTER THE SECOND ADVENT OF CHRIST]

"Then shall the Lord go forth, and fight against those nations as when he fought in the day of battle." And his feet shall stand in that day upon the mount of Olives, which is before Jerusalem on the east, and the mount of Olives shall cleave in the midst thereof toward the east and toward the west, and there shall be a very great valley; and half of the mountain shall remove toward the north and half of it toward the south. And ye shall flee to the valley of the mountains; for the valley of the mountains shall reach unto Azal: yea, ye shall flee, like as ye fled from before the earthquake in the days of Uzziah king of Judah: and the Lord my God shall come, and all the saints with thee. And it shall come to pass in that day, that the light shall not be clear, no dark: But it shall be one day which shall be known to the Lord, not day, nor night: but it shall come to pass, that at evening time it shall be light. And it shall be in that day, that living waters shall go out from Jerusalem; half of them toward the former sea, and half of them toward the hinder sea, and in summer and in winter shall it be.

And the Lord shall be king over all the earth: in that day shall there be one Lord and his name one. All the land shall be turned as a plain from Gerba to Rimmon south of Jerusalem: and it shall be lifted up, and inhabited in her place, from Benjamin's gate unto the place of the first gate, unto the corner gate, and from the tower of Hananeel unto the king's winepresses. And men shall dwell in it and there shall be no more utter destruction; but Jerusalem shall be safely inhabited."
(Zechariah 14:3-11)

New Jerusalem

After the Second Advent of Christ/The Tribulation (Revelation 6:1-18:24); the Millennium (Revelation 19:11-20:15); the Renovation of the Earth (Hebrew 1:1; 12:26; II Peter 3:10); New Jerusalem is coming down to earth and there will be a New Heavens and New Earth (Isaiah 65-66; Revelation 21-22); also known as the AGE of Ages (Ephesians 2:7 and 3:11).

Moreover, further examination of the **"celestial city"** *(New Jerusalem)* is required. God will do a new thing! "And he that sat upon the throne said, Behold, I make all things new. *And he said unto me, Write: for these words are true and faithful. And He said unto me, It is done. I am Alpha and Omega, the beginning and the end.*" (Revelation 21:5-6) Presently, God is building a **"celestial city"** that will come down from Heaven to a New Earth!

Chapter 18

Ezekiel's Prophecies of Aholah & Aholibah

(The Professor's comments)

There is no way to talk about the captivity of Southern Tribe of Judah without mentioning Ezekiel's Prophecies! Ezekiel *(means = God strengthens)* was both a priest and prophet to Judah about 606-538 B.C. Initially, Ezekiel was among the captives with king Jehoiachin (Ezekiel 1:2; II Kings 24:6-17).

Ezekiel was a powerful *major* prophet who lived among the captives in Tel-abib *(by the River Chebar)*. **Yahweh** called Ezekiel to minister to Judah *(during the seventy years of exile)* and to the captives in Babylon. *"The word of the Lord came* expressly ***unto Ezekiel the priest, the son of Buzi, in the land of the Chaldeans by the river Chebar; and the hand of the Lord was there upon him."*** (Ezekiel 1:3)

As his name implies, Ezekiel was sent *"...as a* watchman ***unto the house of Israel..."*** (Ezekiel 3:17) to strengthen, speak, and to give warnings to the captives about **Yahweh and His judgments** against them. *"**Thus Ezekiel is unto you a sign: according to all that he hath done shall ye do: and when this cometh, ye shall know that I am the Lord GOD."*** (Ezekiel 24:24)   Many of the Hebrews came to seek Ezekiel's advice, *"**And the people said unto me, Wilt thou not tell us what*** *these things are to us, that thou doest so?"* (Ezekiel 24:19) However, the Hebrews did not listen and they were disobedient throughout their captivity.

The *wise old Hittite owl* said that God called on poor Ezekiel out of the blue. Ezekiel's visions, prophecies, and commissions were to aid and strengthen the *stiff-necked* captives in Judah. God knew in advance that the people were not going to listen to Ezekiel! As typical, people *know* they are wrong but they *refused* to do right! The more people sin the easier it is to commit sin! So, people keep on sinning (and sinning) until their behavior is the acceptable norm. Thus, they call wrong right and right wrong!

Throughout the **Book of Ezekiel**, a three-word phrase is echoed over and over,

"...*a rebellious house*..." (Ezekiel 2:5-6, 8; 3:9, 27; 12:2-3, 9, 25; 17:12; 224:3; 44:6) In Ezekiel 2:3-5, Judah is referred to as ***a rebellious nation***,

"And he said unto me, Son of man, I send thee to the children of Israel, to a <u>rebellious nation</u> that hath rebelled against me; they and their fathers have transgressed against me, even unto this very day. For they are impudent children and stiffhearted. I do send thee unto them; and thou shalt say unto the, Thus saith the Lord GOD. And they, whether they will hear, or whether they will forbear, (<u>for they are a rebellious house</u>), yet shall know that there hath been a prophet among them."

(Movie Material: Ezekiel's Visions)
Modern men would pay millions *(maybe billions)* of dollars to see Ezekiel's visions of: **God, the brightness of His Glory, and His Throne expressed in miraculous living colors of the rainbow and the aurora borealis of lights; the firmament; the heavens opened; the whirlwind; the four living creatures with four faces, wings, and hands; the entire living, breathing transportation system (wheel within a wheel and full of eyes); their obedience to the Spirit of God; their speed**

of movement; and the coals of fire between the wheels and under the cherub, and so on.

In fact, the Holy Book (Ezekiel 3:1-3) that was given to Ezekiel would be a priceless commodity on EBAY; except, Ezekiel ate it! Too bad, Ezekiel did not have a digital camera, cam recorder, and access to the worldwide web! *That would be something to tweet about!*

Yahweh assigned so many tasks to Ezekiel such as *multiple* pantomimes (being bound and tied up, *unable to go out*; struck with dumbness, *unable to speak*; using a tile as a city and making siege against it; using an iron pan as a wall or iron; lying on the right and left sides of his body for countless days; eating unclean food and drinking water by measure *in representation of the famine in Jerusalem*; shaving his hair and beard with a sharp knife and a barber's razor; dividing his hair and beard into three parts *(burning one-third; smite one-third with a knife; scatter one-third in the wind; and God will draw out a sword after them)*; judgments against seven the gentile nations (*Ammon, Moab, Edom, Philistia, Tyre, Zidon, and Egypt*); and predictions regarding: king Nebuchadnezzar; the Prince of Tyre (Lucifer, the anointed cherub); the *nine* precious stones given to Lucifer *(plus the gold)*; the Valley of Dry Bones; the Parable of the Two Sticks = One Stick *(the House of Judah and the House of Joseph, Ephraim)*; Israel's re-gathering, restoration, and conversion; the New Covenant of Peace; and Armageddon, etc.

Furthermore, Yahweh placed the duties of Ezekiel's office (as prophet and priest) above the prophet's personal life. Ezekiel was married but they had no children. However, Ezekiel's wife died *(about the ninth year of his banishment)* suddenly and God forbade him to mourn the death of his own wife, **"Also, the word of the Lord came unto me, saying, Son of man, behold, I take away from thee the desire of thine eyes with a stroke: yet neither shalt thou mourn nor weep, neither shall thy tears run down. Forbear to cry, make no mourning for the dead, bind the tire of thine head upon thee, and put on thy shoes upon thy feet, and cover not thy lips, and eat not the bread of men."** (Ezekiel 24:15-17) The prophet preached to the people in the morning, **"...*at even my wife died and I did in the morning as I was commanded.*"** (Ezekiel 24:18)

Ezekiel's Call, Visions, and Commissions

(Ezekiel 1:1-4)

"Now it came to pass in the thirtieth year, in the fourth month, in the fifth day of the month, as I was among the captives by the river of Chebar, <u>that the heavens were opened, and I saw visions of God</u>. The word of the Lord came <u>expressly</u> unto Ezekiel the priest, the son of Buzi, in the land of the Chaldeans by the river Chebar; and the hand of the Lord was there upon him. And I looked, and, behold a whirlwind came out of the north, a great cloud, and a fire infolding itself, and a brightness was about it, and out of the midst thereof as the color of amber, out of the midst of the fire."

(Four Living Creatures, Faces, Wings, Hands, Feet, Color, Speed)

(Ezekiel 1:5-14)

"Also out of the midst came the likeness of four living creatures. And this was their appearance; they had the likeness of a man. And everyone had four faces, and every one had four wings. And their feet were straight feet; and the sole of their feet was like the sole of a calf's foot: and they sparkled like the color of burnished brass.

And they had the hands of a man under their wings on their four sides; and they four had their faces and their wings. Their wings were joined one to another; they turned not, when they went; they went every one straight forward.

As for the likeness of their faces, they four had the face of a man, and the face of a lion, on the right side: and they four had the face of an ox on the left side; they four also had the face of an eagle.

Thus were their faces: and their wings were stretched upward;

two wings of every one were joined one to another, and two covered their bodies.

And they went every one straight forward: whither the spirit was to go, they went; and they turned not when they went. As for the likeness of living creatures, their appearance was like burning coals of fire, and like the appearance of lamps: it went up and down among the living creatures; and the fire was bright, and out of the fire went forth lightning. And the living creatures ran and returned as the appearance of a flash of lightning."

(The Wheels, Eyes, Color, One Likeness)
(Ezekiel 1:15-21)

"Now as I beheld the living creatures, behold one wheel upon the earth by the living creatures, with his four faces: The appearance of wheels and their work was like unto the color of a beryl: and they four had one likeness and their appearance and their work was as it were a wheel in the middle of a wheel.

When they went, they went upon their four sides: and they turned not when they went. As for their rings, they were so high that they were dreadful; and their rings were full of eyes round about them four. And when the living creatures went, the wheels went by them: and when the living creatures were lifted up from the earth, the wheels were lifted up.

Whithersoever the spirit was to go, they went, thither was their spirit to go; and the wheels were lifted up over against them: for the spirit of the living creature was in the wheels."

(The Firmament)
(Ezekiel 1:22-25)

"And the likeness of the firmament upon the heads of the living

creature was as the color of the terrible crystal, stretched forth over their heads above.

And under the firmament were their wings straight, the one toward the other: every one had two, which covered on this side, and everyone had two, which covered on that side, their bodies.

And when they went, I heard the noise of their wings, like the noise of great waters as the voice of the Almighty, the voice of speech, as the noise of an host: when they stood they let down their wings.

And there was a voice from the firmament that was over their heads, when they stood, and had let down their wings."

(The Throne & The Glory of the Lord)
(Ezekiel 2:26-28)
"And above the firmament that was over their heads was the likeness of a throne, as the appearance of sapphire stone: and upon the likeness of the throne was the likeness as the appearance of a man above upon it. And I saw as the color of amber, as the appearance of fire round about within it, from the appearance of his loins even upward, and from the appearance of his loins even downward, I saw as it were the appearance of fire, and it had brightness round about.

As the appearance of the bow that is in the cloud in the day of rain, so was the appearance of the brightness round about. This was the appearance of the likeness of the glory of the Lord. And when I saw it, I fell upon my face, and I heard a voice of one that spake."

(Ezekiel's Actual Commission & Infilling of the Spirit)
(Ezekiel 2:1-5)
"And he said unto me, Son of man, stand upon they feet, and I will speak unto thee. And the spirit entered into me when he spake

unto me, and set me upon my feet, that I heard him that spake unto me. And he said unto me, Son of man, I send thee to the children of Israel, to a rebellious nation that hath rebelled against me: they and their fathers have transgressed against me, even unto this very day. For they are impudent children and stiffhearted. I do send thee unto them; and thou shalt say unto them; Thus saith the Lord God. And they, whether they will hear, or whether they will forbear, (for they are a rebellious house) yet shall know that there hath bee a prophet among them. And thou, son of man, be not afraid of them, neither be afraid of their words, though briers and thorns be with thee, and thou dost dwell among scorpions: be not afraid of their words, nor be dismayed at their looks, though they be a rebellious house. And thou shalt speak my words unto them, whether they will hear, or whether they will forbear: for they are most rebellious."

(Ezekiel Eats the Holy Book)

(Ezekiel 2:8-10; 3:1-3)

"But thou, son of man, hear what I say unto thee; Be not thou rebellious like that rebellious house: open they mouth, and eat that I give thee. And when I looked, behold, an hand was sent unto me; and, lo a roll of a book was therein; and he spread it before me; and it was written within and without: and there was written therein lamentations and mourning, and woe. Moreover he said unto me, Son of man, eat that thou findest; eat this roll, and go speak unto the house of Israel. So I opened my mouth, and he caused me to eat that roll. And he said unto me, Son of man, cause thy belly to eat, and fill thy bowels with this roll hat I give thee. Then did I eat it; and it was in my mouth, as honey for sweetness."

God Reiterates To Ezekiel

(Ezekiel 3:4-11)

God told Ezekiel, *"Son of man, go, get thee unto the house of*

200

Israel, and speak with my words unto them. For thou are not sent to a people of a strange speech and of an heard language, but to the house of Israel; Not to many people of a strange speech and of an hard language, whose words thou canst ot understand. Surely, had I sent thee to them, they would have hearkened unto thee. But the house of Israel will not hearken unto thee; for they will not hearken unto me: for all the house of Israel are impudent and hardhearted. Behold I have made thy face strong against their faces, and thy forehead strong against their foreheads. As an adamant harder than flint have I made thy forehead: fear the not, neither be dismayed at their looks, though they be a rebellious house.

Moreover He said unto me, son of man, all my words that I shall speak unto thee receive in thine heart, and hear with thine ears. And go, get thee to them of the captivity, unto the children of thy people, and speak unto them, and tell them, Thus saith the Lord God; whether they will hear, or whether they will forebear."

(The Spirit Lifted up Ezekiel)

(Ezekiel 3:12-16)

Because Ezekiel did not ask to be disturbed or for the commissions, he was mad and bitter.

"Then, the spirit took me up,[52] and I heard behind me a voice of a great

---

52   The same *Spirit* took up Philip the Evangelist from Gaza to Azotus. Departing Jerusalem, Philip traveled through the desert of Gaza and there he baptized an Ethiopian eunuch (of great authority) over Queen Candace's treasury. The story goes as follows: the eunuch was reading aloud the writings of Prophet Isaiah, *"He was led as a sheep to the slaughter; and like a lamb dumb before his shearer, so opened he not his mouth..."* (Isaiah 53:7) Hearing this, Philip ran over to the eunuch and asked, *"Understandest thou what thou readest?"* The eunuch answered, *"How can I, except some man should guide me? And he desired Philip that he would come up and sit with him."* (Acts 8:31) The eunuch said, *"I pray thee, of whom speaketh the prophet this? Of himself or of some other man? Then Philip opened his mouth, and began at the same scripture, and preached unto him Jesus. And as they went on their way,*

rushing, Blessed be the glory of the Lord from his place. I heard also the noise of the wings of the living creatures that touched one another, and the noise of the wheels over against them, and a noise of a great rushing. <u>*So the spirit lifted me up and took me away, and I went in bitterness, in the heat of my spirit; but the hand of the Lord was strong upon me.*</u> *Then I came to them of the captivity at Tel-abib that dwelt by the river of Chebar, and I sat where they sat, and remained there astonished among them seven days. And it came to pass at the end of seven days, that the word of the Lord came unto me..."*

Angels Assisted the Army of Babylon

The **Lord GOD** came down to Babylon. The <u>**Bible**</u> states, <u>**"the glory of God was there in Babylon ..."**</u> (Ezekiel 9:3) And, the **Lord GOD** assisted the Babylonian soldiers. **Ezekiel saw:** SIX MEN *(angels)* [53] appear from no where with slaughter weapons in their hands and one man clothed in

---

they came unto a certain water: and the eunuch said, See, here is water: what doth hinder me to be baptized? And Philip said, If thou believest with all thine heart, thou mayest. And he answered and said, I believe that Jesus Christ is the Son of God. And he commanded the chariot to stand still: and they went down both into the water, both Philip and the eunuch; and he baptized him. "And when they were come up out of the water, <u>*the Spirit of the Lord caught away Philip,*</u> *that the eunuch saw him no more: and he went on his way rejoicing. But Philip was found at Azotus* [25 miles]*; and passing through he preached in all the cities til he came to Caesarea."* (Acts 8:34-40); In the Book of II Corinthians 12:1b-4, Apostle Paul was caught up in the *Spirit,* *"...I will come to visions and revelations of the Lord. I knew a man in Christ above fourteen years ago, (whether in the body, I cannot tell; or whether out of the body, I cannot tell: God knoweth;) such an one caught up to the third heaven...*<u>*How that he was caught up into paradise,*</u> *and heard unspeakable words, which it is not lawful for a man to utter."*

53   The appearance of these six angels is similar to the story of Abraham in the plains of Mamre, *"And the Lord appeared unto him in the plains of Mamre: and he sat in the tent door in the heat of the day; And he lift up his eyes and looked, and, lo three men stood by him: and when he saw them he ran to meet them from the tent door, and bowed himself toward the ground."* (Genesis 18:1)

linen (with a writer's inkhorn on his side) <u>and these men came directly to the brasen altar and stood awaiting their orders!</u> ***"And, the glory of the God of Israel was gone up from the cherub, whereupon he was, to the threshold of the house…"*** (Ezekiel 9:3) The man (angel) *clothed in linen* was told to mark the righteous and faithful men on their foreheads (as a <u>*sign of protection*</u>) because they detested the *abominable sins* of Jerusalem. Apparently, these righteous men abhorred Judah's sins and they were not stiffnecked as the sinful men in Judah. Therefore, they would escape death!

(Ezekiel 9:1-2)

"He [Yahweh] *cried also in mine ears with a loud voice, saying Cause them that have charge over the city to draw near, even every man with his destroying weapon in his hand. <u>And BEHOLD six men came from the way of the higher gate which lieth toward the north, every man a slaughter weapon in his hand; and one man among them was clothe with linen, with a writer's inkhorn by his side: and they went in, and stood beside the brasen altar.</u>"*

(The Angel in Linen with the Writer's Inkhorn)
(Ezekiel 9:3-4)

<u>***"And the glory of the God of Israel was gone up from the cherub, whereupon he was, to the threshold of the house. And he called to the man clothed with linen, which had the writer's inkhorn by his side;***</u>

<u>***And the Lord said unto him, Go through the midst of the city, through the midst of Jerusalem, and set a mark upon the foreheads of the men that sign and that cry for all the abominations that be done in the midst thereof."***</u>

(Five Angelic Executioners)
(Ezekiel 9:5-6)

"And to the others he said in mine hearing, Go ye after him through the city, and smite: let not your eye spare, neither have ye pity: Slay utterly old and young, both maids, and little children, and women:

but come not near any man upon whom is the mark; and begin at my sanctuary. Then they began at the ancient men which were before the house."

The Glory of God Departed from Jerusalem

(Ezekiel 10:1-15, 19-22)

"Then I looked, and, behold in the firmament that was above the head of the cherubims there appeared over them as it were a sapphire stone, as the appearance of the likeness of a throne. And he spake unto the man clothed with linen [angel], and said, Go in between the wheels even under the cherub, and fill thine hand with coals of fire from between the cherubims, and scatter them over the city. And he went in in my sight. Now the cherubims stood on the right side of the house, when the man went in; and the cloud filled the inner court. Then the glory of the Lord went up from the cherub, and stood over the threshold of the house; and the house was filled with the cloud, and the court was full of the brightness of the Lord's glory.

And the sound of the cherubims' wings was heard even to the outer court, as the voice of the Almighty God when he speaketh. And it came to pass, that when he had commanded the man clothed with linen, saying, Take fire from between the cherubims; then he went in, and stood beside the wheels.

And one cherub stretched forth his hand from between the cherubims unto the fire that was between the cherubims, and took thereof, and put it into the hands of him that was clothed with linen: who took it, and went out.

And there appeared in the cherubims the form of a man's hand under their wings. And when I looked, behold the fourth wheels by the cherubims, one wheel by one cherub, and another wheel by another cherub; and the appearance of the wheels was as the color of a beryl stone. And as for their appearances, they four had one likeness, as if a wheel had been in the midst of a wheel. When they went, they went upon their four sides; they turned not as they went, but to the place whither the head looked they followed it; they turned not as they went.

<u>And their whole body, and their backs, and their hands, and their wings, and the wheels, were full of eyes round about, even the wheels that they four had. As for the wheels, it cried unto them in my hearing, O wheel.</u>

And everyone had four faces; the first face was the face of a cherub, and the second face was the face of a man, and the third the face of a lion, and the fourth the face of an eagle. And the cherubims were lifted up. <u>This is the living creature that I saw by the river of Chebar</u>…<u>Then the glory of the Lord departed from off the threshold of the house</u>, and stood over the cherubims. And the cherubims lifted up their wings, and mounted up from the earth in my sight: when they went out, the wheels also were beside them, and every one stood at the door of the east gate of the Lord's house; and the glory of the God of Israel was over them above.

<u>This is the living creature that I saw under the God of Israel by the river of Chebar; and I knew that they were the cherubims</u>. Every one had four faces apiece, and every one four wings; and the likeness of the hands of a man was under their wings. And the likeness of their faces was the same face which I saw bay the river of Chebar, their appearances and themselves: they went every one straight forward."

(Ezekiel 11:22-25)

"Then did the cherubims lift up their wings, and the wheels beside them; and the glory of the God of Israel was over them above. And the glory of the Lord went up from the midst of the city, and stood upon the mountain which is on the east side of the city. Afterwards the spirit took me up, and brought me in a vision by the Spirit of God into Chaldea, to them of the captivity. So the vision that I had seen went up from me. Then I spake unto them of the captivity all the things that the Lord had shewed me."

(Ezekiel 43:2-5)

"And, behold, the glory of the God of Israel came from the way of the east; and his voice was like a noise of many waters: and the earth shined with his glory. And if was according to the appearance of the vision which I saw, even according to the vision that I saw when I came to destroy the city: and the vision s were like the vision that I saw by the river Chebar; and I fell upon my face. And the glory of the Lord came into the house by the way of the gate whose prospect is toward the east. So the spirit took me up, and brought me into the inner court; and, behold, the glory of the Lord filled the house."

(The Millennium: Glory of the Lord to Return)

(Ezekiel 43:6-7)

"And I heard him speaking unto me out of the house; and the man stood by me. And he said unto me, Son of man, the place of my throne, and the place of the soles of my feet, <u>**where I will dwell in the midst of the children of Israel for ever, and**</u> <u>**my holy name shall the house of Israel no more defile**</u>, neither they, nor their kings, by their whoredom, nor by the carcases of their kings in their high place."

Jerusalem's Abominations

(Ezekiel 16:1-6)

"Again the word of the Lord came unto me, saying, Son of man, cause Jerusalem to know her abominations. And say, thus saith the Lord God unto Jerusalem; Thy birth and thy nativity is of the land of Canaan; thy father was an Amorite, and thy mother an Hittite.

And as for thy nativity, in the day thou wast born thy naval was *not cut, neither wast thou washed in water to supple thee; thou wast not salted at all, nor swaddled at all.*

None eye pitied thee, to do any of these unto thee, to have compassion upon thee but thou wast cast out in the open field, to the loathing of thy person, in the day that thou wast born.

And when I passed by thee, and saw thee polluted in thine own blood, I said unto thee when thou wast in thy blood, Live; yea, I said unto thee when thou wast in thy blood, Live."

Jerusalem is Blessed

(Ezekiel 16:7-14)
"I have caused thee to multiply as the bud of the field, and thou hast increased and waxen great, and thou art come to excellent ornaments: thy breasts are fashioned, and thine hair is grown, whereas thou wast naked and bare.

Now when I passed by thee, and looked upon thee, behold thy time was the time of love; and I spread my skirt over thee, and covered thy nakedness: yea, I sware unto thee, and entered into a covenant with thee, saith the Lord God, and thou became mine.

Then washed I thee with water; yea, I thoroughly washed away thy blood from thee, and I anointed thee with oil. I clothed thee also with broidered work, and shod thee with badgers' skin, and I girded thee about with fine linen, and I covered thee with silk.

I decked thee also with ornaments, and I put bracelets upon thy hands, and a chain on they neck. And I put a jewel on thy forehead, and earrings in thine ears, and a beautiful crown upon thine head. Thus wast thou decked with gold and silver; and thy raiment was of fine linen, and silk, and broidered work; thou didst eat fine flour, and honey, and oil: and thou was exceeding beautiful, and thou didst prosper into a kingdom. And thy renown went forth among the heathen for thy beauty: for it was perfect through my comeliness, which I had put upon thee, saith the Lord God."

Aholah and Aholibah

(Ezekiel 23:1-4)
"The word of the Lord came again unto me, saying, Son of man, there were two women, the daughters of one mother: And they committed whoredoms in Egypt; they committed whoredoms in their youth: there were their breasts pressed , and there they bruised the teats of their virginity. And the names of them were Aholah the elder, and the Aholibah her sister: and they were mine, and they bare sons and daughters. Thus were their names; Samaria is Aholah, and Jerusalem Aholibah."

(Samaria's Harlotry with Assyria)
(Ezekiel 23:5-10)
"And Aholah played the harlot when she was mine; and she doted on her lovers, on the Assyrians her neighbors, Which were clothed with blue, captains and rulers, all of them desirable young men, horsemen riding upon horses. Thus she committed her whoredoms with them, with all them that were the chosen men of Assyria, and with all on whom she doted: with all their idols she defiled herself. Neither left she her whoredoms brought from Egypt: for in her youth they lay with her, and they bruised the breasts of her virginity, and poured their whoredom upon her. Wherefore I have delivered her into the hand of her lovers, into the hand of the Assyrians, upon whom she doted. These discovered her nakedness: they took her slew her with the sword: and she became famous among women; for thy hand executed judgment upon her."

(Judah's Harlotry with Assyria)
(Ezekiel 23:11-12)

"And when her sister Aholibah saw this, she was more corrupt in her inordinate love than she, and in her whoredoms more than her sister in her whoredoms. She doted upon the Assyrians her neighbors, captains and rulers clothed most gorgeously, horsemen, riding upon horses, all of them desirable young men."

(Judah's Harlotry with Assyria and Babylon)
(Ezekiel 23:11-12)

"Then I saw that she was defiled, that they took both one way. And that she increased her whoredoms: for when she saw men portrayed upon the wall, the images of the Chaldeans portrayed with vermillion, Girded with girdles upon their loins, exceeding in dyed attire upon their heads, all of them princes to look to, after the manner of the Babylonians of Chaldea, the land of their nativity: And as soon as she saw them with her eyes, she doted upon them, and sent messengers unto them into Chaldea. And the Babylonians came to her into the bed of love, and they defiled her with their whoredom, and she was polluted with them, and her mind was alienated from them. So she discovered her whoredoms, and discovered her nakedness: then my mind was alienated from her, like as my mind was alienated from her sister. Yet she multipled her whoredoms, in calling to remembrance the days of her youth, wherein she had played the harlot in the land of Egypt. For she doted upon their paramours, whose flesh is as the flesh of asses, and whose issue is like the issue of horses. Thus thou callest to remembrance the lewdness of thy youth, in bruising thy teats by the Egyptians, for the paps of thy youth."

(Judgment against Aholibah, Judah)
(Ezekiel 23:22-35)

"Therefore, O Aholibah, thus saith the Lord God; Behold, I will raise up thy lovers against thee, from whom thy mind is alienated, and I will bring them against thee on every side; The Babylonians, and

all the Chaldeans, Pekod, and Shoa, and Koa, and all the Assyrians, with them: all of them desirable young men, captains and rulers, great lords and renowned, all of them riding upon horses. And they shall come against thee with chariots, wagons, and wheels, and with an assembly of people, which shall set against thee buckler and shield and helmet round about: and I will set judgment before them, and they shall judge thee according to their judgments.

And I will set my jealousy against thee and they shall deal furiously with thee: they shall take away thy nose and thine ears; and thy remnant shall fall by the sword: they shall take thy sons and thy daughters; and thy residue shall be devoured by the fire. They shall also strip thee out of thy clothes, and take away thy fair jewels. Thus will I make thy lewdness to cease from thee, and thy whoredom brought from the land of Egypt: so that thou shalt not lift up thine eyes unto thee, nor remember Egypt any more.

For thus saith the Lord God; Behold I will deliver thee into the hand of them who thou hatest, into the hand of them from whom thy mind is alienated. And they shall deal with thee hatefully, and shall take away all thy labor, and shall leave thee naked and bare: and the nakedness of thy whoredoms shall be discovered, both thy lewdness and thy whoredoms. I will do these things unto thee, because thou hast gone a whoring after the heathen, and because thou art polluted with their idols.

Thou hast walked in the way of thy sister; therefore will I give her cup into thine hand. Thus said the Lord God; thou shalt drink of thy sister's cup deep and large: thou shalt he laughed to score and had in derision; it containeth much. Thou shalt be filled with drunkenness and sorrow, with the cup of astonishment and desolation, with the cup of thy sister Samaria.

Thou shalt even drink it and suck it out, and thou shalt break the sherds (shard) thereof, and pluck off thine own breast: for I have spoken it, saith the Lord God. Therefore thus saith the Lord God; Because thou hast forgotten me, and cast me behind thy back, therefore bear thou also thy lewdness and thy whoredoms."

(Eight Sins of Aholah & Aholibah)
(Ezekiel 23:36-44)

"The Lord said moreover unto me; Son of man wilt thou judge Aholah and Aholibah? Yea, declare unto them their abominations; They that have committed adultery, and blood is in their hands, and with their idols have they committed adultery, and have also caused their sons, whom they bare unto me, to pass through the fire, to devour them. Moreover this they have done unto me: they have defiled my sanctuary in the same day, and have profaned my Sabbaths. For when they had slain their children to their idols, then they came the same day into my sanctuary to profane it; and, lo, thus have they done in the midst of mine house. And furthermore, that ye have sent for men to come from far, unto whom a messenger was sent; and lo they came: for whom thou didst wash thyself, painted thy eyes, and decked thyself with ornaments, And sat upon a stately bed, and a table prepared before it, whereupon thou hast set mine incense and mine oil. And a voice of a multitude being at ease was with her: and with the men of the common sort were brought Sabeans, from the wilderness, which put bracelets upon their hands, and beautiful crowns upon their heads. Then I said unto her that was old in adulteries, Will they now commit whoredoms with her, and she with them?

Yet they went in unto her, as they go in unto a woman that played the harlot: so went they in unto Aholah and unto Aholibah, the lewd women."

(Summary of Eight Sins Committed by Aholah & Aholibah)
(Ezekiel 23:22-35)
1. *Adultery;*
2. *Murders;*
3. *Idolatry;*
4. *Burned their children to idols;*
5. *Defiled God's sanctuary;*
6. *Profaned Holy Sabbaths;*
7. *Allied with heathens; and*
8. *Guilty of idolatry & adultery with heathens.*

Chapter 19

Israel's Two Kingdoms: North & South

Theocracy Rejected

Just as **Yahweh** rule in Heaven, He intended to rule on Earth. However, *Lucifer* interfered with both planets and started two wars: *the first in Heaven and the second on Earth!* So, **Yahweh** selected a small group of people *(called the Chosen Ones)* to worship Him on Earth and the lineage He chose to bring forth the Redeemer, Jesus *(son of the Living God)*. **Yahweh** planned to rule with Divine Authority, Theocracy.

But, **Yahweh's** *Chosen people* wanted to be like the other nations and they rejected **Yahweh's** government! The *Chosen Ones* preferred to bow down before lifeless gods and to serve a mortal man, *someone they could see and touch.* Bluntly, the *Chosen Ones* didn't care that the man could not cast fleas or ticks off a dog, heal the sick, raise the dead, or turn water into wine! *They still wanted to look upon a mortal king as he aged with gray hairs, white whiskers, flat feet, knock-knees, loose teeth, broken teeth, loss of hearing and eyesight, leaning upon a walking cane or an aide, and suffering from memory loss!* They forgot about the miraculous crossing of the *Red Sea;* their deliverance out of four hundred (400) years of servitude; the spectacular *Cloud* that covered them from the dry, blazing heat of the

Sun (in the wilderness of Sin); the *Pillar of Fire* that heated them during the freezing temperatures at night; God sent quails for them to eat; God rained manna (bread from heaven) for them to eat; water that poured out of the rock; bitter water was made sweet; their clothes and shoes never waxed old; the *Mosaic Laws* given at Mt. Sinai; victory over warring nations that hated them; the miraculous crossing of the *Jordan River*; the Battle of Jericho and the walls of the city fell down; and so many, many other deliverances and wonderful things **Yahweh** did for them!

There were many events leading up to the culmination of the Chosen Ones' unrest with their judges. This one particular incidence concerned two people, Joel and Abiah, (Prophet Samuel's two wicked sons). Like any other Father, Samuel wanted his sons to carry his mantle for Children of Israel. However, Joel and Abiah were cohorts in crime and they did not walk in Samuel's footsteps. In fact, they were liars, dishonest, took bribes, perverted judgment, and disobeyed the Mosaic Laws. Thus, the elders unanimously demanded of Samuel (now up in age), ***"...make us a king to judge us like all the nations."*** (I Samuel 8:5) Question: How in the world was Samuel going to make them a king? Answer: Maybe, Samuel planned to pick a king off an apple tree? Perhaps, Samuel had a special formula to manufacture kings! However, the elders could have called for the resignations of Joel and Abiah, but they did not! Truthfully, the elders used the failures of these *two judges* as an excuse to demand a king! All along, they wanted to be like the other nations! Their request broke Samuel's heart and he prayed against it, ***"And the Lord said unto Samuel, Hearken unto the voice of the people in all that they say unto thee: for they have not rejected thee, but they have rejected me, that I should not reign over them."*** (I Samuel 8:5)

Prophet Samuel's Words to Israel

"And Samuel called the people together unto the Lord to Mizpeh. And said unto the children of Israel, Thus saith the Lord God of Israel, I brought up Israel out of Egypt, and delivered you out of the hand of the Egyptians, and out of the hand of all the kingdoms, and of them that oppressed you. And ye have

this day rejected your God, who himself saved you out of all your adversities and your tribulations; and ye have said unto him, Nay, but set a king over us. Now therefore present yourselves before the Lord by your tribes, and by your thousands. And when Samuel had caused all the tribes of Israel to come near, the tribe of Benjamin was taken. When he had caused the tribe of Benjamin to come near by their families, the family of Matri was taken, and <u>Saul the son of Kish was taken</u>: and when they sought him, he could not be found. Therefore they enquired of the Lord further, if the man should yet come thither. And the Lord answered, Behold, he hath hid himself among the stuff. And they ran and fetched him thence; and when he stood among the people, he was higher than any of the people from his shoulders and upward. And Samuel said to all the people, <u>See ye him whom the Lord hath chosen, that there is none like him among all the people</u>? And all the people shouted, and said, God save the king." (I Samuel 10:17-24)

Israel's First King, Saul

"*Now there was a man of Benjamin, whose name was Kish, the son of Abiel, the son of Zeror, the son of Bechorath, the son of Aphiah, a Benjamite, a mighty man of power. <u>And he had a son, whose name was Saul, a choice young man, and a goodly: and there was not among the children of Israel a goodlier person than he: from his shoulders and upward he was higher than any of the people</u>. And the asses of Kish Saul's father were lost. And Kish said to Saul his son, Take now one of the servants with thee, and arise, go seek the asses.*" (I Samuel 9: 1-3)

"*Now the Lord had told Samuel in his ear a day before Saul came, saying, Tomorrow about this time I will send thee a man out of the land of Benjamin, and thou shalt anoint him to be captain over my people Israel that he may save my people out of the hand of the Philistines: for I have looked upon my people, because their cry is come unto me. And when Samuel saw Saul, the Lord said unto him,*

Behold the man whom I spake to thee of! This same shall reign over my people." (I Samuel 9: 15-17)

(Samuel Anointed Saul)

"Then Samuel took a vial of oil, and poured it upon his [Saul] *head, kissed him, and said, Is it not because the Lord hath anointed thee to be captain over his inheritance?"* (I Samuel 10:1)

(Saul's Former Occupation)

The man chosen as Israel's first king (Saul) was **a keeper of asses**, *nice, handsome to look at, and taller than the average person.* Saul's former employment was to keep up with his Father's <u>asses</u>, *not the sheep!* At least, David watched over his Father's sheep, a foreshadowing of his assignment to come (by **Yahweh**) *as the Shepherd over Israel!* But, we first meet Saul *(and one of his Father's servants)* on mission impossible *"...go seek the asses."* (I Samuel 9: 1-3) Certainly, two servants could have looked for the missing asses. Wasn't there something more substantial for Saul to do? Notice, there is nothing said about Saul's heart, military ability, endeavors, education, spiritual convictions, etc. But, the **_Bible_** states that Saul <u>"... from his shoulders and upward he was higher than any of the people.</u> Well now, the shoulders are above the heart, so (at this point) we still don't know anything about the intents of Saul's heart!

Saul was nothing like Kish (his Father) who was a mighty man of power! <u>What is wrong with this picture?</u> For whatever reason, **Yahweh <u>did not</u> select Kish to be king over Israel!** <u>Why</u> not? Perhaps, Israel would have trusted in Kish's military strength rather than **Yahweh's power and might!** As we know, **Yahweh is a jealous God and He will not share His pedestal with another!** Or, **Yahweh** wanted to build up simple Simon, *Saul as king.*

(Saul's Transformation)

Later, **Yahweh** transformed Saul into a spiritual man with gifts. Samuel said to Saul, *"...thou shalt come to the hill of God, where is the garrison of the Philistines: and it shall come to pass, when thou art come thither to the city, that thou shalt meet a company of prophets coming down from the high place with a psaltery, and a tabret, and a pipe, and a harp, before them: and they* shall prophesy: <u>*And the Spirit of the Lord will come upon thee,*</u> <u>*and thou shalt prophesy with them,*</u> *and shalt be turned into another* <u>*man.*</u> *And let it be when these signs are come unto thee, that thou do as* <u>*occasion serve thee; for God is with thee*</u>*...And it came to pass, when all that knew him beforetime saw that, behold, he prophesied among the prophets, then the people said one to another, What is this that is come unto the son of Kish? Is Saul also among the prophets? And one of the same place answered and said, But who is their father? Therefore it became a proverb, Is Saul also among the prophets."*

(I Samuel 10:5-13)

(Saul's Spiritual Inability)

Saul was not operating in the office of his spiritual gifts and authority. Positively, Prophet Samuel told Saul, <u>*"And the Spirit of the Lord will come upon*</u> <u>*thee, and thou shalt prophesy with them, and shalt be turned into another man.*</u> <u>*And let it be when these signs are come unto thee, that thou* **do as occasion**</u> **serve thee***; for God is with thee.*" (I Samuel 10:6-7) The Prophet Samuel meant for Saul to use his spiritual gifts with authority (prophesying and speaking things into existence under the anointing of God). That's what is meant by "***do*** ***as occasion serve thee.***"

Lets look back at Saul's Coronation. Saul's lack of spiritual authority and confidence in **Yahweh** was *fully* revealed at his Coronation. Saul was hiding from Samuel and the people, "***When he*** [Samuel] ***had caused the tribe of*** ***Benjamin to come near by their families, the family of Matri was taken, and*** ***Saul the son of Kish was taken:*** ***and when they sought him, he could*** ***not be found***. *And the Lord answered, Behold,* <u>*he hath hid himself among*</u> <u>*the stuff*</u>. *And they ran and fetched him thence...*" (I Samuel 10: 21-22) Lets think about this for a moment. When God calls you, strengthens you, fills you with His *Holy Spirit*, rewards you with gifts, sets you up on high, delivers you, anoints you, tells everyone "he's the man," do you run and hide under the bed? Well, that's what Saul did! Throughout, Saul's kingship, his old ways, demons, lack of faith, jealousies, envies, failures to submit to the prophets *(Samuel and Nathan)*, and disobedience to **Yahweh** became his downfall. In the end, Saul committed suicide! That's a big no, no in Scripture!!!

David, king of Hebron

During the seven years David was king over Hebron *(located in the hill country of Judah)* and just before he was made king over the United Kingdom, *Judah and Israel*, there was so much drama and tragedy in Israel: **(1)** the suicide of king Saul and the death of three sons, Jonathan *(David's best friend)*, Abinadab, and Melchishua, *at the battle of Mount Gilboa* (I Samuel 31:1-13); **(2)** ***"...there was long war between the two houses of Saul and David: but the house of David waxed stronger and stronger and the house of Saul waxed weaker and weaker."*** (II Samuel 3:1); **(3)** many lies manufactured and spread among friends and foes; **(4)** Ishbosheth, a surviving son of king Saul was appointed king (II Samuel 2:8) by Abner *(Israel's Commander-in-Chief of the Army)*; **(5)** Abner killed Asahel [54] *(brother of Joab and Abishai)*; **(6)** due to false rumors, General Abner *defects* from serving king Ishbosheth and *makes peace* with king David (II Samuel 3:17-21); **(7)** Joab *(Judah's Commander-in-Chief of the Army)* and Abishai avenged *Asahel's death* by killing Abner *(in spite of David's clemency to Abner)*; **(8)** Joab killed two captains of the host (Abner and Amasa) shed *blood of war* in the *time of peace* and smeared the blood on his girdle and filled his shoes with blood (I Kings 2:5-6); **(9)** David mourned for General Abner and cursed Joab (II Samuel 2:31); **(10)** king Ishbosheth of Israel was assassinated by his own captains, Baanah and Rechab *(the sons of Rimmon a Beerothite of the children of Benjamin)*, who cut-off the head of king Ishbosheth and took it to king David; **(11)** Absalom *(king David's son)* murdered his half-brother, Amnon, for raping Tamar, *his sister* (II Samuel 13:28-29); **(12)** Absalom covets the throne and king David's flees (II Samuel 13-18); **(13)** Ahithophel *(means = brother of foolishness; grandfather to Bathsheba; and counselor to king David)* allies with Absalom (II Samuel 16:15); **(14)** Absalom appoints

---

54   Asahel, a fast runner (like a roe); the youngest brother to Joab and Abishai; *all three are sons of Zeruiah (sister of king David)*. Joab is *Commander of Judah's Army*. General Abner *(Commander of Israel's Army)* warned Asahel not to follow him but Asahel did not listen. Unfortunately, Abner killed Asahel. In retaliation, Joab and Abishai killed Abner!

Amasa as his Captain (II Samuel 17:25); **(15)** General Joab murdered Absalom, *against David's orders* (II Samuel 18:14); **(16)** Joab is dismissed as Judah's Commander-in-Chief; **(17)** Amasa *(son of Abigail, sister of king David)* is offered the post as Judah's *Commander-in-Chief* (II Samuel 19:13); **(18)** Joab *(not willing to give up his post)* killed his cousin, Amasa (II Samuel 20:10); **(19)** Joab supports Adonijah *(one of king David's son)* self-appointed for the throne (I Kings 1:5); **(20)** king Solomon ordered the death of Adonijah (I Kings 2:25); (21) David gave Solomon an order to get rid of Joab (I Kings 2:5; 28-34); and so on.

David the Just

Before David's Inauguration, he *vindicated* the house of late king Saul. David slew the murderers of Ishbosheth *(king Saul's son)*. In the matter concerning captains Baanah and Rechab, they were very proud of themselves for cutting off king Ishbosheth's head. However, David did a flip-flop on these captains for their misconduct! King David disgustingly said, ***"As the Lord liveth, who hath redeemed my soul out of all adversity, when one told me, saying behold Saul is dead, thinking to have brought good tidings, I took hold of him, and slew him in Ziklag…How much more, when wicked men have slain a righteous person in his own house upon his bed shall I not therefore now require his blood of your hand, and take you away from the earth? And David commanded his young men, and they slew them, and cut off their hands, and their feet, and hanged them up over the pool in Hebron. But they took the head of Ishbosheth, and buried it in the sepulcher of Abner in Hebron."*** (II Samuel 4: 9-12)

King David remembered his covenant with Jonathan (king Saul's son). In fact, king David honored his covenant with Jonathan (deceased) who was his best friend. The king summoned for Mephibosheth (Jonathan's son who was lame in his feet) to appear and said, ***"Fear not for I will surely shew thee kindness for Jonathan thy father's sake, and will***

restore thee all the land of Saul thy father; and thou shalt eat bread at my table continually." (II Samuel 9:7)

United Kingdoms of Israel, David

(The Professor's comments)

According to the **_Bible_**, the Nation of Israel (under king David) was the first nation on record to be called the UK (United Kingdom) and King David reigned in honor, **"And David reigned over all Israel; and David executed judgment and justice unto all his people."** (II Samuel 8:15)

"Then came all the tribes of Israel to David unto Hebron, and spake, saying, Behold, we are thy bone and thy flesh. Also in time past, when Saul was king over us, thou wast he that leddest out and broughtest in Israel: and the Lord said to thee, Thou shalt feed my people Israel, and thou shalt be a captain over Israel. So all the elders of Israel came to the king to Hebron; and king David made a league with them in Hebron before the Lord: and they anointed David king over Israel. David was thirty years old when he began to reign, and he reigned forty years. In Hebron he reigned over Judah seven years and six months: and in Jerusalem he reigned thirty and three years over all Israel and Judah." (II Samuel 5: 1-5)

Divided Kingdoms of Israel – North & South

After the death of king David, the United Kingdom was split into *two independent states* (North and South) as follows: **(1) the Northern Kingdom:** [55] consisted of ten (10) tribes: Rueben, Simeon, Levi, Dan,

---

55   The Northern Kingdom of Israel is also known as the *House of Joseph* * because Reuben (Jacob and Leah's first born) laid with Bilah *(Rachel's handmaid)* his Father's concubine **"...and his birthright was given to the sons of Joseph."** (I Chronicles 5:1) *The House of Joseph consisted of two tribes, Manasseh and Ephraim, *the youngest.*

Naphtali, Gad, Asher, Issachar, Zebulon, and Joseph; and **(2) the Southern Kingdom:** consisted of two (2) tribes: Judah and Benjamin.

King Solomon, Southern Kingdom of Judah

Although, king Solomon (David's son) ascended to the throne, **Yahweh** took most of the kingdom from Solomon and gave it to another, Jeroboam I *(the first king of the divided kingdom, the Northern Tribe of Israel)*. Jeroboam I (reigned about 931-910 B.C.) was the son of Nebat, an Ephrathite of Zereda, Solomon's servant not of the Davidic line. (I Kings 11:26-40) By chance Jeroboam (a mighty man) was offered 10 tribes by Prophet Ahijah the Shilonite who ripped his new garment into 12 pieces and gave 10 to Jeroboam I. Also Jeroboam was the third adversary of king Solomon the Lover.

(I Kings 11:1-13)

"But king Solomon loved many strange women, together with the daughter of Pharaoh, women of the Moabites, Ammonites, Edomites, Zidonians, and Hittites. Of the concerning which the Lord said unto the children of Israel, Ye shall not go in to them, neither shall they come in unto you: for surely they will turn away your heart after their gods: Solomon clave unto these in love. And he had seven hundred wives, princesses, and three hundred concubines: and his wives turned away his heart.

For it came to pass when Solomon was old, that his wives turned away his heart after other gods: and his heart was not perfect with the Lord his God, as was the heart of David his father. For Solomon went after Ashtoreth, the goddess of the Zidonians, and after Milcom the abomination of the Ammonites. And Solomon did evil in the sight of the Lord, and went not fully after the Lord, as did David his father. Then did Solomon build an high place for Chemosh, the abomination of Moab, in the hill that is before Jerusalem, and for

Molech, the abomination of the children of Ammon. And likewise did he for all his strange wives, which burnt incense and sacrificed unto their gods.

And the Lord was angry with Solomon, because his heart was turned from the Lord God of Israel, which had appeared unto him twice, And had commanded him concerning this thing, that he should not go after other gods: but he kept not that which the Lord commanded. Wherefore the Lord said unto Solomon, Forasmuch as this is done of thee, and thou hast not kept my covenant and my statutes, which I have commanded thee, I will surely rend the kingdom from thee, and will give it to thy servant. Northwistanding in thy days I will not do it for David thy father's sake: but I will rend it out of the hand of thy son. Howbeit I will not rend away all the kingdom; but will give one tribe to thy son for David my servant's sake, and for Jerusalem's sake which I have chosen."

(First Adversary to king Solomon)

"And the Lord stirred up an adversary unto Solomon, __Hadad__ the Edomite: he was of the king's seed in Edom. For it came to pass, when David was in Edom, and Joab the captain of the host was gone up to bury the slain, after had smitten every male in Edom; For six months did Joab remain there with all Israel until he cut off every male in Edom. That Hadad fled, he and certain Edomites of his father's servants with him, to go into Egypt; Hadad being yet a little child. And they arose out of Midian, and came to Paran: and they took men with them out of Paran, and they came to Egypt, unto Pharaoh king of Egypt; which gave him an house, and appointed him victuals, and gave him land. And Hadad found great favor in the sight of Pharaoh...And when Hadad heard in Egypt that David slept with his fathers, and that Joab the captain of the host was dead, Hadad said to Pharaoh, Let me depart, that I may go to mine own country..." (I Kings 11:14-22)

(Second Adversary to king Solomon)

"And God stirred him up another adversary, __Rezon__ the son of Eliadah, which fled from his lord Hadadezer, king of Zobah: And he gathered men unto

him, and became captain over a band, when David slew them of Zobah: and they went to Damascus, and dwelt therein and reined in Damascus. And he was an adversary to Israel all the days of Solomon, beside the mischief that Hadad did: and he abhorred Israel, and reigned over Syria." (I Kings 11:23-24)

(Third Adversary to king Solomon)
"And **Jeroboam** *the son of Nebat, an Ephrathite of Zereda, Solomon's servant...even he lifted up his hand against the king."* (I Kings 11:26)

King Jeroboam, Northern Kingdom of Israel

"And **Jeroboam** *the son of Nebat, an Ephrathite of Zereda, Solomon's servant...even he lifted up his hand against the king.*

And this was the cause that he lifted up his hand...Solomon built Millo and repaired the breaches of the city of David his father. And the man Jeroboam was a mighty man of valor: and Solomon seeing the young man that he was industrious, he made him ruler over all the charge of the house of Joseph. And it came to pass at that time when Jeroboam went out of Jerusalem, that the prophet Ahijah the Shilonite found him in the way; and he had clad himself with a new garment; and they two were alone in the field: And Ahijah caught the new garment that was on him and rent it in twelve pieces: And he said to Jeroboam, Take thee ten pieces: for thus saith the Lord, The God of Israel, behold, I will rend the kingdom out of the hand of Solomon, and will give ten tribes to thee...Because that they have forsaken me, and have worshipped Ashtoreth the goddess of the Zidonians, Chemosh the god of the Moabites, and Milcom the god of the children of Ammon, and have not walked in my ways, to do that which is right in mine eyes, and to keep my statutes and my judgments as did David his father. Howbeit, I will not take the whole kingdom out of his hand..." (I Kings 11:26-34)

223

The Chosen Ones, Israel's Northern and Southern Tribes

However, the two Hebrew nations (North & South) were extremely disobedient and rebellious. And, they would not turn from their wicked ways. Like a boxer hits, beats up, and throws multiples blows on a punching bag, the **Lord GOD** brought several warring nations *(i.e., Philistines; Syrians; Ammonites; Moabites; Hittites; Egyptians; Giant Nations (Anakims, Avims, Emims, Horims, Rephaims, Zamzummins, Canaanites); Assyrians; Babylonians; and others)* to fight against His Chosen Ones However, this did not knock any sense into their heads! Finally, the Lord selected and strengthened the two most ruthless nations to capture His people.

Allow me a little time to explain what I mean. The Chosen Ones are the Northern and Southern Tribes of Israel. **Yahweh** selected a small group to worship Him, "***Now the Lord had said unto Abram*** [the son of Terah, the son of Nahor, the son of Serug, A.K.A. Saruch, the son of Re'u, the son of Peleg, the son of Eber, the son of Salah, the son of Arphaxad, the son of Shem, the son of Noah] ***Get thee out of thy country, and from thy kindred and from thy father's house, unto a land that I will shew thee: and I will make of thee a great nation, and I will bless thee, and make thy name great; and thou shalt be a blessing: And I will bless them that bless thee, and curse them that curseth thee: and in thee shall all families of the earth be blessed.***" (Genesis 12:1-3)

Eventually, the Hebrews *(Abraham's descendents)* got beside themselves because they were *Chosen*. As they multiplied in number, their sins got bigger and bigger! In other words, they said *(within themselves,* "We're bad,56 we're bad, we can do whatever we want... Our Fathers are Noah and Abraham!" So, they mimicked the sins and copied the cults and

---

56   In slang, the word "bad" is interchangeably used for the words *good, tough,* and/ or *out-of-sight..*

abominations of the ungodly nations in Canaan. The more **Yahweh** pleaded with the Children of Israel to put-off their whoredoms, the more sins they committed. Often times, the Chosen Ones sinned then repented, then sinned again and repented, then sinned again and repented, and the vicious process kept repeating itself. *They refused to make an about-face to* **Yahweh!** They rebelled against **Yahweh**, murdered **His** prophets, priests, and scribes, bankrupt all of the *Mosaic Laws*, transgressed the covenants, hired *non-Levitical* priests and put them over the people, fashioned themselves gods made of wood and stone to serve, sacrificed their own children on idol altars, guilty of necromancy, worshipped the host of heaven *(sun, moon, and stars)*, and *committed other abominations not proper to discuss.*

Yahweh's Forewarnings to His People

Captivity was not a cheap trick or play thing because the **Lord GOD** warned His people through Moses, *"**And it shall come to pass that as the Lord rejoiced over you to do you good, and to multiply you;** so the Lord will rejoice over you to destroy you, and to bring you to nought; and ye shall be plucked from off the land whither thou goest to possess it.*

(Deuteronomy 28:63)

Without question, there were two choices: (a) do good and be multiplied; or (b) do wrong and be destroyed! Once again, God wanted the world (including His people) to witness His greatness and His demand for righteousness without respect of persons!

Animal Dialog

(Koos' comments)

By now, Koos *(the little humming bird)* wanted to say something important – he was tired of humming and flying from tree to tree! So

225

Koos said, "Gee, Professor Baykus, you're so smart, full of wisdom, and you have so much Biblical knowledge!"

(Sinjop's comments)
    After hearing that, Sinjop (*the fat furry squirrel*) said, "Koos, Koos, you're just trying to flatter Professor Baykus but this is serious business! If you have nothing concrete to say, SHUT UP!"

(The Professor's comments)
    The *old Hittite owl* said, "Fellows it's ok, I know this is a lot of information to swallow!" Then, the Professor said to the wolf-man, "I know your voice is exasperated so allow me to give everybody a short history lesson about **Yahweh's** Covenant with the Children of Israel."

Prelude to the Palestinian Covenant

(The Professor's comments)
    The *wise old Hittite Owl* said that there are certain events leading up to the Palestinian Covenant. **Yahweh** didn't just pounce judgment on His people. Instead, He gave forewarnings to the Children of Israel. Lets go back to their Exodus from Egypt. God made important covenants with them: (1) the Mosaic Law (given on Mt. Horeb, A.K.A. Mt. Sinai); and (2) The Palestinian Covenant (given in the plains of Moab). Both of these covenants were extremely important, but the latter one was a renewal of the first covenant (given at Mr. Horeb/Mt. Sinai) with critical warnings to Israel!

    Right after Moses sent out the twelve spies to search the Promised Land, the children of Israel murmured to Moses. They considered themselves *grasshoppers* in comparison to the sons of Anak (giants) in the Promised Land. **Yahweh** was extremely tired of Israel's unbelief, complaining, and provocations. Again, He wanted to smite them with the pestilence, disinherit them, and make a greater nation through Moses. But, Moses protested and begged God to pardon them! And, **Yahweh said,** *"I have pardoned according to thy word."* (Numbers 14:20)

However, God has the last word, *"Because all those men which have seen my glory, and my miracles, which I did in Egypt and in the wilderness, and have tempted me now these ten time, and have not hearkened to my voice; Surely they shall not see the land which I sware unto their fathers, neither shall any of them that provoked me see it..."* (Numbers 14:22-23) *"Doubtless ye shall NOT come into the land, concerning which I sware to make you dwell therein, save Caleb the son of Jephunneh, and Joshua the son of Nun. But your little ones which ye said should be a prey, them will I bring in, and they shall know the land which ye have despised. But as for you, your carcases, they shall fall in this wilderness. And your children shall wander in the wilderness forty years, and bear your whoredoms, until your carcases be wasted in the wilderness. After the number of the days in which ye searched the land, even forty days, each day for a year, shall ye bear your iniquities, even forty years, and ye shall know my breach of promise. I the Lord have said, I will surely do it unto all this evil congregation, that are gathered together against me: in this wilderness they shall be consumed, and there they shall die."* (Numbers 14:30-35)

The Palestinian Covenant, Land of Moab

The Book of Deuteronomy 29:1-15, introduces the Palestinian Covenant that was made in the plains of Moab. It is not a new covenant. Instead, it is a renewed covenant with the surviving children of the *Children of Israel who left Egypt* and with the strangers and workers who were in the camp of Israel.

This covenant was made in the plains of Moab many years (thirty-nine) after the Sinai *(Mt. Horeb)* Covenant (Exodus Chapters 20-24). Furthermore, there is more historical reference to its inception. The Palestinian Covenant was made on Moses' one hundred and twentieth (120th) birthday, the day he died! From the mountaintop, Moses saw the Promised Land, but he was not allowed to enter into it!

(Parties of the Covenant)

(Deuteronomy 29:1-15)

"These are the words of the covenant, which the Lord commanded Moses to make with the children of Israel in the land of Moab, <u>beside the covenant which he made with them in Horeb</u>. And Moses called unto all Israel, and said unto them, Ye have seen all that the Lord did before your eyes in the land of Egypt unto Pharaoh, and unto all his servants, and unto all his land…Yet the Lord hath ot given you an heart to perceive, and eyes to see, and ears to hear, unto this day…and I have led you forty years in the wilderness: your clothes are not waxen old upon you, and thy shoe is not waxen old upon thy foot…Keep therefore the words of this covenant, and do them, that ye may prosper in all that ye do…Ye stand this day all of you before the Lord your God; your captains of your tribes, your elders, and your officers, with all the men of Israel, Your little ones, your wives, and thy stranger that is in thy camp, from the hewer of thy wood unto the drawer of thy water: That thou shouldest enter into covenant with the Lord thy God, and into his oath, which the Lord thy God maketh with thee this day: That he may establish thee to day for a people unto himself, and that he may be unto thee a God, as he hath said unto thee, and as he hath sworn unto thy fathers he hath sworn unto thy fathers, to Abraham, to Isaac, and to Jacob. Neither with you only do I make this covenant and oath; But with him that standeth here with us this day before the Lord our God, and also with him that is not here with us this day."

(Palestinian Covenant Curses)

"For ye know how we have dwelt in the land of Egypt and how we came through the nations which ye passed by. And ye have seen their abominations, and their idols, wood and stone, silver and gold, which were among them: Lest there should be among you man, or woman, or family, or tribe, whose heart turneth away this day from the Lord our God, to go and serve the gods of these nations; lest there shall be among you a root that beareth gall and wormwood…The Lord will

not spare him, but then the anger of the Lord and his jealousy shall smoke against that man, and all the curses that were written in this book shall lie upon him, and the Lord shall blot out his name from under heaven...And that the whole land thereof is brimstone, and salt, and burning, that is not sown, nor beareth, nor any grass groweth therein, like the overthrow of Sodom, and Gomorrah, Admah, and Zeboim, which the Lord overthrew in his anger, and in his wrath: Even all nations shall say, Wherefore hath the Lord done thus unto this land? What meaneth the heat of this great anger? Then men shall say, because they have forsaken the covenant for the Lord God of their fathers, which he made with them when he brought them forth out of the land of Egypt: For they went and served other gods, and worshipped them, gods whom they knew not, and whom, he had not given unto them. And the anger of the Lord was kindled against this land to bring upon it all the curses that are written in this book: And the Lord rooted them out of their land in anger, and in wrath, and in great indignation, and cast them into another land, as it is this day." (Deuteronomy 29:16-28)

(Ultimate Punishment)

"And it shall come to pass that as the Lord rejoiced over you to do you good, and to multiply you; so the Lord will rejoice over you to destroy you, and to bring you to nought; and ye shall be plucked from off the land whither thou goest to possess it. **And the Lord shall scatter thee among all people, from the one end of the earth even unto the other; and there thou shalt serve other gods, which neither thou nor thy fathers have known, even wood and stone.** *And among these nations shalt thou fine no ease, neither shall the sole of thy foot have rest; but the Lord shall give thee there a trembling heart, and failing of eyes, and sorrow of mind: And thy life shall hang in doubt before thee; and thou shalt fear day and night, and shalt have none assurance of thy life..."* (Deuteronomy 28:63-66)

Chapter 20

Assyria vs. Northern Tribe of Israel

(The Professor's comments)

The Northern Tribe of Israel (A.K.A. the House of Joseph) consisted of the following tribes: Ephraim and Manasseh *(sons of Joseph, the son of Israel)*; Reuben, Simeon, Zebulun, Issachar, Dan, Gad, Asher, and Naphtali *(brothers of Joseph and all sons of Israel)*. These ten tribes of the twelve were taken (Genesis 11:35) from Rehoboam (king Solomon's son) and given to Jeroboam (who eventually fell from grace to worship false idols).

Assyrian Roots in Asshur

The **Lord GOD** used the Assyrians to take down the Northern Tribe of Israel. At that time, Assyria was much stronger than Babylon! In fact, the Assyrians thought very highly of themselves. Assyria's progenitor, Asshur, (the son of Shem, *son* of Noah) was the second generation to Noah.

By God's saving grace, Shem (the second son of Noah) was an icon (in his own rights) and he had five sons: Elam, Assur, Arphaxad, Lud, and Aram. As brothers, Assur and Arphaxad's were tied by bloodline and their descendants were tied by bloodline as well!

As stated earlier, the City of Nineveh (built by Noah's grandson) was the second capital of ancient Assyria but the first capital was named after its founder, *Asshur*, **"Out of that land went forth Asshur** *[the son of Shem, the son of Noah]* **and built Nineveh, Rehoboth, Calah, and Resen."** (Genesis 10:11-12) The descendants of Asshur *(the Assyrians, i.e., derivative of Asshur)* became the largest empire to *quickly* expand and conquer the other nations. This fact alone made them feel superior to all else.

However, there are several theories for the Assyrians' enormous egos. **Firstly**, their line of descent from Noah was much closer than the Babylonians who were their second cousins. Their paternal connection to Noah gave them the right to say, *"My Father Noah and My Father Shem;"* and thus believed themselves greater than their ancestors.

Secondly, the Assyrians believed Noah's honorary position *(through grace)* with **The Almighty GOD** gave them preferential treatment but they did not want to serve Noah's **GOD**. Considering themselves greater than Noah and Shem, they outgrew **"The Almighty God of Noah and Shem."** In this respect, the Assyrians *(believing themselves wiser)* were weaker! Therefore, they decided to worship the *Host of Heaven*. This term is associated and used interchangeably with: (A) *The Host in Heaven* (God's army of mighty angelic warriors); and (B) *The Army of the Skies* (the sun as king; the moon as vice-regent; and the stars & planets as the attendants) ordained and commissioned (by God) to watch over the Earth, to do His Will, and to fight on behalf of His people as in the Old Testament and other times. The Assyrians worshiped the latter definition of "B," the Army of the Skies. Regardless, God warned mankind not to worship the Host of Heaven.[57] Furthermore, God is a jealous God, **"Thou shalt have no other gods before me. Thou shalt not make unto**

---

57   See book entitled: *RAHAB of Jericho* by Constance Lee.

thee any graven image, or any likeness of any thing that is in heaven above, or that is in the earth beneath, or that is in the water under the earth. Thou shalt not bow down thyself to them, nor serve them: for I the Lord thy God am a jealous God, visiting the iniquity of the father upon the children unto the third and fourth generation of them that hate me..." (Exodus 20:4-5)

Thirdly, the first mention of Assyria is associated with two great rivers of *Biblical antiquity*. The Bible mentions four rivers (Pison, Gihon, Hiddekel, and the Euphrates) flowing from **ONE RIVER** in the **Garden of Eden**, "*And a river went out of Eden to water the garden; and from thence it was parted, and became into four heads. The name of the first is Pison: that is it which compasseth the whole land of Havilah, where there is gold; And the gold of that land is good: there is bdellium and the onyx stone. And the name of the second river is Gihon: the same is it that compasseth the whole land of Ethiopia. And the name of the third river is Hiddekel [A.K.A., Tigris]; that is it which goeth toward the east of Assyria. And the fourth river is Euphrates.*" (Genesis 2:10-14) Geographically, Assyria was located closer to the Tigris River in the northern part of Mesopotamia *(the land between the two ancient rivers, the Tigris and the Euphrates).*

Fourthly, the **Lord GOD** covenanted this land to Abraham, Isaac, and Jacob, "*Unto thy seed have I given this land, from the river of Egypt unto the great river, the river Euphrates: The Kenites, the Kenizzites, the Kadmonites, the Hittites, the Perizzites, the Rephaims [giants], Amorites, the Canaanites, the Girgashites, and the Jebusites.*" (Genesis 15:18b-21) The Bible states that the **Lord GOD** cares for the Land of Canaan, "*For the land, whither thou goest in to possess it, is not as the land of Egypt, from whence ye came out, where thou sowedst thy seed, and wateredst it with thy foot, as a garden of herbs: But the land whether ye go to possess it, is a land of hills and valleys, and drinketh water* of the rain of heaven: *<u>A land which the Lord thy God careth</u>* *<u>for: the eyes of the Lord thy God are always upon it, from</u>* *<u>the beginning of the year even unto the end of the year.</u>*" (Deuteronomy 11:10-12) Furthermore, the **Lord GOD** swore to give Abraham, Isaac, and Jacob great and goodly cities which they did not build, *"And houses full of all good things, which thou filledst not, and wells digged, which thou diggedst not, vineyards and olive trees, which thou plantedst not..."* (Deuteronomy 6:11) To date, this real estates is extremely priceless!

Ruthless Terrorists

The Assyrian Race was nobody to play *tick-tack-toe* with and there was no compromising. They were ruthless killers, murderers, and terrorists! Actually, they were quite the contrast to their *gentle* grandfather, Noah (who planted vineyards and drank the wine!) Without blinking and without remorse: the Assyrians ripped out unborn children from their Mother's wombs; leveled cities; sacked cities; attacked defenseless cities; raped women and maidens; confiscated gold, silver, jewels, and other treasures. They completely forgot their National origins. The Almighty God of Heaven used the Assyrian's tyranny to *unleash horror and to conquer* the Northern Tribe of Israel (about 722 B.C.).

ASSYRIA vs. Northern Tribe of Israel

And so, little by little, here a little and there a little, the Assyrians chipped away at the Northern Ten Tribes of Israel and carried them into exile.

FIRST ASSYRIAN INVASION vs. king Menahem of Israel

Menahem[58] paid tribute (one thousand talents of silver) to the Assyrians led by king Tiglath-Pileser III (II Kings 15:19) to leave; variant spellings for Tiglath-Pileser, A.K.A., Tigath-Pilneser (I Chronicles 5:6; II Chronicles 28:20); and A.K.A, Pul (II Kings 15:19; I Chronicles 5:26);

SECOND ASSYRIAN INVASION vs. king Pekah of Israel

Again king Tiglath-Pileser led another invasion against king Pekah [59] and this time he did not back down, *"In the days of Pekah king of Israel came Tiglath-Pileser king of Assyria and took I-jon, Abel-beth-maach, Janoah, Kedesh, Hazor, Gilead, Galilee, all the land of Naphtali, and carried them captive to Assyria."* (II Kings 15:29)

According to I Chronicles 5:3-8, many Reubenite descendants were taken into Assyrian captivity, *"The sons, I say, of Reuben the firstborn of Israel were, Hanoch, and Pallu, Hezron, and Carmi. The sons of Joel: Shemiah and his son, Gog, his son, Shimei, his son, Micah his son, Reaia his son, Baal his son, Beerah his son whom Tilgath-pilneser king of Assyria carried away captive: he [Beerah] was prince of the Reubenites. And his brethren by their families, when the genealogy of their generations was reckoned, were the chief, Jeiel and Zechariah. And Bela the son of Azaz, the son of Shema, the son of Joel, who dwelt in Aroer, even unto Nebo and Baal-meon."*

---

58   Menahem became king of Israel (about 752-742 B.C.) after murdering king Shallum (about 752 B.C.) who murdered the previous king, *Zachariah** (reigned for six months about 752 B.C.) was son of Jeroboam II; and the last wicked descendant of Jehu* (II Kings 15:8-12). *According to II Kings 10:30, God promised Jehu (about 841-814 B.C.) for punishing the house of Ahab that four generations of his descendants would sit on the throne of Israel: <u>*Jehoahaz*</u> *(about 814-798 B.C.);* <u>*Joash*</u>*, A.K.A. Jehoash* (about 798-782 B.C.); <u>*Jeroboam II*</u> *(about 782-753 B.C.);* and <u>Zachariah</u> (about 752 B.C.) the last one.

59   *Pekah* became king of Israel about 742-740 B.C., after murdering king Pekahiah (who ascended to the throne after his father, king *Menahem*).

234

THIRD ASSYRIAN INVASION vs. king Pekah of Israel and king Rezin of Syria During this invasion, wicked king Ahaz of Judah (about 736-716 B.C.) allied with the Assyrian king against two kingdoms, *"Ahaz sent messengers to Tiglath-Pileser king of Assyria saying, I am thy servant and thy son: come up and save me out of the hand of the king of Syria, and out of the hand of the king of Israel which rise up against me. And Ahaz took the silver and gold that was found in the house of the Lord, and in the treasures of the king's house and sent it for a present to the king of Assyria. And the king of Assyria hearkened unto him: for the king of Assyria went up against Damascus, and took it, and carried the people of it captive to Kir, and slew Rezin."* (II Kings 16:7-9);

FOURTH ASSYRIAN INVASION vs. king Hoshea of Israel *"And the king of Assyria found conspiracy in Hoshea[60] for he had sent messengers to Sō king of Egypt, and brought no present to the king of Assyria, as he had done year by year: therefore the king of Assyria shut him up and bound him in prison. Then the king of Assyria came up throughout all the land, and went up to Samaria, and besieged it three years. In the ninth year of Hoshea, the king of Assyria too Samaria, and carried Israel away into Assyria and placed them in Halah, Habor by the river of Gozan, and in the cities of the Medes."* (II Kings 17:4-6) Another passage relating to the captivity of the Northern Tribes reads, *"And it came to pass in the fourth year of king Hezekiah, which was the seventh year of Hoshea son of Elah king of Israel, that Shalmaneser king of Assyria came up against Samaria, and besieged it. And at the end of three years they took it: even in the sixth year of Hezekiah, that is the ninth year of Hoshea king of Israel, Samaria was taken. And the king of Assyria did carry away Israel unto Assyria, and put them in Halah and in Habor by the river of Gozan, and in the cities of the Medes: Because they obeyed not the voice of the Lord their God, but transgressed his covenant, and all*

[60]   *Hoshea* (reigned 732-722 B.C.; was the son of Elah; the last king of Israel before Assyrian captivity) murdered king *Pekah*. Hoshea was a puppet king Israel to the Assyrian king, Tiglath-Pileser.

that Moses the servant of the Lord commanded, and would not hear them, nor do them." (II Kings 18:9-12)

FIFTH ASSYRIAN INVASION vs. king Hoshea, Northern Kingdom of Israel After the death of Tiglath-Pileser, Shalmaneser king of Assyria (reigned about 726-722 B.C.) finished the attack of Samaria and captured the Ten Tribes of Israel, *"For the children of Israel walked in all the sins of Jeroboam which he did; they departed not from them; Until the Lord removed Israel out of his sight, as he had said by all his servants the prophets. So was Israel carried away out of their own land to Assyria. And the king of Assyria* [Shalmaneser] *brought men from Babylon, Cuthah, Ava, Hamath, and from Sepharvaim, and placed them in the cities of Samaria instead of the children of Israel: and they possessed Samaria, and dwelt in the cities thereof."* (II Kings 17:22-24)

According to II Kings 18:9-12 (in the fourth year of Hezekiah, king of Judah), *"**Shalmaneser king of Assyria came up against Samaria, and besieged it**. And at the end of three years they took it: even in the sixth year of Hezekiah, that is the ninth year of Hoshea king of Israel, Samaria was taken. And the king of Assyria did carry away Israel unto Assyria, and put them in Halah, and in Habor by the river of Gozan, and in the cities of the Medes: Because they obeyed not the voice of the Lord their God but transgressed his covenant, and all that Moses the servant of the Lord commanded, and would not hear them, nor do them."*

Samaria's New Residents

The king of Assyria [Shalmaneser] replenished Samaria like a cattleman brings new *cows and bulls* into the corral. Shalmaneser didn't care one way or the other about the cities of Northern Kingdom of Israel. Literally, he went out, grabbed people (*undesirables, deadbeats, broken teeth, missing teeth, flat feet, and bow legged)*, up-rooted them and their families, and ordered them to live over yonder! So, he created a melting pot, fiasco, and fusion of people, ethnicities, religions, and ideologies, ***"And the king of Assyria brought men from Babylon, Cuthah, Ava, Hamath, and from Sepharvaim, and placed them in the cities of Samaria instead of the children of Israel, and they possessed Samaria, and dwelt in the cities thereof."*** (II Kings 17:22-24)

Well, well, well, well, well, God sent lions to destroy the new residents of Samaria and its surrounding cities,

"And so it was at the beginning of their dwelling there that they feared not the Lord: therefore the Lord sent lions among them, which slew some of them. Wherefore they spake to the king of Assyria [Shalmaneser] saying, The nations which thou hast removed, and placed in the cities of Samaria, know not the manner of the God of the land: <u>therefore he [God] hath sent lions among them, and, behold they slay them, because they know not the manner of the God of the land.</u>" (II Kings 17:24-26)

(A Religious Man sent to Samaria)

Because of the judgment God executed upon Samaria, the citizens begged the king of Assyria for help. How unfortunate, they did not seek the face of God! So, the king of Assyria *(Shalmaneser)*a heathen said, ***"Carry one of the priest whom ye brought thence and let them go and dwell there and let him teach them <u>the manner of the God of the land.</u>"*** (II Kings 17:27)

(Idolatry Continued)

All of the residents in Samaria and the surrounding cities were hypocrites and lived dubious lifestyles. The priest taught them the true way to live, but they wanted to live according to ***"…<u>the manner of the god of the land</u>."*** (II Kings 17:27)

"Then one of the priests whom they had carried away from Samaria

237

came and dwelt in Bethel and taught them how they should fear the Lord. ***Howbeit every nation made gods of their own, and put them in the houses of the high places which the Samaritans had made, every nation in their cities where they dwelt.***" (II Kings 17:27)

And the men of Babylon made a Succoth-benoth [means booth of the daughters who rendered themselves to men]***...the men of Cuth made Nergal*** [the god of hunting or chase]***...the men of Hamath made Ashima*** [goat figure without wool like the Greek god, Pan]***...Avites made Nibhaz*** [dog with a man's head] ***and Tartak*** [perhaps an ass]***... and Sepharvites burnt their children in the fire to Adram-me-lech*** [god of Ammon]***, and A-nam-me-lech*** [a different god like a horse] ***the gods of Sepharvaim.***

<u>So they feared the Lord, and served their own gods, after the manner of the nations whom they carried away from thence.</u>" (II Kings 17:29-32)

Two Last Kings, Northern Kingdom of Israel

Professor Baykus said that all of the kings from Jeroboam I [61] *(the first king of the divided Northern Tribe of Israel)* to Hoshea *(the last king of the Northern Tribe of Israel)* including the Children of Israel [62] sinned

---

61   Jeroboam I (about 931-910 B.C.) was the son of Nebat, an Ephrathite of Zereda, Solomon's servant not of the Davidic line. (I Kings 11:26-40) By chance Jeroboam (a mighty man) was offered 10 tribes by Prophet Ahijah the Shilonite who ripped his new garment into 12 pieces and gave 10 to Jeroboam I who became the third adversary of Solomon who was serving false gods, *Ashtoreth, Chemosh, Milcom.*

62   Although the Northern Kingdom was terribly wicked, this does not mean that their sister, *the* Southern Kingdom, were little saints. However, the Southern Kingdom had more righteous kings (who had a repenting heart after king David's heart) than the kings of the Northern Kingdom. Unlike their Southern sister, king Jeroboam became the role model for subsequent kings of the Northern Kingdom. The ***Bible*** states: (a) ***"...and his heart was not perfect with the Lord his God, as the heart of David his father...."*** (I Kings 15:3); and/or (b) ***"But he walked in the way of the kings of Israel...made his son to pass through the fire, according to the abominations of the heathen whom the***

against God! In fact, the Northern Kingdom of Israel were still sinning right down to the last two kings *(Pekah and Hoshea)* of Israel to the very second their captivity.

(king Pekah)

"And he [Pekah [63] the Israeli king] *did that which was evil in the sight of the Lord: <u>he departed not from the sins of Jeroboam the son of Nebat who made Israel to sin.</u>"* [64] (II Kings 15:28; II Kings 3:3; II Kings 13:2, 11; II Kings 15:18; 28, etc.) Also, Pekah *"smote and killed Pekahiah (king of Israel) and reigned in his room."*

(king Hoshea)

"In the twelfth year of Ahaz king of Judah began Hoshea the son of Elah to reign in Samaria over Israel nine years. <u>And he did that which was evil in the sight of the Lord, but not as the kings of Israel that were before him.</u>" (II Kings 15:30; 17:1) However, Hoshea was still a sinner. He took murder for his crown because he *"smote and slew Pekah (king of Israel) and reigned in his stead."* (II Kings 15:25)

Baykus said that God got tired of the ways of the kings and the people, *"For the children of Israel walked in all the sins of Jeroboam* [the first king of the ten tribes of Israel] *which he did; they departed not from them; Until the Lord removed Israel out of his sight, as he had said by all his servants the prophets. So was Israel carried away out of their own land to Assyria..."* (II Kings 17:22)

Lord cast out from before the children of Israel...sacrificed and burnt incense in the high places, and on the hills, and under every green tree." (II Kings. 16:3-4)

63   Pekah, the son of Remaliah, reigned about 740-732 B.C.; he murdered Pekahiah who reigned about 742-740 B.C.

64   *Jeroboam II** (about 782-753 B.C.; son of Jehu*) followed in the wicked footsteps of Jeroboam I (the first king of the Northern Kingdom of Israel). God used Jeroboam I as a "grading base" for all of the wicked kings of Israel (including kings of Judah) who followed Jeroboam's apostasy and abominations.

The Lord's Covenant Broken

There was and is no justification for the disobedience of the Ten Tribes of Israel,

(II Kings 17:34-41)
*"Unto this day, they do after the former manners: they fear not the Lord, neither do they after their statutes, or after their own ordinances, or after the law and commandment which the Lord commanded the children of Jacob, whom he named Israel. With whom the Lord had made a covenant, and charged them, saying, **<u>Ye shall not fear other gods, nor bow yourselves to them, nor serve them, nor sacrifice to them</u>**:*

But the Lord, who brought you up out of the land of Egypt with great power and a stretched out arm, him shall ye fear, and him shall ye worship, and to him shall ye do sacrifice.

And the statues, and the ordinances, and the law, and the commandment, which he wrote for you, ye shall observe to do for evermore; and ye shall not fear other gods.

<u>And the covenant that I have made with you ye shall not forget; nether shall ye fear other gods. But the Lord your God ye shall fear; and he shall deliver you out of the hand of all your enemies. Howbeit they did not hearken, but they did after their former manner.</u>

So these nations feared the Lord, and served their graven images, both their children, and their children's children; as did their fathers, so do they unto this day."

Chapter 21

Assyria vs. Southern Tribe of Israel

(The Professor's comments)

The Southern Tribe of Israel are the descendants of Shem (generally considered Noah's first son to receive a blessing) and a celebrity in his own rights. As stated earlier, Shem was one of the four men God spared during Noah's Deluge! Shem had five sons: Elam, Assur, Arphaxad, Lud, and Aram. His third son, Arphaxad, is the progenitor of the Israelites, Arabians, Edomites, Moabites, Ishmaelites, Ammonites, Midianites, and other tribes. (Genesis 11:10-32; 17:20; 25:1-18; 36:1-43)

(Nebuchadnezzar's comments)

Nebuchadnezzar (*the former wolf-man*) said that the big-bad Assyrians wolfed at the *Southern Kingdom of Israel*. At that time, Hezekiah was king of Judah and his luck turned for the worse: **(1)** Hezekiah became extremely ill; **(2)** Prophet Isaiah brought bad omens: (a) told the king to prepare himself to die; (b) all of Judah's treasures would be carried off to Babylon; and (c) Hezekiah's sons (*descendants, not yet born*) would be taken into captivity and made eunuchs; and **(3)** The Assyrians (*who captured the Ten Northern Tribes of Israel*) were outside knocking at Hezekiah's gate: (a) ***In the fourteenth year of king Hezekiah did Sennacherib king of Assyria come up against all the fenced cities of Judah and***

took them.*" (II Kings 18:13); (b) they did not wait for the **Lord GOD to commission them!**

Of course, this troubled the Judean king and it weakened the *faith* of the people of Southern Kingdom of Judah. They were terrified of the Assyrians. However, the threatened attack on the Southern Kingdom could have been avoided. They should have studied the reasons for their sister's *(the Northern Tribe)* captivity. They were full of apostasies, abominations, disbeliefs, transgressions, etc. Moreover, the Northern Kingdom refused to take heed to **Yahweh's** warnings and His prophets.

However, none of this mattered to the Southern Tribe of Judah. They were in the same pitiful condition as the Northern Tribe. Like their sister, the Southern Tribe did not believe the prophets that were sent by **Yahweh.** In fact, they insulted, ridiculed, punished, banished, mutilated, imprisoned, and killed the **Yahweh's** prophets (just as the Northern Tribe). To understand the Southern Tribe, a brief review of their previous king's (Ahaz) administration is necessary *(because he made Judah to sin)*!

King Ahaz, Wicked Reign in Judah

(The Professor's comments)
Professor Baykus interrupted Nebuchadnezzar and said,

"Ahaz was twenty years old when he began to reign, and he reigned sixteen years in Jerusalem: <u>**but he did not that which was right**</u> *in the sight of the Lord, like David his father:*

<u>For he walked in the ways of the kings of Israel, and made molten images for Baalim. Moreover he burnt incense in the valley of the son of Hinnom, and burnt his children in the fire, after the abominations of the heathen whom the Lord had cast out before the children of Israel.</u>

He sacrificed also and burnt incense in the high places, and on the hill, and under every green tree." (II Chronicles 28:2-4)

By this time, Professor Baykus *(was <u>hooting</u> as if he had lost his mind and <u>flapping his feathery wings</u> as if he was a jet airplane preparing to take-off flying through the air!)* said that king Ahaz was a fool, **"...king Ahaz took away a portion out of the house of the Lord, and out of the house of the king, and of the princes, and gave it unto the king of Assyria** [Tilgath-pil-ne-ser]; **but he helped him not. And in the time of his distress did he** [Ahaz] **trespass yet more against the Lord: this is that king Ahaz. For he sacrificed unto the gods of Damascus which smote him: and he said, Because the gods of the kings of Syria help them, therefore will I sacrifice to them, that they may help me. But they were the ruin of him, and of all Israel. And Ahaz gathered together the vessels of the house of God, and cut in pieces the vessels of the doors of then house of the Lord, and he made him altars in every corner of Jerusalem. And in every several city of Judah he made high places to burn incense unto other gods, and provoked to anger the Lord God of his fathers."** (II Chronicles 28:20-25)

King Hezekiah's, Righteous Reign in Judah

(The Professor's comments)

The *wise old Hittite owl* yelled out, "King Hezekiah was not a Freddy-cat,"

"And the Lord was with him [Hezekiah]; and he prospered whithersoever he went forth: and he rebelled and refused to serve the king of Assyria, and served him not." (II Kings 18:7)

(king Hezekiah's Ferocious Revival)

The Bible states,

(II Kings 18:4-7)
"Again," said Professor Baykus, **<u>"King Hezekiah removed the high</u>**

243

places and brake the images and cut down the groves, and brake in pieces the brasen serpent that Moses had made for unto those days the children of Israel did burn incense to it: and he called it Nehushtan. He trusted in the Lord God of Israel; so that after him was none like him among all the kings of Judah, nor any that were before him. For he clave to the Lord and departed not from following him, but kept his commandments which the Lord commanded Moses. And the Lord was with him [king Hezekiah; and he prospered whethersoever he went forth…"

(II Chronicles 29:1-19)

*"Hezekiah began to reign when he was five and twenty years old (25), and he reigned nine and twenty years in Jerusalem…**And he did that which was right in the sight of the Lord, according to all that David[65] his father had done**. He in the first year of his reign, in the first month, opened the doors of the house of the Lord, and repaired them. And he brought in the priests and the Levites …**And he said unto them, Hear me, ye Levites, sanctify now yourselves and sanctify the house of the Lord God of your fathers, and carry forth the filthiness out of the holy place**. For our fathers have trespassed, and done that which was evil in the eyes of the Lord our God, and have forsaken him, and have turned away their faces from the habitation of the Lord, and turned their backs. Also they have shut up the doors of the porch, and put out the lamps, and have not burned incense nor offered burnt offerings in the holy place unto the God of Israel.*

Wherefore the wrath of the Lord was upon Judah and Jerusalem, and he hath delivered them to trouble, to astonishment, and to hissing, as ye see with your eyes. For lo, our fathers have fallen by the sword, and our sons and our daughters and our wives are in captivity for this.

Now it is in mine heart to make a covenant with the Lord God of Israel that his fierce wrath may turn away from us. My sons, be not

---

65   All of the kings of Judah were compared to king David (a man after God's own heart) and/or to the wicked king of Israel, *Jeroboam I (son of Nebat)*.

now negligent: for the Lord hath chosen you to stand before him, to serve him, and that ye should minister unto him and burn incense.

Then the Levites arose, Mahath the son of Amasai, and Joel the son of Azariah, of the sons of the Kohathites: and of the sons of Merari, Kish the son of Abdi, and Azariah the son of Jehalelel: and of the Gershonites; Joah the son of Zimmah, and Eden the son of Joah:

And of the sons of Elizaphan; Shimri, and Jeiel: and of the sons of Asaph; Zechariah, and Mattaniah: And of the sons of Heman; Jehiel, and Shimei: and of the sons of Jeduthun; Shemaiah, and Uzziel.

And they gathered their brethren, and sanctified themselves, and came, according to the commandment of the king, by the words of the Lord, to cleanse the house of the Lord. And the priests went into the inner part of the house of the Lord, to cleanse it, and brought out all the uncleanness that they found in the temple of the Lord into the court of the house of the Lord. And the Levites took it, to carry it out abroad into the brook Kidron.

Now they began on the first day of the first month to sanctify, and on the eighth day of the month came they to the porch of the Lord: so they sanctified the house of the Lord in eight days; and in the sixteenth day of the first month they made an end.

Then they went in to Hezekiah the king, and said, We have cleansed all the house of the Lord, and the altar of burnt offering, with all the vessels thereof, and the shewbread table, with all the vessels thereof.

Moreover all the vessels which king Ahaz in his reign did cast away in his transgression, have we prepared and sanctified, and, behold, they are before the altar of the Lord."

(Temple Worship Restored)

"Then Hezekiah the king rose early and gathered the rulers of the city, and went up to the house of the Lord." (II Chronicles 29:20)

(II Chronicles 29:34-35)

They praised the Lord. **"And he set the Levites in the house of the Lord with cymbals, psalteries, harps…according to the commandment of David, of Gad the king's seer, and Nathan the prophet: for so was the commandment of the Lord by his prophets…And the Levites stood with the instruments of David, and the priests with the trumpets… And all the congregation worshipped, and the singers sang, and the trumpeters sounded: and all this continued until the burnt offering was finished. And when they made an end of offering, the king and all that were present with him bowed themselves, and worshipped. Moreover Hezekiah the king and the princes commanded the Levites to sing praise unto the Lord with the words of David, and of Asaph the seer. And they sang praises with gladness, and they bowed their heads and worshipped. Then Hezekiah answered and said, Now ye have consecrated yourselves unto the Lord, come near and bring sacrifices and thank offerings in to the house of the Lord. And the congregation brought in sacrifices and thank offerings; and as many as were of a free heart burnt offerings."**

According to their customs, the priests sacrificed animals (bullocks, rams, sheep, lamb, oxen, and goats) totaling three thousand and six hundred or more *(3,600)* on the altar. There were so many animals,

(II Chronicles 29:34-35)

"…the priests were too few, so that they could not flay all the burnt offerings: wherefore their brethren the Levites did help them, till the work was ended, and until the other priests had sanctified themselves: for the Levites were more upright in heart to sanctify themselves than the priests. And also the burnt offering were in abundance, with

the fat of the peace offerings, and the drink offerings for every burnt offering. So the service of the house of the Lord was set in order."

(All Rejoiced)
"And Hezekiah rejoiced and all the people, that God had prepared the people: for the thing was done suddenly."   (II Chronicles 29:36)

(The Passover Restored)
Both the Southern Tribe and the Northern Tribe *(the remnants of the Ten Tribes left after the captivity)* re-assembled for the Passover,

(II Chronicles 30:1-5)

"And Hezekiah sent to all Israel and Judah, and wrote letter also to Ephraim and Manasseh, that they should come to the house of the Lord at Jerusalem, to keep the Passover unto the Lord God of Israel. For the king had taken counsel, and his princes, and all the congregation in Jerusalem, to keep the Passover in the second month. For they could not keep it at that time, because the priests had not sanctified themselves sufficiently, neither had the people gathered themselves together to Jerusalem. And the thing pleased the king and all the congregation. So they established a decree to make proclamation throughout all Israel, from Beersheba even to Dan, that they should come to keep the Passover unto the Lord God of Israel at Jerusalem: for they had not done it of a long time in such sort as it was written."

(Pony Express Letters Sent)
(II Chronicles 30:6-14)

"So the Posts *[Pony Express Riders] went with the letters from the king and his princes throughout all Israel and Judah, and according to the commandment of the king saying, Ye children of Israel, turn again unto the Lord God of Abraham, Isaac, and Israel, and he will return to the remnant of you, that are escaped out of the hand of the kings of Assyria. And be not ye like your fathers, and like your brethren, which trespassed against the Lord God of*

their fathers, who therefore gave them up to desolation, as ye see. Now be ye not stiffnecked as your fathers were, but yield yourselves unto the Lord, and enter into his sanctuary, which he hath sanctified for ever: and serve the Lord your God, that the fierceness of his wrath may turn away from you. For if ye turn against unto the Lord, your brethren and your children shall find compassion before them that lead them captive, so that they shall come against into this land: for the Lord your God is gracious and merciful, and will not turn away his face from you, if ye return unto him.

So the Posts **passed from city to city through the country of Ephraim and Manasseh even unto Zebulun:** but they laughed them to scorn, and mocked them. **Nevertheless divers of Asher and Manasseh and of Zebulun humbled themselves, and came to Jerusalem. Also in Judah the hand of God was to give them one heart to do the commandment of the king and of the princes, by the word of the Lord. And there assembled at Jerusalem much people to keep the feast of unleavened bread in the second month, a very great congregation. And they arose and took away the altars that were in Jerusalem, and all the altars for incense took they away, and cast them into the brook Kidron."**

(king Hezekiah Defeated the Philistines)
"And one more thing," stated the Professor, **"...king Hezekiah defeated the Philistines."** (II Kings 18:8)

Hezekiah's Test of FAITH Compared

(Hezekiah's Faith Tested)

After Hezekiah's great religious reforms, sanctification of the priests, revivals, and the Unitarian *Call to Worship*, the devil *still came knocking at the door of Judah's Kingdom.* It seems totally unfair! King Hezekiah overcame his corrupt Father *(king Ahaz)* and proved to be a *"righteous ruler after king David's heart."* Yet, king Hezekiah's faith was tested! After all the good he did, finally, peace came to the Southern Tribe of

Judah. *Then, the enemy came knocking at their door!* Why did **Yahweh** allow this to happen? There are multiple reasons for **Yahweh's** actions. **Yahweh** wanted to see if the people would call on Him or trust in their own strength. Also, He planned to punish the Assyrians.

(The Just Shall Live By Faith)

Yet, the *waters of faith* must be tested, ***"THE JUST SHALL LIVE BY FAITH!"*** (Romans 1:17) GOD IS UNIVERSAL, *"Where is boasting then? It is excluded. By what law? Of works? Nay: but by the law of faith. Therefore we conclude that a man is justified by faith without the deeds of the law. Is he the God of the Jews only? Is he not also of the Gentiles? Yes, of the Gentiles also: Seeing it is one God which shall justify the circumcision by faith, and uncircumcision through faith. Do we then make void the law through faith? God forbid: yea, we establish the law."* (Romans 3:27-31)

(Abraham's Faith Tested)

(Romans 4:1-3, 13-16, 17-21)

"What shall we say then the that Abraham our father, as pertaining to the flesh, hath found? For if Abraham were justified by works, he hath whereof to glory; but not before God. For what saith the scripture? Abraham believed God, and it was counted unto him for righteousness...For the promise, that he should be the heir of the world, was not to Abraham, or to his seed, through the law, but through the righteousness of faith. For if they which are of the law be heirs, faith is made void, and the promise made of none effect: Because the law worketh wrath: for where no law is, there is no transgression. Therefore it is of faith, that it might be by grace; to the end the promise might be sure to all the seed; not to that only which is of the law, but to that also which is of the faith of Abraham; who is the father of us all...As it is written, I have made thee a father of many nations before him whom he believed, even God, who quickeneth the dead, and called those things which be not as though they were. Who against hope believed in hope, that he might become the father

of many nations according to that which was spoken, So shall they see be. And being not weak in faith, <u>he considered not his own body now dead</u>, when he was about an hundred years old neither yet the <u>deadness of Sarah's womb</u>: He staggered not at the promise of God through unbelief; but was strong in faith giving glory to God. And being fully persuaded that, what he had promised, he was able also to perform."

(David's Faith Tested)

(Romans 4:6-8; Psalm 32:1-2; 51:1-13; 91:16; 103:3)

"Even as David also describeth the blessedness of the man, unto whom God imputeth righteousness without works, Saying, Blessed are they whose iniquities and whose sins are forgiven, and whose sins are covered. Blessed is the man to whom the Lord will not impute sin." (Romans 4:6-8) According to the Scriptures, David was a man after God's own heart which means that David had a penitent heart. Openly, he cried out for forgiveness and mercy.

Assyria's Attack on the Southern Tribe of Judah

Sennacherib the Assyrian king (reigned about 704-681 B.C.) succeeded in an attack on the fenced cities (about 46 cities)[66] of Judah. As a result of this victory, the Assyrians launched a campaign against Jerusalem (under king Hezekiah of Judah). It was no small matter!

---

66   Sennacherib's invasion of the 46 fenced cities* *(of the Southern Tribe of Judah)* is described on one of the three clay Prisms belonging to Sennacherib: *the Taylor Prism (in the British Museum; the Sennacherib Prism (in the Oriental Institute of Chicago; and one other Prism (in the Israel Museum in Jerusalem). The Prisms are written in Akkadian (six paragraphs of cuneiform); made of red baked clay; hexagonal; approximately 38.0 centimeters in height by 14.0 centimeters in width. Each prism is a record of Sennacherib's lists dates, sieges, campaigns and victories against Israel and Judah as dictated by Assyrian historians. As expected, there are similarities and slight variations between the Sennacherib's prisms and stories in the Old Testament.

(Rabshakeh's Hard Speech to Judah)

King Sennacherib had his bigmouth spokesman (Rabshakeh) threaten Jerusalem in the Hebrew language, rather than in the Assyrian tongue, so all of Judah would understand his threats! Rabshakeh made a sacrilegious speech against **Yahweh** and Judah,

(II Kings 18:17-25)

"And the king of Assyria sent Tartan and Rabsaris and Rabshakeh and Rabshakeh from Lachish to king Hezekiah with a great host against Jerusalem. And they went up and came to Jerusalem. And when they were come up, they came and stood by the conduit of the upper pool, which is in the highway of the fuller's field. And when they had called to the king, there came out to them Eliakim the son of Hilkiah, which was over the household, and Shebna the scribe, and Joah the son of Asaph the recorder.

And Rabshakeh said unto them, Speak ye now to Hezekiah, Thus saith the great king, the king of Assyria, <u>What confidence is there where in thou trustest</u>? *Thou sayest, (but they are vain words,) I have counsel and strength for the war. Now on whom doest thou trust that thou rebellest against me?*

Now, behold, thou trustest upon the staff of this bruised reed, even upon Egypt, on which if a man lean, it will go into his hand, and pierce it: so is Pharaoh king of Egypt unto all that trust on him. But if ye say unto me, We trust in the Lord our God: is not that he, whose high places and whose altars Hezekiah hath taken away, and hath said to Judah and Jerusalem, Ye shall worship before this altar in Jerusalem?

Now therefore, I pray thee, give pledges to my lord the king of Assyria, and I will deliver thee two thousand horses, if thou be able on thy part to set riders upon them. How then wilt thou turn away the face of one captain of the least of my master's servants, and put thy trust on Egypt for chariots and for horsemen?

Am I now come up without the Lord against this place to destroy it? The Lord said to me, Go up against this land, and destroy it."

(Eliakim Begs Rabshakeh To Speak Assyrian)
(II Kings 18:26)

"Then said Eliakim the son of Hilkiah, and Shebna, and Joah, unto Rabshakeh, Speak, I pray thee to thy servants in the Syrian language; for we understand it: and talk not with us in the Jews' language in the ears of the people that are on the wall."

(Rabshakeh Refuses To Speak Hebrew)
(II Kings 18:27-32)

"But Rabshakeh said unto them, Hath my master sent me to thy master, and to thee, to speak these words? Hath he not sent me to the men which sit on the wall, that they may eat their own dung, and drink their own piss with you?

Then Rabshakeh stood and cried with a loud voice in the Jews' language, and spake saying, Hear the word of the great king, the king of Assyria:

Thus saith the king, Let not Hezekiah deceive you: for he shall not be able to deliver you out of his hand: Neither let Hezekiah make you trust in the Lord, saying, The Lord will surely deliver us, and this city shall not be delivered into the hand of the king of Assyria.

Hearken not to Hezekiah: for thus saith the king of Assyria, Make an agreement with me by present, and come out to me, and then eat ye every man of his own vine, and every one of his fig tree, and drink ye every one the waters of his cistern:

Until I come and take you away to a land like your own land or bread and vineyards, a land of oil olive and of honey, that ye may live, and not die: and hearken not unto Hezekiah, when he persuadeth you, saying, The Lord will deliver us."

(Rabshakeh's Great Boastings)

(II Kings 18:33-37)

"Hath any of the gods of the nations delivered at all his land out of the hand of the king of Assyria? Where are the gods of Hamath, and of Arpad? Where are the gods of Sepharvaim, Hena, and Ivah? Have they delivered Samaria out of mine hand? Who are they among all the gods of the countries, that have delivered their country out of mine hand, that the Lord should deliver Jerusalem out of mine hand?

But the people held their peace, and answered him not a word: for the king's commandment was, saying, Answer him not.

Then came Eliakim the son of Hilkiah, which was over the household, and Shebna the scribe, and Joah the son of Asaph the recorder, to Hezekiah with their clothes rent, and told him the words of Rabshakeh."

(Hezekiah Believes in Yahweh)

(II Kings 19:1-5a)

"And it came to pass, when king Hezekiah heard it, that he rent his clothes, and covered himself with sackcloth, and went into the house of the Lord. And he sent Eliakim...to Isaiah the prophet the son of Amoz.

And they said unto him, Thus saith Hezekiah, This day is a day of trouble, and of rebuke, and blasphemy: for the children are come to the birth, and there is not strength to bring forth.

It may be the Lord thy god will hear all the words of Rabshakeh, whom the king of Assyria his master hath sent to reproach the living God; and will reprove the words which the Lord thy God hath heard:

wherefore lift up thy prayer for the remnant that are left. So the servants of king Hezekiah came to Isaiah."

(Hezekiah's Prayer)

(II Kings 19:15-19; Isaiah 37:16-17)

"And Hezekiah prayed before the Lord, and said, O Lord God of Israel, which dwellest between the cherubims, thou art the God, even thou alone, of all the kingdoms of the earth; thou hast made heaven and earth. Lord, bow down thine ear, and hear: open, Lord, thine eyes, and see: and hear the words of Sennacherib, which hath sent him to reproach the living God. Of a truth, Lord, the kings of Assyria have destroyed the nations and their lands, And have cast their gods into the fire: for they were no gods, but the work of men's hands, wood and stone: therefore they have destroyed them. Now therefore, O Lord our God, I beseech thee, save thou us out of his hand, that all the kingdoms of the earth may know that thou are the Lord God, even thou only."

(Yahweh's Answer to king Hezekiah)

(II Kings 19:5b-7)

"And Isaiah said unto them, Thus shall ye say to your master, Thus saith the Lord, Be not afraid of the words which thou hast heard, with which the servants of the king of Assyria have blasphemed me. Behold, I will send a blast upon him, and he shall bear a rumor, and shall return to his own land; and I will cause him to fall by the sword in his own land."

(Yahweh's Lengthier Answer to king Hezekiah)

(II Kings 19:20-34)

"Then Isaiah the son of Amoz sent to Hezekiah, saying, Thus saith the Lord God of Israel, That which thou hast prayed to me against Sennacherib king of Assyria I have heard. This is the word that the Lord hath spoken concerning him;

The virgin the daughter of Zion hath despised thee, and laughed thee to scorn; the daughter of Jerusalem hath shaken her head at thee. Whom thou reproached and blasphemed? And against whom hast thou exalted thy voice, and lifted up thine eyes on high? Even against the Holy One of Israel.

By thy messengers thou hast reproached the Lord, and hast said, With the multitude of my chariots I am come up to the height of the mountains, to the sides of Lebanon, and will cut down the tall cedar trees thereof, and the choice fir trees thereof: and I will enter into the lodgings of his borders, and into the forest of his Carmel.

I have digged and drunk strange waters, and with the sole of my feet have I dried up all the rivers of besieged places. Hast thou not heard long ago how I have done it, and of ancient time that I have formed it? Now have I brought it to pass, and thou shouldest be to lay waste fenced cities into ruinous heaps.

Therefore their inhabitants were of small power, they were dismayed and confounded; they were as the grass of the field, and as the green herb, as the grass on the house tops, and as corn blasted before it be grown up.

But I know thy abode and thy going out, and thy coming in, and thy rage against me. Because thy rage against me and thy tumult is come up into mine ears, therefore I will put my hook in thy nose, and my bridle in thy lips, and I will turn thee back by the way by which thou camest.

And this shall be a sign unto thee, Ye shall eat this year such things as grow of themselves, and in the second year that which springeth of the same; and in the third year sow ye, and reap, and plant vineyards, and eat the fruits thereof.

And the remnant that is escaped of the house of Judah shall yet against take root downward, and bear fruit upward. For out of Jerusalem shall go forth a remnant, and they that escape out of mount Zion: the zeal of the Lord of hosts shall do this.

Therefore thus saith the Lord concerning the king of Assyria. He shall not come into this city, and shoot an arrow there, no come before it with shield, nor cast a bank against it. By the way that he came by the same shall he return and shall into come into this city, saith the Lord. For I will defend this city to save it, for mine own sake, and for my servant David's sake."

(Yahweh's Rebuke Against Sennacherib)
Again, the Prophet Isaiah was sent to king Hezekiah saying,

(Isaiah 37:21-29)
"Thus saith the Lord God of Israel, Whereas thou hast prayed to me against Sennacherib king of Assyria: This is the word which the Lord hath spoken concerning him; The virgin, the daughter of Zion, hath despised thee, and laughed thee to scorn; the daughter of Jerusalem hath shaken her head at thee. Whom has thou reproached and blasphemed? And against whom has thou exalted thy voice, and lifted up thing eyes on high? Even against the Holy One of Israel. By thy servants has thou reproached the Lord, and hast said, By the multitude of my chariots am I come up to the height of the mountains, to the sides of Lebanon; and I will cut down the tall cedars thereof, and the choice fir trees thereof: and I will enter into the height of his border, and the forest of his Carmel. I have digged, and drunk water; and with the sole of my feet have I dried up all the rivers of the besieged places. Hast thou not heard long ago, how I have done it; and of ancient times, that I have formed it? Now have I brought it to pass, that thou shouldest be to lay waste defenced cities into ruinous heaps. Therefore their inhabitants were of small power, they were dismayed and confounded: they were as the grass of the field, and

as the green herb, as the grass on the housetops, and as corn blasted before it be grown up. But I know thy abode, and thy going out, and thy coming in, and thy rage against me. <u>Because thy rage against me, and thy tumult, is come up into mine ears, therefore will I put my hook in thy nose, and my bridle in thy lips, and I will turn thee back by the way by which thou camest.</u>"

(The Rumor)

(II Kings 19:8-9)

"So Rabshakeh returned, and found the king of Assyria warring against Libnah: for he had heard that he was departed from Lachish. And when he heard say of Tirhakah king of Ethiopia, Behold, he is come out in fight against thee..."

(Angel of the Lord Slays 185,000 Assyrians)

Most likely, the Assyrians coined the phrase "Do you want a piece of this?" The Assyrians' egos were over-baked, fried, and barbequed in conceit, arrogance, and pride. The **Lord GOD** grew weary of their boasting, and He would not use them to chastise the Southern Tribe of Israel. However, this did not stop the *haughty* Assyrians and they took themselves into the Southern Kingdom. BUT THEIR SUCCESS AGAINST JERUSALEM WAS NOT WRITTEN IN THE STARS, *"Thus saith the Lord, concerning the king of Assyria, He shall not come into this city, or shoot an arrow there, no come before it with shields, no cast a bank against it. By the way that he came, by the same shall he return, and shall not come into this city, saith the Lord. For I will defend this city to save it for mine own sake, and for my servant David's sake."* (Isaiah 37:33-35) Because of **Yahweh's Word**, the Assyrian's siege against the Southern Tribe of Judah was a total flop and disgrace!

(II Kings 19:35)

"And it came to pass that night, that the angel of the Lord went out, and smote in the camp of the Assyrians an hundred fourscore and five thousand (185,000): and when they arose early in the morning, behold they were all dead corpses."

(king Sennacherib's Death)

(II Kings 19:36-37)

"So Sennacherib king of Assyria departed, and went and returned, and dwelt at Nineveh. As a result, king Sennacherib fled to Nineveh and prayed to his god, *Nisroch*. While the king was praying, his two sons (Adrammelech and Sharezer) murdered him and they fled to the land of Armenia. Apparently, the two brothers, families, and followers were pursued and punished with death. Esarhaddon (about 681-669 B.C.) the youngest son of the late Sennacherib took the throne. (II Kings 19:36-37) Later, it seems that Esarhaddon died suddenly and Ashurbanipal became the last king of Assyria!

Hezekiah's Sickness, Healing, & Sign

Again, king Hezekiah's faith in **Yahweh** came forth victoriously! During the Assyrian crisis, king Hezekiah was *terminally ill*. As stated much earlier, Prophet Isaiah told king Hezekiah, **"*Set thine house in order for thou shalt die and not live.*"** (Isaiah 38:2; II Kings 20:1)

It must have been difficult for the king who struggled with *failing health* and Rabshakeh *(the Assyrian dog)* at his heel! Yet, Hezekiah's faith endured the test.

With all this turmoil, Hezekiah did not forget how to pray! He got away from the Queen, his chancellors, staff, servants, and he turned his face to the wall to pray, **"*Remember now O Lord, I beseech thee, how I have walked before thee in truth and with a perfect heart, and have done that which is good in thy sight. And Hezekiah wept sore.*"** (Isaiah 38:1-3; II Kings 20:1-5)

<u>A DIVINE MIRACLE</u>: After king Hezekiah's sincere prayer and within a blink of an eye, God struck Isaiah with an answer, **"*And it came to pass, afore Isaiah was gone out into the middle court, that the*</u>**

__word of the Lord came to him, saying, Turn again, and tell Hezekiah the captain of my people, Thus saith the Lord, the God of David thy father, I have heard thy prayer, I have seen thy tears...__" (II Kings 20:1-5)

(Hezekiah's Frame of Mind)
King Hezekiah was deeply troubled,

"Mine age is departed and removed from me...my life is cut off because of sickness...I am chattering like a crane [67] and swallow... mourning like a dove, eyes failing to look upward...oppressed... bitter...." (Isaiah 38:12-14)

(Yahweh's Answer)
"Then came the word of the Lord to Isaiah, saying, Go, and say to Hezekiah, Thus saith the Lord, the God of David thy father: **(A)** *I have heard thy prayer I have seen thy tears;* **(B)** *Behold, I will add unto thy days fifteen years;* **(C)** *__And I will deliver thee and this city out of the hand of the king of Assyria__;* **(D)** *__And I will defend this city__;* **(E)** *And Hezekiah said unto Isaiah, what shall be the sign that the Lord will heal me, and that I shall go up into the house of the Lord the third day?* (II Kings 20:8); **(F)** Healing with natural fruit, *For Isaiah had said, Let them take a lump of figs, and lay it for a plaister upon the boil, and he shall recover. Hezekiah also had said, What shall be the sign that I shall*

---

67   The crane birds have big bodies, long legs, long necks, fly with their necks out stretched, and they look very regal. *The cranes are broadcasters!* They are known for their loud grievous and melancholy calls. They seem to hold their *notes* for a lengthy time *(about the same length as their long legs)* and they repeat the calls getting louder and louder making three to four more calls and flapping their wings. Frankly, cranes don't care who or what hears them and their sounds will wake-up the dead. In contrast, the swallow is a little short-legged bird with a short beak. Frankly, they make continuous noise, chatter, and they tell everything! They are the CNN (news reporters) in the animal kingdom and they yap about everything and everybody! Nothing is hidden from their cameras. Like the dove (a sweet bird, faithful, nonresistant), Hezekiah felt helpless against his enemies.

go up to the house of the Lord? (Isaiah 38:21); and **(G)** *THE SIGN: And this shall be a sign unto thee from the Lord, that the Lord will do this thing that he hath spoken: Behold, I will bring again the shadow of the degrees which is gone down in the sundial of Ahaz, ten degrees backward. So the sun returned ten degrees, by which degrees it was gone down."* (Isaiah 38:4-8)

(Hezekiah Allows Babylonian Spies into the City)

In summary, king Hezekiah opened up the gates and let the Babylonians into his palace. In reality, the Babylonians were stunned (like the rest of the world) regarding *"...the shadow of the degrees which went down in the sundial of Ahaz, by ten degrees..."* They knew that the Hebrew God wrought this miracle and that king Hezekiah was healed on his death bed. Moreover, they were spying (checking-out) the Kingdom of Judah! *And, Hezekiah fell into the trap with "his eyes wide open."* Under the flag *of brotherhood, these demons came to wish a great king wellness!* Does this remind you of any one you know? And, Hezekiah gave them The 411 Tour of the White House, *"At that time, Merodach-Baladan, the son of Baladan, king of Babylon, sent letters and a present to Hezekiah: for he had heard that he had been sick and was recovered. And Hezekiah was glad of them and shewed them the house of his precious things, silver, gold, spices, and the precious ointment, and all the house of his armor, and all that was found in his treasures: there was nothing in his house, nor in all his dominion, that Hezekiah shewed them not."* (Isaiah 39: 1-3) Soon, the Babylonians would return under the umbrella, *Winner Takes It All!*

Chapter 22

Babylon vs. Southern Tribe of Judah

(Nebuchadnezzar's comments)

King Nebuchadnezzar said, "This story <u>is not</u> just about me. Let me give you a *quick snapshot* on these four kingdoms. It's about <u>*Assyria vs. the Northern Tribe of Israel*</u> and <u>*Babylon vs. the Southern Tribe of Judah*</u>. I am just one of the vessels *(used of God)* to chastise the Chosen people of Judah. It seems that everyone wants to point the finger at me. Until God called me to be His servant, I had no issues with the Nation of Judah. Babylonia was too busy fighting with Assyria. However, the **Lord GOD** commissioned the Babylonians to take down the Southern Tribe of Israel.

Babylonian Roots in Nimrod

As discussed earlier, Babylon's progenitor (Nimrod) was the <u>third</u> generation to Noah (the son of Cush, the son of Ham, the son of Noah). The Bible states, ***"Nimrod was a mighty hunter and the beginning of his kingdom was <u>Babel</u>, Erech, Accad, Calneh, in the land of Shinar.*** (Genesis 10:8-11) Like the Assyrians, the Babylonians did not relish their National origins stemming from Noah who found grace from God, before the flood. They no more believed Noah or the stories he told about God than a man on the moon!

261

(The Babylonia Reality Television Show)

The Babylonians waded up to their necks in the waters of arrogance and pride! It makes no difference that they were the third generation to Noah. Technically, they could have been with Noah in the Ark and they still would not live right! The fact that they were used of God and their names recorded in the Bible is significant. However, the final outcome of the matter is more important than their beginning. Of course, their link to the infamous Noah and his son, Ham, makes them celebrities. This link alone qualified them for a number one T.V. Reality Show! Imagine watching the daily Babylonian Saga: building projects, temples, aqueducts, motifs, paintings, wars, conquests, deportation process, city structure, government process, military procedures, human bondage, prisons, the fiery furnace, and more. This entire program would be far more interesting than the Atlanta Wives Reality Show!

Let's pretend, Nebuchadnezzar (one of Nimrod's descendents) has a "live television broadcast." The following is a make-believe dialog but it captures the essence of Nebuchadnezzar's arrogance,

(Nebuchadnezzar' Statement)

"We come from a proud heritage beginning with Grandpas Noah and Ham, their descents, our fathers, and uncles! Unfortunately, Grandpa Noah and Grandpa Ham were old fashioned. Grandpa Noah just sat in the sunlight everyday just to warm his old bones! He repeated so many old stories (over and over and over) about the ancient wicked cultures, people living to be 1,000 years old, a flood that he called "Noah's Deluge," God, and how his family was saved from a worldwide flood! He said that people were screaming, scratching, and banging on the door of the Ark (some big ship he and his sons built for one hundred and twenty-years). Then, Grandpa Noah said that he preached for 120 years to wicked people who laughed and mocked at him. Well, I can imagine people laughing at Grandpa Noah, but I cannot imagine that he preached and built an Ark for 120 years. That's ridiculous! Man, when grandpa Noah said that I knew he was off his rocker! He said that the ship was bigger than a football field!

Really, I think Grandpa Noah was senile and he meant well, but there was no flood! You see, Grandpa Noah was about 950 years old when he died. I'll always love him and I will never forget him! He was good, all good! Truthfully, Grandpa Noah use to sip wine, get drunk, pass-out (in the dirt bed of his vineyards). One day Grandpa Noah woke-up to his old donkey licking his face. The donkey's tongue was so thick and full of slime that gramps just thought he was drowning! He was drowning! But it was in saliva! You know how it is when you get 950 years old!

Also, Grandpa Ham (the youngest son of Noah) was so busy drinking and chasing Canaanite women that he could not keep up with the signs of the times! In fact, Grandpa Noah cursed Grandpa Ham him for laughing at him while he was passed out from liquor! Because of their ages, I often worried about those two.

As children (on the other side of Noah's Deluge), Grandpa Noah and Grandpa Ham heard many folklore stories that they started getting the stories mixed up! That's why the Babylonians were polytheists! They did not want to offend any of the gods! Besides, if one god doesn't work, the Babylonians just made another one. It's too boring to serve One God because the world is a melting pot! We have a right to do as we please! I could never understand why Grandpa Noah believed in the concept of One True Living God!

Technically, the continuation of our bloodline and survival are the real issues not Grandpa Noah or Grandpa Ham's mystical stories. There stories are fine as bedtime stories for the kids, but not in reality.

My Father, Nabopolassar and I had to put Babylonia back on the map! Times were changing! Our second cousins, the Asshurites (Ninevites) were monsters! They were taking over all the nations and it was time to put an end to their madness! Although their bloodline was much closer to Grandpa Noah than ours, we did not let that fact hinder our warfare against them. We continued fighting for over two hundred (200) years before we won our independence from Assyria!

Surely, I can talk about being lifted-up in pride; because I was just as boisterous, arrogant, and conceited as my cousins, the Assyrians. I was just as boisterous, arrogant, and conceited as my cousins, the Assyrians. In spite of my character flaws, the **Lord GOD** commissioned Babylon to accomplish His Will against His Chosen, Judah. **GOD** allowed Babylon to succeed the ruthless Assyrians through a great military feat. Looking back on history, **GOD** knew that Babylon would overtake Jerusalem and that Babylon would be lifted up in pride as well! Nonetheless, **GOD** used us **to chastise His people, Judah.** In this respect, Babylon succeeded in their task and they conquered Judah.

After my victorious conquests, accumulated wealth, and enormous building projects, I got lifted up in conceit! I walked around like <u>Bruce Almighty</u>! Just look what happened to me. I lost my mind and the officials ran me out of my own palace and Babylon the Great (the city I made fabulous and famous!) My mental state of mind and my physical being was altered. I could no longer live with humans and maintain my regency! I could no longer sleep with my beautiful wife, Amytis, and stroll through the Hanging Gardens! Amytis could not stand my animalistic behavior!! Furthermore, the women in my harem wouldn't even look at me! I was disgusting! Surely, the **Lord GOD** passed rightful judgment upon me. Moreover, the **Lord GOD** judged all of us.

Signed, Nebuchadnezzar

<u>Isaiah's Prophecy to king Hezekiah,</u> CAPTIVITY

Prophet Isaiah told king Hezekiah that the Southern Tribe would go into captivity and that God would send fierce and mighty nations from the North. Here is part of Isaiah's dialog,

<u>Prophet Isaiah asked king Hezekiah,</u> **"What said these men? And from whence came they unto thee?"** (Isaiah 39:3)

<u>And Hezekiah said</u>, *"They are come from a far country unto me, even from Babylon."* (Isaiah 39:3)

<u>Prophet Isaiah asked</u>, *"What have they seen in thine house?* (Isaiah 39:4)

<u>And Hezekiah answered</u>, *"All that is in mine house have they seen: there is nothing among my treasures that I have not shewed them."* (Isaiah 39:4)

<u>Prophet Isaiah said to Hezekiah</u>, *"Hear the word of the Lord of hosts: Behold the days come, that all that is in thine house, and that which thy fathers have laid up in store until this day, shall be carried to Babylon: nothing shall be left, saith the Lord. And of thy sons that shall issue from thee, which thou shall beget, shall they take away; and they shall be eunuchs in the palace of the king of Babylon."* (Isaiah 39:5-8)

<u>Then said Hezekiah to Isaiah</u>, *"**Good** is the word of the Lord which thou hast spoken. He said moreover, for there shall be peace and truth in my days."* (Isaiah 39:5-8)

Habakkuk's Words, A Burden

Habakkuk *(means = to embrace)* was a contemporary prophet during the last years of Judah, "The burden which Habakkuk the prophet did see." (Habakkuk 1:1) Like Prophet Jeremiah *(dubbed, the weeping prophet)*, Habakkuk <u>hollered</u> for Judah, *"<u>O Lord, how long shall I cry, and thou wilt not hear even cry out to thee of violence, and thou wilt not save!</u> Why dost thou shew me iniquity, and cause me to behold grievance? For spoiling and violence are before me: and there are that raise up strife and contention. Therefore the law is slacked and judgment doth never go forth: for the wicked doth compass about the righteous; therefore wrong judgment proceedeth."* (Habakkuk 1:2-4)

Constance Lee

Habakkuk's Words, Chaldean/Babylonians

Habakkuk gives an excellent character description of the Babylonian-Chaldeans and their war machines,

(Habakkuk 5:10)
"Behold ye among the heathen, and regard, and wonder marvelously: for I will work a work in your days, which ye will not believe, though it be told you. <u>*For, lo, I raise up the Chaldeans, that bitter and hasty nation, which shall march through the breadth of the land to possess the dwelling places that are not theirs. They are terrible and dreadful: their judgment and their dignity shall proceed of themselves. Their horses also are swifter than the leopards, and are more fierce than the evening wolves: and their horsemen shall spread themselves and their horsemen shall come from far; they shall fly as the eagle that hasteth to eat. They shall come all for violence: their faces shall sup up as the east wind, and they shall gather the captivity as sand. And they shall scoff at the kings, and the princes shall be a scorn unto them: they shall deride every strong hold; for they shall heap dust, and take it.*</u>*"*

Habakkuk's Words, king Nebuchadnezzar

The Prophet Habakkuk prophesized about <u>Nebuchadnezzar's madness</u>, *" Then shall his mind change, and he shall pass over and offend, imputing this his power unto his god."* (Habakkuk 1:11)

Ezekiel's, Jerusalem Captured

(Ezekiel 33:21)
"And it came to pass in the twelfth year of our captivity, in the

tenth month, in the fifth day of the month, that one that had escaped out of Jerusalem came unto me, saying, the city is smitten. Now the hand of the Lord was upon me in the evening, afore he that was escaped came; and had opened my mouth, until he came to me in the morning; and my mouth was opened, and I was no more dumb."

Difference Between Babylonian & Assyrian Captivities

There are notable differences between the two captivities of the *Northern Tribe of Israel* and *the Southern Tribe of Judah*. One of the most notable differences involves the number of people taken captive. The Assyrians deported about twenty seven thousand and three hundred (27,300) people both upper and lower classes. And they *"…carried Israel away into Assyria and placed them in Halah, Habor by the river of Gozan, and in the cities of the Medes."* (II Kings 17:5) The Assyrians made approximately *five* invasions on the Northern Tribe of Israel until the fall of Samaria, about 722.B.C. They replaced the deportees with outsiders *(men from Babylon, Cuthah, Ava, Hamath, and Sepharvaim).* Samaria became a melting pot of foreigners, non-believers, and polytheistic. (II Kings 17:22-24)

In contrast, the fall of Jerusalem occurred about 586 B.C. The Babylonians made approximately three invasions on the Southern Tribe of Judah and carried away about twelve thousand or more captives (nobles and upper class) to Babylon for seventy years. The captives were allowed to blend in with the Babylonians. In fact, the Hebrews applied their skills (as artists, metal workers, etc.) to many of the construction sites in Babylon. This captivity was not the same as the Hebrews in Egypt for 400 years! However, the Hebrew captives lived in Babylon for seventy years. Like Samaria, the rich homes, temple, and the city was burned and sacked. Many riches, treasures, and holy vessels were taken to Babylon. Unlike their sister's captivity, General Nebuzaradan left the poorer Hebrews in Jerusalem *giving them a chance to make something of themselves.* Spiritually, the Hebrews left behind had a truer understanding of the order of Worship to **Yahweh** *(unlike the new residents in Samaria who has no clue).*

BABYLONIA vs. Southern Tribe of Judah

The Babylonia race grew to be just as mighty as their cousins, *the Assyrians.* As stated earlier, the Babylonian's conquered the Southern Tribe of Judah (about 586 B.C.) and they took the upper class and nobles into captivity approximately twelve thousand or more Hebrews were taken to Babylon.

FIRST BABYLONIAN INVASION vs. king Jehoiakim of Judah

(Judah Defeated and king Jehoiakim's death)
(II Chronicles 36:8-10)
"Jehoiakim (A.K.A. Eliakim was his birth name; king Neco, king of Egypt, changed it to Jehoiakim) was twenty-five years old when he began to reign, and he reigned eleven years in Jerusalem: and he did that which was evil in the sight of the Lord his God. Against him came up Nebuchadnezzar king of Babylon, and bound him in fetters to carry him to Babylon. Nebuchadnezzar also carried of the vessels of the house of the Lord to Babylon and put them in his temple at Babylon. Now the rest of the acts of Jehoiakim, and his abominations, which he did, and that which was found in him, behold, they are written in the book of the kings of Israel and Judah: and Jehoiachin his son reigned in his stead."

(II Kings 24:1-6)
"In his days Nebuchadnezzar king of Babylon came up, and Jehoiakim became his servant three years: then he turned and rebelled against him. And the Lord sent against him bands of the Chaldees, and bands of the Syrians, and bands of the Moabites, and bands of the children of Ammon, and sent them against Judah to destroy it,

according to the word of the Lord, which he spake by his servants the prophets. Surely at the commandment of the Lord came this upon Judah, to remove them out of his sight, for the sins of Manasseh, according to all that he did: And also for the innocent blood that he shed: for he filled Jerusalem with innocent blood; which the Lord would not pardon.

Now the rest of the acts of Jehoiakim, and all that he did, are they not written in the book of the chronicles of the kings of Judah? So Jehoiakim slept with his fathers: and Jehoiachin his son reigned in his stead."

SECOND BABYLONIAN INVASION vs. king Jehoiachin of Judah

(Jerusalem Sacked and the Temple Destroyed)

(II Kings 24:8-16)

"Jehoiachin (A.K.A. Jeconiah and Coniah; was the grandson to the goodly king Josiah) was eighteen years old when he began to reign, and he reigned in Jerusalem three months…And he did that which was evil in the sight of the Lord, according to all that his father had done. At that time the servants of Nebuchadnezzar king of Babylon came up against Jerusalem, and the city was besieged. And Nebuchadnezzar king of Babylon came against the city, and his servant did besiege it. And Jehoiachin the king of Judah went out to the king of Babylon, he and his mother, and his servants, and his princes, and his officers: and the king of Babylon took him in the eighth year of his reign. And he carried out thence all the treasures of the house of the Lord, and the treasures of the king's house, and cut in pieces all the vessels of gold which Solomon king of Israel had made in the temple of the Lord, as the Lord had said. And he carried away all Jerusalem, and all the princes, and all the mighty men of valor, even ten thousand

captives, and all the craftsmen, and smiths: none remained, save the poorest sort of the people of the land. And he carried away Jehoiachin to Babylon, and the king's mother, and the king's wives, and his officers, and the mighty of the land, those carried he into captivity from Jerusalem to Babylon. And all the men of might, even seven thousand, and craftsmen and smiths a thousand, all that were strong and apt for war, even them the king of Babylon brought captive to Babylon."

(king Jehoiachin taken into captivity)
(II Chronicles 36:9-10)

"Jehoiachin was eight years old [the correct age was 18 years old] *when he began to reign, and he reigned three months and ten days in Jerusalem: and he did that which was evil in the sight of the Lord. And when the year was expired, king Nebuchadnezzar sent, and brought him to Babylon, with the goodly vessels of the house of the Lord, and made Zedekiah his brother* [Zedekiah, A.K.A Mattaniah, was not his brother; he was Jehoiachin's uncle, the son of Josiah] *king over Judah and Jerusalem."*

(king Jehoiachin released from prison after 37 years)
(II Kings 25:27-28)

"And it came to pass in the seven and thirtieth year of the captivity of Jehoiachin king of judah, in the twelfth month, on the seven and twentieth day of the month, that Evil-Merodach [Awil-Marduk, son of king Nebuchadnezzar II] *king of Babylon in the year that he began to reign did lift up the head of Jehoiachin king of Judah out of prison. And, he spake kindly to him, and set his throne above the throne of the kings that were with him in Babylon; And changed his prison garments; and he did eat bread continually before him all the days of his life. And his allowance was a continual allowance given him of the kings daily rate for every day, all the days of his life."*

THIRD BABYLONIAN INVASION vs. king Zedekiah of Judah

(Judah Defeated and king Zedekiah captured)

(II Kings 24:17)
"And the king of Babylon made Mattaniah his father's brother king in his stead, and changed his name to Zedekiah." [Mattaniah's name changed to Zedekiah]

(II Kings 25:1-7)
"And it came to pass in the ninth year of his reign, in the tenth month, in the tenth day of the month, that Nebuchadnezzar...came, he, and his host against Jerusalem, and pitched against it; and they built forts against it round about. And the city was besieged unto the eleventh year of king Zedekiah. And on the nine day of the fourth month the famine prevailed in the city, and there was no bread for the people of the land. And the city was broken up, and all the men of war fled by night by the way of the gate between two walls, which is by the king's garden: (now the Chaldees were against the city round about) and the king went the way toward the plain. And the army of the Chaldees pursued after the king and overtook him in the plains of Jericho: and all his army were scattered from him. So they took the king, and brought him up to the king of Babylon to Riblah; and they gave judgment upon him. And they slew the sons of Zedekiah before his eyes, and put out the eyes of Zedekiah, and bound him with fetters of brass, and carried him to Babylon."

(II Kings 25:8-10)
"And in the fifth month, on the seventh day of the month, which is the nineteen year of king Nebuchadnezzar of Babylon, came Nebuzaradan, captain of the guard, a servant of the king of Babylon, unto Jerusalem: And he burnt the house of the Lord, and the king's house, and all the houses of Jerusalem, and every great man's house burnt he with fire. And all the army of the Chaldees, that were with

the captain of the guard, brake down the walls of Jerusalem round about."

Jeremiah Preached Twenty-Three Years to Judah

(Jeremiah 25:1-7)

The Bible states, *"The word that came to Jeremiah concerning all the people of Judah in the fourth year of Jehoiakim the son of Josiah king of Judah, that was the first year of Nebuchadnezzar king of Babylon;*

The which Jeremiah the prophet spake unto all the people of Judah, and to all the inhabitants of Jerusalem, saying from the thirteenth year of Josiah the son of Amon king of Judah even unto this day, that is the three and twentieth year, the word of the Lord hath come unto me, and I have spoken unto you, rising early and speaking; but ye have not hearkened.

And the Lord hath sent unto you all his servants the prophets, rising early and sending them; but ye have not hearkened, nor inclined your ear to hear.

They said, Turn ye again now every one from his evil way, and from the evil of your doing, and dwell in the land that the Lord hath given unto you and to your fathers for every and ever: And go not after other gods to serve them, and to worship them, and provoke me not to anger with the works of your hands; and I will do you no hurt. Yet ye have not hearkened unto me, saith the Lord; that ye might provoke me to anger with the works of your hands to your own hurt."

Seventy (70) Years of Captivity

Yahweh commissioned king Nebuchadnezzar as His servant to punish the Southern Tribe of Judah. And **Yahweh** *gave* Judah to king Nebuchadnezzar for 70 years. Frankly, Nebuchadnezzar had no choice in the matter! Whatever **Yahweh** says goes! **Basically, Yahweh told Judah, "You won't be on holiday, singing, dancing, partying, drinking, toasting, entertaining, celebrating, or doing the mashed potatoes!**

(Jeremiah 25:8-11)
"Therefore thus saith the Lord of hosts; Because ye have not heard my words,

Behold, I will send and take all the families of the north, and Nebuchadnezzar the king of Babylon, my servant, *and will bring them against this land, and against the inhabitants thereof, and against all these nations round about, and will utterly destroy them, and make them an astonishment, and an hissing, and perpetual desolations.* Moreover I will take from them the voice of mirth, and the voice of gladness, the voice of the bridegroom, and the voice of the bride, the sound of the millstones, and the light of the candle. And this whole land shall be a desolation, and an astonishment; and these nations shall serve the king of Babylon seventy years."

Ezekiel's Vision: Angels Helped Babylon

Prophet Ezekiel saw the glory of the Lord lift up from the cherub and move the threshold of the house.

(Ezekiel 9:1-2)
"He **[Yahweh]** *cried also in mine ears with a loud voice, saying Cause them that have charge over the city to draw near, even every man with his destroying weapon in his hand.* And BEHOLD six men [angels] came from the way of the higher gate which lieth toward the north, every man a slaughter weapon in his hand; and one man among them was clothe with linen, with a writer's inkhorn by his side: and they went in, and stood beside the brasen altar."

273

(The Angel in Linen with the Writer's Inkhorn)

(Ezekiel 9:3-4)

"And the glory of the God of Israel was gone up from the cherub, whereupon he was, to the threshold of the house. And he called to the man clothed with linen, which had the writer's inkhorn by his side. And the Lord said unto him, Go through the midst of the city, through the midst of Jerusalem, and set a mark upon the foreheads of the men that sigh and that cry for all the abominations that be done in the midst thereof."

(Five Angelic Executioners)

(Ezekiel 9:5-6)

"And to the others he said in mine hearing, Go ye after him through the city, and smite: let not your eye spare, neither have ye pity: Slay utterly old and young, both maids, and little children, and women: but come not near any man upon whom is the mark; and begin at my sanctuary. Then they began at the ancient men which were before the house."

A Message of HOPE during Captivity

(Jeremiah 29:4-14)

"Thus saith the Lord of hosts, the God of Israel, unto all that are carried away captives, <u>whom I have caused to be carried away from Jerusalem unto Babylon</u>;

Build ye houses, and dwell in them; and plant gardens, and eat the fruit of them; Take ye wives, and beget sons and daughters; and take wives for your sons, and give your daughters to husbands, that they may bear sons and daughters; that ye may be increased there, and not diminished. And seek the peace of the city whither I have caused you to be carried away captives and pray unto the Lord for it: for in the peace thereof shall ye have peace...

For thus saith the Lord, that after seventy years be accomplished at Babylon I will visit you, and perform my good word toward you, in causing you to return to this place.

For I know the thoughts that I think toward you, saith the Lord, thoughts of peace, and not of evil, to give you an expected end. Then shall ye call upon me, and ye shall go and pray unto me, and I will hearken unto you. And ye shall seek me, and find me, when ye shall search for me with all your heart. And I will be found of you, saith the Lord: and I will turn away your captivity, and I will gather you from all the nations, and from all the places whither I have driven you, saith the Lord; and I will bring you again into the place whence I caused you to be carried away captive. "

False Prophets

(Jeremiah 29:8-9)
"For thus saith the Lord of hosts, the God of Israel; Let not your prophets and your diviners, that be in the midst of you, deceive you, neither hearken to your dreams which ye cause to be dreamed. <u>For they prophesy falsely unto you in my name: I have not sent them, saith the Lord</u>."

Punishment on False Prophets

During Judah's captivity in Babylon, there were many false prophets,

(Jeremiah 29:20-32)

"Hear ye therefore the word of the Lord, all ye of the captivity, whom I have sent from Jerusalem to Babylon:

Thus saith the Lord of hosts, the God of Israel, of Ahab the son of Kolaiah *and* Zedekiah the son of Maaseiah, *which prophesy a lie unto you in my name;* Behold, I will deliver them into the hand of Nebuchadnezzar king of Babylon; and he shall slay them before your eyes:

And of them shall be taken up a curse by all the captivity of Judah which are in Babylon, saying, <u>The Lord make thee like Zedekiah and like Ahab whom the king of Babylon roasted in the fire</u>;

Because they have committed villainy in Israel, and have committed adultery with their neighbors' wives and have spoken lying words in my name, which I have not commanded them; even I know and am a witness, saith the Lord.

Thus shalt thou also speak to Shemaiah the Nehelamite, *saying, Thus speaketh the Lord of Hosts...Because thou hast sent letter in thy name unto all the people that are at Jerusalem and to Zephaniah the son of Maaseiah the priest, and to all the priests, saying,*

The Lord hath made thee priest in the stead of Jehoiada the priest, that ye should be officers in the house of the Lord, for every man that is mad, and maketh himself a prophet, that thou shouldest put him in prison, and in the stocks [referring to Prophet Jeremiah].

Now therefore why hast thou not reproved Jeremiah of Anathoth, which maketh himself a prophet to you? For therefore he sent unto us in Babylon, saying, This captivity is long: build ye houses, and dwell in them; and plant gardens, and eat the fruit of them. And Zephaniah the priest read this letter in the ears of Jeremiah the prophet.

Then came the word of the Lord unto Jeremiah, saying, Send to all them of the captivity, saying, Thus saith the Lord, concerning Shemiah the Nehelamite; Because that Shemaiah hath prophesied unto you, and I sent him not, and he caused you to trust in a lie; Therefore thus saith the Lord: Behold, I will punish Shemaiah the Nehelamite and his seed: he shall not have a man to dwell among this people; neither shall he behold the good that I will do for my people, saith the Lord; because he hath taught rebellion against the Lord."

Chapter 23

The Fall of Assyria

(The Professor's comments)

The *wise old Hittite Owl* said, "Oddly enough, **Yahweh's** people were not the only ones lifted up in pride, idolatry, greed, covetous, unholy living, abominations, human sacrifice, torture, and the like. It should have been an honor for Assyria to be used of God. **Yahweh** used the Assyrians as an instrument of correction against the Northern Tribe of Israel. **The more Yahweh empowered the Assyrians, the more they labeled themselves an invincible SUPERPOWER!** In fact, they discredited and disgraced themselves. So, God had to take them down to dirt level! **God is so merciful!** Before God destroyed Assyria, He sent prophets to warn the Assyrian Empire that destruction was coming.

Prophet Zephaniah (an Ethiopian)

(The Professor's comments)

Zephaniah *(means = the Lord has hidden)* was a minor prophet with great big OPINIONS about a lot of heavy topics (Judah, Assyria, Moab, Ammon, Ethiopia, the last days - Armageddon, conversion of all the nations, and the Messiah's reign on Earth). The ***Bible*** states, "***The word of the Lord which came unto Zephaniah the son of Cushi, the son of Gedaliah, the son of Amariah, the son of Hizkiah*** [A.K.A. king

Hezekiah of Judah]***, in the days of Josiah the son of Amon, king of Judah.***" (Zephaniah 1:1)

Zephaniah's Identity and Roots

It is extremely important to establish Zephaniah's identity, roots, and lineage. Firstly, Zephaniah the son of Cushi *(translated, Cush; II Samuel 18:21-32; Jeremiah 36:14; Zephaniah 1:1)* is listed in the **Table of Nations** (Genesis 10:8; I Chronicles 1:8-10; Isaiah 11:11); Secondly, Cush is the son of Ham, the son of Noah. The land of Cush is also known as the land of Nubia *(residents are called Nubians)* parts of Sudan, Cushites, Ethiopians = dark skinned people; Black); Thirdly, Zephaniah's lineage goes back to king Hezekiah of Judah and he is the great grandson; and Fourthly, Zephaniah prophesized during the reign of king Josiah of Judah. (Zephaniah 1:1)

Scriptures Regarding the Egyptians, Ethiopians, Nubians

Egyptians: Basically, Egypt is located in the northeastern part of Africa *(the second largest continent on Earth)*. Mizraim (means = double and is the Hebrew name for Egypt) was the son of Ham, the son of Noah. Mizarim is the progenitor of the Egyptian tribes (upper and lower Egypt). In addition, Mizarim is the brother of Cush *(son of Ham)*.

The Pharaohs and upper classes were extremely wealthy. In ancient times, their land was fertile, rich in minerals and metals. In general, the Egyptians were great mathematicians, architects, and builders, strong in military power, and great traders. Historically, Egyptians are known for many things including the great pyramids, palaces, the River Nile, hieroglyphics, worshipping idols, embalming, and mostly, for enslaving the Hebrews. [68]

The Nubians were from northern Sudan, southern Egypt, Arabia *(the land of Cush, A.K.A. Kush)*, Babylonia, and India. Significantly, the Nubians were descendants of Cush the progenitor of various Ethiopian tribes. Obviously, each group (Egyptians, Nubians, and Sudanese) had their own characteristics (customs, traditions, attire, music, beliefs, dances, and language). BUT, they had one common denominator, their very dark skin.

(Job 28:12-19) Job talked about the topaz of Ethiopia,
"But where shall wisdom be found? And where is the place of understanding? Man knoweth not the price thereof; neither is it found in the land of the living. The depth saith, It is not in me; and the sea saith, It is not with me. It cannot be gotten for gold neither shall silver be weighed for the price thereof. It cannot be valued with the gold of Ophir, with the precious onyx, or the sapphire. The gold, and the crystal cannot equal it: and the exchange of it shall not be for jewels of fine gold. No mention shall be made of coral, or of pearls: for the price of wisdom is above rubies. <u>The topaz of Ethiopia shall not equal it, neither shall it be valued with pure gold</u>. Whence then cometh wisdom? And where is the place of understanding? Seeing it is hid from the eyes of all living, and kept close from the fowls of the air. Destruction and death say, We have heard the fame thereof with our ears. God understandeth the way thereof, and he knoweth the place thereof. For he looketh to the ends of the earth, and seeth under the whole heaven...<u>And unto man he said, Behold, the fear of</u>

---

68   The Hebrew bondage was not a surprise. God told Abraham, *"...<u>Know of surety that thy seed shall be a stranger in a land that is not theirs, and shall serve them; and they shall afflict them four (400) hundred years; And also that nation, whom they shall serve, will I judge: and afterward they shall come out with great substance.</u>"* (Genesis 15:13-14)

the Lord, that is wisdom; and to depart from evil is understanding."
PRAISE THE LORD!

(Isaiah 11:11) God will regather Israel from Cush and other places,
"*And it shall come to pass in that day, that the Lord shall set his hand again the second time to recover the remnant of his people, which shall be left from Assyria, and from Egypt, and from Pathros, and from Cush, and from Elam, and from Shinar, and from Hamath, and from the island of the sea. And he shall set up an ensign for the nations, and shall assemble the outcasts of Israel, and gather together the dispersed of Judah from the four corners of the earth.*"

(Isaiah 18:2, 7) Isaiah's burden and woe to Ethiopia,
"*Woe to the land shading with wings, which is beyond the rivers of Ethiopia: That sendeth ambassadors by sea, even in vessels of bulrushes upon the waters, saying, Go, ye swift messengers, to a nation scattered and peeled, to a people terrible from their beginning hitherto; a nation meted out and trodden down, who land the rivers have spoiled!*"

(Zephaniah 2:12) Woe to the Ethiopians,
"*Ye Ethiopians, also, ye shall be slain by my sword.*"

(Jeremiah 13:23) Regarding the color of the Ethiopian,
"Can the Ethiopian change his skin, or the leopard his spots? *Then may ye also do good, that are accustomed to do evil.*"

(Psalm 68:31-35) Ethiopian and Egyptian Princes,
"*Princes shall come out of Egypt; Ethiopia shall soon stretch out her hands unto God. Sing unto God, ye kingdoms of the earth; O sing praises unto the Lord; Selah. To him that rideth upon the heavens of heavens, which were of old; lo, he doth send out his voice, and that a mighty voice. Ascribe ye strength unto God: his excellency is over Israel, and his strength is in the clouds. O God, thou art terrible out*

of thy holy places: the God of Israel is he that giveth strength and power unto his people. Blessed be God."

(Daniel 11:43) Referring to the Antichrist in the end time,
"But he shall have power over the treasures of gold and of silver, and over all the precious things of Egypt: and the Libyans, and the Ethiopians shall be at his steps."

A Few Famous Blacks in the Bible

Moses' First Wife: Her name, *Zipporah a Midianite* who lived in Midian located in Arabia *(the land of Cush also known as Ethiopia).* Naturally, Jethro the Midianite Priest *(Zipporah's Father)* was a descendant of Midian *the son of Abraham*[69] *and Keturah who bore Abraham six sons, i.e., the Arab side of the family: Zimran, Jokshan (who begat Sheba and Dedan,) Medan,* **Midian***, Ishbak, and Shuah.* (Genesis 25:1-4). However, the **_Bible_** does not say Zipporah was a Nubian but it does say that she was a descendant of Midian *(son of Abraham and Keturah).* Explicitly, the **_Bible_** says that Zipporah lived in the land of Midian. Therefore, she was a Midianite who lived in Midian located in Arabia *(also known as the land of Cush also known as Ethiopia).* Furthermore, Moses met Zipporah in the land of Midian by the *Well of Jethro* (Exodus 2:15). There are other names for Jethro the Midian Priest: **(a)** Reuel, Exodus 2:18; **(b)** Raguel, Numbers 10:29; and **(c)** Hobab, (Judges 4:11).

(Exodus 2:16-22) *"Now the priest of Midian* [Jethro] *had seven daughters and they came and drew water, and filled the troughs to water their father's flock. And the shepherds came and drove them away: but Moses stood up and helped them, and watered their flock... And Moses was content to dwell with the man:* and he gave Moses, Zipporah his daughter."

---

69   The Bible says, *"Abraham gave all that he had unto Isaac. But unto the sons of the concubines, which Abraham had, Abraham gave gifts, and sent them away from Isaac his son, while he yet lived, eastward unto the east country."* (Genesis 25:5-6) God's covenant was with Abraham, Isaac, and Jacob.

<u>**Moses' Second Wife:**</u> No name given. Numbers 12:1, *"And Miriam and Aaron spake against Moses because of the <u>Ethiopian woman whom he had married</u>..."*

Ebed-Melech: The Black eunuch from Ethiopia (working for king Zedekiah of Judah) was extremely courageous and begged for Jeremiah's release from the dungeon,

(Jeremiah 38:7) *"Now when Ebed-Melech the Ethiopian, one of the eunuchs which was in the king's house, heard that they had put Jeremiah in the dungeon: the king then sitting in the gate of Benjamin; Ebed-Melech went forth out of the king's house, and spake to the king, saying, My lord the king, these men have done evil in all that they have done to Jeremiah the prophet, whom they have cast into the dungeon; and he is like to die for hunger in the place where he is: for there is no more bread in the city..."*

Queen Candace: A title given to the *wealthy* Queen(s) of Ethiopia (Acts 8:27); and the,

Black Treasurer: The Ethiopian eunuch (Treasurer to Queen Candace of Ethiopia) was baptized in the Gaza desert by Philip the Evangelist,

(Acts 8:26-40) *"And the angel of the Lord spake unto Philip, saying, Arise and go toward the south unto the way that goeth down from Jerusalem unto Gaza which is desert. And he arose and went: and, behold, a man of Ethiopia, an eunuch of great authority under Candace queen of the Ethiopians, who had the charge of all her treasure, and had come to Jerusalem for to worship, was returning, and sitting in his chariot read Esaias (Isaiah) the prophet..."*

Queen Sheba: An extremely wealthy Black female sovereign from Ethiopia. She was a descendant of *"Sheba son of Raamah (A.K.A. Raama), the son of Cush, the son of Ham."* (Genesis 10:7) Furthermore,

Queen Sheba was extremely intelligent, challenging, and highly favored by king Solomon of Judah.

(I Kings 10:1-13) *"And when the queen of Sheba heard of the fame of Solomon concerning the name of the Lord, she came to prove him with hard questions. And she came to Jerusalem with a very great train, with camels that bare spices, and very much gold, and precious stones; and when she was come to Solomon, she communed with him of all that was in her heart. And Solomon told her all her questions: there was not any thing hid from the king, which he told her not. And when the queen of Sheba had seen all Solomon's wisdom, and the house that he had built…and she said to the king, It was a true report that I heard in mine own land of thy acts and of thy wisdom. Howbeit I believed not the words, until I came, and mine eyes have seen it: and, behold the half was not told me: thy wisdom and prosperity exceedeth the fame which I heard…And king Solomon gave unto the queen of Sheba all her desire, whatsoever she asked, beside that which Solomon gave her of his royal bounty. So she turned and went to her own country, she and her servants."*

(Matthew 12:42) In the *New Testament*, **Jesus Our Lord** mentioned the Queen of South, *"The queen of the south* [referring to the Queen of Sheba] *shall rise up in the judgment with this generation, and shall condemn it: for she came from the uttermost parts of the earth to hear the wisdom of Solomon; and, behold, a greater than Solomon is here."*

Sabeans: The Sabeans are descendants of Sheba, the son of Raamah, (A.K.A. Raama)**,** *the son of Cush, the son of Ham."* (Genesis 10:7) Furthermore, the Sabeans stole Job's oxen and killed his servants.

(Job 1:14-15) *"And there came a messenger unto Job, and said, The oxen were plowing, and the asses feeding beside them: And the Sabeans fell upon them, and took them away; yea, they have slain the servants with the edge of the sword; and I only am escaped alone to tell thee."*

(Ezekiel 27:22; 38:13) The people of Sheba and Raamah are mentioned. *"The merchants of Sheba and Raamah, they were thy merchants: they occupied in they fairs with chief of all spices, and with all precious stones, and gold."*

(Joel 3:3-8) Concerning the judgment against the nations, God said, *"I will gather all nations, and will bring them down into the valley of Jehoshaphat, and will plead with them there for my people and for my heritage Israel, whom they have scattered among the nations, and parted my land. and they have cast lots for my people; and have given a boy for an harlot, and sold a girl for wine, that they might drink. ...Because ye have taken my silver and my gold, and have carried into your temples my goodly pleasant things: The children also of Judah and the children of Jerusalem have y sold unto the Grecians, that ye might remove them far from their border. Behold, I will raise them out of the place whether ye have sold them, and will return your recompence upon your own head: And I will sell your sons and your daughters into the hand of the children of Judah, and they shall sell them to the Sabeans, to a people far off: for the Lord hath spoken it."*

Prophecies Against the Assyrian Empire

(The Professor's comments)

Essentially, Zephaniah was sent to the Southern Tribe of Judah (about 627 B.C.). The wise old Hittite owl said, "Listen to Zephaniah's message to Assyria! See what happens when people get lifted up!"

(Zephaniah's Prophecy)

(Zephaniah 2:13-15)

"And he [God] will stretch out his hand against the north, and destroy Assyria; and will make Nineveh a desolation and dry like a wilderness. And flocks shall lie down in the midst of her, all the beasts

of the nations: both the commorant and the bittern shall lodge in the upper lintels of it; their voice shall sing in the windows; desolation shall be in the thresholds: for he shall uncover the cedar work. <u>This is the rejoicing city that dwelt carelessly, that said in her heart, I am, and there is none beside me:</u> how is she become a desolation, a place for beasts to lie down in! every one that passeth by her shall hiss, and wag his hand."

Nebuchadnezzar's Success & Assyria's Demise

(The Professor continues)

It was not luck that triumph the Babylonians over the Assyrians. **Yahweh** used the Assyrians as a rod of chastening (Isaiah 10:5-6) against the Northern Tribe of Israel (a hypocritical nation). And, He allowed the Assyrians to stretch their egos at length from Earth to Heaven for one reason! **Yahweh planned to reward the Assyrians for their eccentric behavior and monstrosities regarding the nations.** Without help from anyone, the Assyrians doomed themselves because they were overly proud, boisterous, arrogant, and terrorists!

Prophecies Against Nineveh, Assyria

An excellent Word for all who are lifted up in pride,

"Shall the ax boast itself against him that heweth therewith? Or shall the saw magnify itself against him that shaketh it? As if the rod should shake itself against them that lift it up, or as if the staff should lift up itself, as if it were no wood." (Isaiah 10:15)

Prophet Isaiah

(Isaiah's Prophecy Against Assyria)

Before the Assyrians captured Israel (the Northern Tribe) and other nations, Prophet Isaiah *(about the 8 century B.C.; name means = the Lord is salvation)* prophesied Assyria's downfall and that the king of Assyria would be lifted up in pride and fall,

(Isaiah 10:12-14)

"Wherefore <u>it shall come to pass</u> that when the Lord hath performed his whole work upon mount Zion and on Jerusalem, <u>I will punish the fruit of the stout heart of the king of Assyria and the glory of his high looks</u>…For he saith, by the strength of my hand I have done it, and by my wisdom; for I am prudent: and I removed the bounds of the people, and have robed their treasures, and I have put down the inhabitants like a valiant man: And my hand hath found as a nest the riches of the people: and as one gathered all the earth; and there was none that moved the wing, or opened the mouth, or peeped."

(Isaiah 10:16-18)

"Therefore shall the Lord, the Lord of hosts, send among his fat ones, leanness: and under his glory he shall kindle a burning like the burning of a fire. And the light of Israel shall be for a fire, and his Holy One for a flame; and it shall burn and devour his thorns and his briers in one day: and shalt consume the glory of his forest, and of his fruitful field, both soul and body: and they shall be as when a standardbearer [person who carries the flag] *fainteth."*

Prophet Jonah

(Jonah's Prophecy Against Nineveh)

Moreover, Jonah's *(about 8 century B.C.; name means = dove)* prophecies contributed to the overthrow and doom of Nineveh (Assyria's capital).

The Assyrians were Babylon's *number one* enemy. The story of Jonah is one of the greatest stories in the **<u>Bible</u>** concerning *Nineveh* and cannot be overlooked. Naturally, all prophecies against Assyria contributed to the success of Nabopolassar, Nebuchadnezzar, and the Medes. God told Jonah, ***"Arise, go to Nineveh, that great city, and cry against it for their wickedness is come up before me."*** (Jonah 1:2)

(Jonah's Bigotry)

Because of *hatred*, Jonah refused to deliver God's message to the Ninevites. Instead, he went down to Joppa, priced the fare to Tarshish, jumped on the ship, and sailed away! But, God cornered Jonah and his bigotry: a tempestuous storm arose; *the men in the boat were exceedingly afraid*; questions were asked; Jonah confessed his nationality as a Hebrew and fear of the Lord. *Then, Jonah said that because of me this great tempest is upon you, so throw me overboard.* But the men did not want to throw Jonah overboard. Nevertheless, the men rowed harder and harder to get to the land, but they failed. With no other choice, the men cried out unto the Lord to save them. Finally, they cast Jonah into the sea! (Jonah 1:3-15)

(Jonah's Voyage to the Bottom of the Sea)

Mercifully, God made a way of escape for Jonah. The Word states that God will always make a way of escape! Sometimes the way of escape may not be the road the escapee desires to travel. Disobedience to God's Will creates delays to: recovery, healing, reconciliation, restitution, righteousness, promotion, and growth. Moreover, disobedience can lead to the road of destruction, more sin, and even death! (Romans 6:23)

"Now the Lord had prepared a great fish to swallow up Jonah. And Jonah was in the belly of the fish three days and three nights. (Jonah 1:17)

Well Jonah paid for a boat ride but he got more than he bargained.

Jonah was transferred from one boat to another! The first boat ride was above sea level and the second the second boat ride was below sea level. Jonah had a wild adventure on a living, breathing submarine beneath sea level.

And, Jonah paid dearly for that boat ride! In fact, it cost his life! The lesson to learn from Jonah's episode is: Be very careful when you refused to obey God!

After Jonah's *Voyage to the Bottom of the Sea*, he was ready to deliver **Yahweh's** message! *"Jonah prayed unto the Lord his God out of the fish's belly…out of the belly of hell cried I, and thou heardest my voice. And said, I cried by reason of mine affliction unto the Lord, and he heard me; out of the belly of hell cried I, and thou heardest my voice. For thou hadst cast me into the deep, in the midst of the seas; and the floods compassed me about: all thy billows and thy waves passed over me. Then I said, I am cast out of thy sight; yet I will look again toward thy holy temple. The waters compassed me about even to the soul: the depth closed me round about, the weeds were wrapped about my head. I went down to the bottoms of the mountains; the earth with her bars was about me for ever: yet hast thou brought up my life from corruption, O Lord my God. When my soul fainted within me I remembered the Lord: and my prayer came in unto thee, into thine holy temple.* " (Jonah 2:1-7)

(Jonah, Ready to Preach)

By Jonah 2:10, Jonah was ready to preach, "And the Lord spake unto the fish, and it vomited out Jonah upon the dry land." While in the belly of the whale for three days and three nights, [70] Jonah had three

---

70   In the New Testament, Jesus talked about Jonah's ordeal to the scribes and Pharisees, *"But he answered and said unto them, an evil and adulterous generation seeketh after a sign; and there shall be no sign given to it, but the sign of the prophet Jonas: For as Jonas was three days and three nights in the whale's belly; so shall the Son of man be three days and three nights in the heart of the earth."* (Matthew 12:40; Luke 11:29)

days to prepare his text and he memorized it. Afterwards, it took Jonah one day to arrive at the entrance of Nineveh. (Jonah 3:4) In fact, Jonah's early arrival was a miracle, because Nineveh was about a three (3) day journey. Apparently, Jonah did not take the time to wash himself, change clothes, and probably, he still had seaweed wrapped around his head and neck.

(All Nineveh Repented)

No wonder the Ninevites repented. [71] They were frightened out of their breeches, because Jonah was a visual, walking, talking, and smelly example of God's justice! "And the people of Nineveh believed God, proclaimed a fast, and put on sackcloth from the greatest of them even to the least of them. For word came unto the king of Nineveh, and he arose from his throne, and he laid his robe from him, and covered him with sackcloth, and sat in ashes. And he caused it to be proclaimed and published through Nineveh the decree of the king and his nobles, saying, Let neither man nor beasts, herd nor flock, taste any thing: let them not feed, nor drink water. But let man and beast be covered with sackcloth, and cry mightily unto God: yea, let them turn every one from his evil way, and from the violence that is in their hands. Who can tell if God will turn and repent, and turn away from his fierce anger that we perish not? And God repented of the evil, that he had said that he would do unto them; and he did it not." (Jonah 3:5-10)

Prophet Nahum

(Nahum's Prophecy, Nineveh)

Nahum *(means = comfort or encourage)* was sent to encourage **Yahweh's** *people* and to pronounce judgment on Nineveh, *their cousin-enemies.* Under Prophet Jonah's revival (about 7th century B.C.), Nineveh's king,

---

71   In the ***New Testament*** Jesus said, *"**The men of Nineveh shall rise in judgment with this generation, and shall condemn it: because they repented at the preaching of Jonah; and behold a greater than Jonas is here.**"* (Matthew 12:41)

nobles, citizens and their king repented in sackcloth and ashes and no man or beast was allowed to eat, feed, or drink water. One hundred (100) years later, **Yahweh** sent Nahum to pronounce judgment against Nineveh, *the bloody city.* This time, the Ninevites did not take heed to the prophet's warnings! Probably, Nahum had a *big* migraine headache. How do we know this? **Nahum addresses Nineveh as a BURDEN!** He starts the book as follows,

(God's Omnipotence)

"*The Burden of Nineveh. The book of the vision of Nahum the Elkoshite. <u>God is jealous, and the Lord revengeth; the Lord revengeth, and is furious; the Lord will take vengeance, and he reserveth wrath for his enemies.</u> The Lord is slow to anger, and great in power, and will not at all acquit the wicked: the Lord hath his way in the whirlwind and in the storm, and the clouds are the dust of his feet... THE LORD IS SLOW TO ANGER, AND GREAT IN POWER, AND WILL NOT AT ALL ACQUIT THE WICKED...Who can stand before his indignation? And who can abide in the fierceness of his anger? His fury is poured like fire, and the rocks are thrown down by him.*" (Nahum 1:1-3, 6)

(God the Destroyer)

(Nahum 2:13)

"*Behold, I am against thee, saith the Lord of hosts, and I will burn her chariots in the smoke, and the sword shall devour thy young lions: and I will cut off thy prey from the earth, and the voice of thy messengers shall no more be heard.*"

(God's Divine Justice on Assyria)

God used king Cyaxares of Media and king Nabopolassar of Babylon to bring down the Assyrians,

(Nahum 2:1-6, 13)

"*He that dashed in pieces is come up before thy face: kept he*

291

munition, watch the way, make thy loins strong, fortify thy power mightily…The shield of his mighty men is made red, the valiant men are in scarlet: the chariots shall be with flaming torches in the day of his preparation, and the fir trees shall be terribly shaken. The chariots shall rage in the streets, they shall justle one against another in the broad ways: they shall seem like torches, they shall run like the lightnings. He shall recount his worthies: they shall stumble in their walk; they shall make haste to the wall thereof, and the defence shall be prepared. The gates of the rivers shall be opened, and the palace shall be dissolved."

(Judgment on Nineveh's Queen)

Nineveh's was burned with fire, but Queen Huzzab escaped with her maids,

(Nahum 2:7)

"And Huzzab shall be led away captive, she shall be brought up, and her maids shall lead her as with the voice of doves, tabering upon their breasts."

(Nineveh's New Profile)

(Nahum 2:8-10

"But Nineveh is of old like a pool of water: yet they shall flee away. Stand, stand, shall they cry; but none shall look back. Take ye the spoil of silver, take the spoil of gold: for there is none end of the store and glory out of all the pleasant furniture. She is empty, and void, and waste: and the heart melteth, and the knees smite together, and much pain is in all loins and the faces of them all gather blackness."

(Where is Nineveh, the Fearless?)

(Nahum 2:11-12)

"Where is the dwelling of the lions, and the feedingplace of the young lions, where the lion, even the old lion, walked, and the lion's whelp, and none made them afraid? The lion did tear in pieces enough

for his whelps, and strangled for his lionesses, and filled his holes with prey, and his dens with ravin."

(God's Wrath)

(Nahum 3:1-4)

"Woe to the bloody city! It is all full of lies and robbery; the prey departeth not; The noise of a whip, and the noise of the rattling of the wheels, and of the pransing horses, and of the jumping chariots.

The horseman lifteth up both the bright sword and the glittering spear: and there is a multitude of slain, and a great number of carcases; and there is none end of their corpses; they stumble upon their corpses:

Because of the multitude of the whoredoms of the well-favoured harlot, the mistress of witchcrafts, that selleth nations through her whoredoms, and families through her witchcrafts."

(God's Judgment)

(Nahum 3:3-7)

"Behold, I am against thee, saith the Lord of hosts; and I will discover thy skirts upon the face, and I will shew the nations thy nakedness, and the kingdoms thy shame. *And I will cast abominable filth upon thee, and make thee vile, and will set thee as a gazingstock. And it shall come to pass, that all they that look upon thee shall flee from thee, and say, Nineveh is laid waste: who will bemoan her? Whence shall I seek comforters for thee?"*

(Get Ready Its Coming)

(Nahum 3:11-14)

"Thou also shalt be drunken: thou shalt be hid, thou also shalt seek strength because of the enemy. All thy strong holds shall be like fig trees with the first-ripe figs: if they be shaken, they shall even fall into the mouth of the eater. Behold, thy people in the midst of thee

are women: the gates of thy land shall be set wide open unto thine enemies: the fire shall devour thy bars. Draw thee waters for the siege, fortify thy strong holds: go into clay, and tread the mortar, make strong the brick-kiln.”

(God's Destruction)

(Nahum 3:15)

“There shall the fire devour thee; the sword shall cut thee off, it shall eat thee up like the cankerworm: make thyself many as the cankerworm, make thyself many as the locusts.”

(God's Utter Destruction)

The great city (Nineveh) was once spared from destruction (during Jonah's revival). By 612 B.C., the Babylonians and the Medes joined forces and destroyed Assyria. Cyaxares *(king of Media)* and Nabopolassar *(king of Babylon)* combined their armies to fight against Assyria.

(Nahum 3:18-19)

“Thy shepherds slumber, O king of Assyria: thy nobles shall dwell in the dust: thy people is scattered upon the mountains, and no man gathereth them. There is no healing of thy bruise; thy wound is grievous: all that hear the bruit of thee shall clap the hands over thee: for upon whom hath not thy wickedness passed continually?”

Assyrian Unrest and Infighting

Another contributing fact to Assyria's downfall is the in-fighting-among the Assyrian princes (jealously, hatred, and vindictiveness), court unrest, and *the murder of* king Sennacherib[72] *slain by his sons.* According to Second

---

72   According to history, Sennacherib was more of a builder than a military general. Sennacherib re-built a breathtaking palace called “The palace without rival” at Nineveh. The discovery was made about 1849 by A. H. Layard, an Englishman, who discovered Sennacherib's palace: about seventy-one rooms (71); two large halls one hun-

Kings 19:36-37, the Angel of the Lord struck down 185,000 Assyrians during their siege against king Hezekiah of Jerusalem. Bewildered, king Sennacherib returned to pray in the *Temple of Nisroch, his god.* Without doubt, there was much discontentment with the king and unrest with the failing kingdom. While the king was praying to Nisroch (who could not hear, see, or speak), Sennacherib's sons (Adrammelech and Sharezer) murdered him and they fled to the land of Armenia. Apparently, the two brothers, families, and followers were pursued and punished with death. Esarhaddon (about 681-669 B.C.) the youngest son of the late Sennacherib took the throne. (II Kings 19:36-37) Later, it seems that Esarhaddon died suddenly and Ashurbanipal became the last king of Assyria!

---

dred and eighty feet long by forty feet wide (180 by 40); fragments of cedar, cypress, silver or cooper casing around doors, alabaster, marble, and ivory, over nine thousand (9,000) reliefs of victories, stories about other ancient cultures; gardens, aqueducts, huge walls surrounding the city, etc.

Chapter 24

The Fall of Babylon

(The Professor's comments)

The wise old Hittite Owl said that the Babylonians had a glorious reign and God used them mightily against Judah, **His Chosen people,** *"Behold ye among the heathen, and regard, and wonder marvelously: for I will work a work in your days, which ye will not believe, though it be told you."* (Habakkuk 1:5) The Babylonians were at the height of their glory and they were killing-machines. *"For, lo, I raise up the Chaldeans, that bitter and hasty nation, which shall march through the breadth of the land to possess the dwelling places that are not theirs. They are terrible and dreadful: their judgment and their dignity shall proceed of themselves. Their horses swifter than the leopards and more fierce than the evening wolves: and their horsemen shall spread themselves and their horsemen shall come from far; they shall fly as the eagle that hasteth to eat. They shall come all for violence: their faces shall sup up as the east wind, and they shall gather the captivity as sand. And they shall scoff at the kings, and the princes shall be a scorn unto them: they shall deride every strong hold; for they shall heap dust, and take it."* (Habakkuk 1:6-10)

What should have been an *honor* to the Babylonians became a *disgrace!* With no other choice, God had to take them down! **Like Assyria, Babylonia was a SUPERPOWER begging for a slap-in-the face and judgment from God!**

Two Legitimate Complaints

(God's Complaint Against Judah)

(Jeremiah 25:8-11)

"Therefore thus saith the Lord of hosts; Because ye [Jerusalem] have not heard my words, Behold, I will send and take all the families of the north, and Nebuchadnezzar the king of Babylon, my servant, *and will bring them against this land, and against the inhabitants thereof, and against all these nations round about, and will utterly destroy them, and make them an astonishment, and an hissing, and perpetual desolations.*

Moreover I will take from them [Judah] the voice of mirth, and the voice of gladness, the voice of the bridegroom, and the voice of the bride, the sound of the millstones, and the light of the candle. And this whole land shall be a desolation, and an astonishment; and these nations shall serve the king of Babylon seventy years."

(Israel's Complaint & Curse Against Babylon)

(Jeremiah 51:34-35)

"Nebuchadnezzar the king of Babylon hath devoured me, he hath crushed me, he hath made me an empty vessel, he hath swallowed me up like a dragon, he hath filled his belly with my delicates, he hath cast me out. The violence done to me and to my flesh be upon Babylon, shall the inhabitant of Zion say; and my blood upon the inhabitants of Chaldea, shall Jerusalem say."

Jeremiah's Prophecies Against Babylon

(The Professor's comments)

The wise owl said that God's mind was made up! Although God

used Babylon to execute judgment against Judah *(His Chosen)* for their disobedience. **Yahweh** planned to inflict judgment on Babylon,

(Punishment on Babylon, after 70 Years)

(Jeremiah 25:12-14)

"And it shall come to pass, when seventy years are accomplished, that I will punish the king of Babylon, and that nation, saith the Lord, for their iniquity, and the land of the Chaldeans, and will make it perpetual desolations. And I will bring upon that land all my words which I have pronounced against it, even all that is written in this book, which Jeremiah hath prophesied against all the nations. For many nations and great kings shall serve themselves of them also: and I will recompense them according to their deed, and according to the works of their own hands."

(All Nations to Drink: The Wine Cup of Fury)

Judah will drink first, then, the other nations will follow,

(Jeremiah 25:15-17)

"For thus saith the Lord God of Israel unto me; Take the wine cup of this fury at my hand, and cause all the nations, to whom I send thee, to drink it. And they shall drink, and be moved, and be mad, because of the sword that I will send among them. Then took I the cup at the Lord's hand, and made all the nations to drink, unto whom the Lord had sent me."

(No Refusals: All Will Drink The Same Wine)

(Jeremiah 25:27b-28)

"…Thus saith the Lord of hosts, the God of Israel; Drink ye, and be drunken, and spue, and fall, and rise no more, because of the sword which I will send among you. And it shall be, if they refuse to take the cup at thine hand to drink, then shalt thou say unto them, thus saith the Lord of hosts; Ye shall certainly drink. For, lo, I begin to bring evil on the city which is called by my name, and should ye be utterly

unpunished? Ye shall not be unpunished: for I will call for a sword upon all the inhabitants of the earth, saith the Lord of hosts."

(God's Word Against Babylon)

(Jeremiah 50:1-3)

"The word of Lord spake against Babylon and against the land of the Chaldeans by Jeremiah the prophet. Declare ye among the nations, and publish, and set up a standard; publish, and conceal not: say, Babylon is taken, Bel is confounded, Merodach is broken in pieces: her idols are confounded, her images are broken in pieces. For out of the north there cometh up a nation against her, which shall make her land desolate, and none shall dwell therein: they shall remove, they shall depart, both man, and beast."

(Medes and Persians Against Babylon)

(Jeremiah 50:41-46)

"Behold, a people shall come from the north, and a great nation, and many kings shall be raised up from the coasts of the earth. They shall hold the bow and the lance: they are cruel and will not shew mercy: their voice shall roar like the sea, and they shall ride upon horses, every one put in array, like a man to the battle, against thee, O daughter of Babylon.

<u>The king of Babylon hath heard the report of them, and his hand waxed feeble: anguish took hold of him, and pangs as of a woman in travail.</u>

Behold, he shall come up like a lion from the swelling of Jordan unto the habitation of the strong: but I will make them suddenly run away from her: and who is a chosen man, that I may appoint over her? For who is like me? And who will appoint me the time? And who is that shepherd that will stand before me?

Therefore hear ye the counsel of the Lord, that he hath taken against

Babylon; and his purposes, that he hath purposed against the land of the Chaldeans: Surely the least of the flock shall draw them out: surely he shall make their habitation desolate with them.

At the noise of the taking of Babylon the earth is moved, and the cry is heard among the nations."

(A Destroying Wind Raised Against Babylon)
(Jeremiah 51:1-4)

*"Thus saith the Lord: **(1)** <u>**Behold, I will raise up against Babylon**</u>, and against them that dwell in the midst of them that rise up against me, <u>a destroying wind;</u>*

*<u>**(2)**</u> <u>**And will send unto Babylon fanners, that shall fan her, and shall empty her land**</u>: for in the day of trouble they shall be against her round about. Against him that bendeth let the archer bend his bow and against him that lifteth himself up in his brigandine [unit of soldiers]: and spare ye not her young men; destroy utterly all her host. **(3)** <u>**Thus the slain shall fall in the land of the Chaldeans, and they that are thrust through in her streets**</u>."*

(God Will Restore Israel)
(Jeremiah 51:6)

"For Israel hath not been forsaken, nor Judah of his God, of the Lord of hosts; though their land was filled with sin against the Holy One of Israel.

Flee out of the midst of Babylon, and deliver every man his soul; be not cut off in her iniquity; for this is the time of the Lord's vengeance; he will render unto her a recompence."

(Babylon: The Golden Cup)
(Jeremiah 51:7-18)

"Babylon hath been a golden cup in the Lord's hand, that made all the earth drunken: the nations have drunken of her wine; therefore the nations are mad.

<u>Babylon is suddenly fallen and destroyed: howl for her; take balm for her pain, if so be she may be healed.</u>

<u>We would have healed Babylon, but she is not healed: forsake her, and let us go every one into his own country: for her judgment reacheth unto heaven, and is lifted up even to the skies.</u>

The Lord hath brought forth our righteousness: come, and let us declare in Zion the work of the Lord our God.

Make bright the arrows; gather the shields: the Lord hath raised up the spirit of the kings of the Medes: for his device is against Babylon, to destroy it; because it is the vengeance of the Lord, the vengeance of his temple.

Set up the standard upon the walls of Babylon, make the watch strong, set up the watchmen, prepare the ambushes: for the Lord hath both devised and done that which he spake against the inhabitants of Babylon.

O thou that dwellest upon many waters, abundant in treasures, thine end is come and the measure of thy covetousness.

The Lord of hosts hath sworn by himself, saying, Surely I will fill thee with men, as with caterpillars; and they shall lift up a shout against thee.

He hath made the earth by his power, he hath established the world by his wisdom, and hath stretched out the heaven by his understanding.

When he uttereth his voice, there is a multitude of waters in the heavens; and he causeth the vapors to ascend from the ends of the earth: he maketh lightnings with rain, and bringeth forth the wind out of his treasures.

Every man is brutish by his knowledge; every founder is confounded by the graven image; for his molten image is falsehood, and there is no breath in them.

They are vanity, the work of errors: in the time of their visitation they shall perish."

(Cyrus The Battle Ax)

(Jeremiah 51:20-25)

"__Thou art my battle axe and weapons of war__: for with thee will I break in pieces the nations, and with thee will I destroy kingdoms; And with thee will I break in pieces the horse and his rider; and with thee will I break in pieces the chariot and his rider;

With thee also I will break in pieces man and woman; and with thee will I break in pieces old and young; and with thee will I break in pieces the young man and the maid;

I will also break in pieces with thee the shepherd and his flock; and with thee will I break in pieces the husbandman and his yoke of oxen; and with thee will I break in pieces captains and rulers.

And I render unto Babylon and to all the inhabitants of Chaldea all their evil that they have done in Zion in your sight, saith the Lord.

Behold I am against thee, O destroying mountain, saith the Lord, which destroyest all the earth: and I will stretch out mine hand upon thee, and roll thee down from the rocks and will make thee a burnt mountain."

(Blow the Trumpet)
(Jeremiah 51:27-28)

"Set up the a standard in the land, blow the trumpet among the nations, prepare the nations against her, call together against her the kingdoms of Ararat, Minni, and Ashchenaz; appoint a captain against her; cause the horses to come up as the rough caterpillars. Prepare against the nations of the Medes, the captains thereof, and all the rulers thereof, and all the land of his dominion."

(Babylon's Mighty Men Are Weak)
(Jeremiah 51:29-33)

"And the land shall tremble and sorrow: for every purpose of the Lord shall be performed against Babylon, to make the land of Babylon a desolation without an inhabitant. The mighty men of Babylon have forborn to fight, they have remained in their holds: their might hath failed; they became as women: they have burned her dwelling places; her bars are broken. One post [Pony Express] shall run to meet another, and one messenger to meet another, to shew the king of Babylon that his city is taken at one end. And that the passages are stopped, and the reeds they have burned with fire, and the men of war are affrighted. For thus saith the Lord of Hosts, the God of Israel; The daughter of Babylon is like a threshing floor, it is time to thresh her: yet a little while and the time of her harvest shall come."

Isaiah's Prophecies Against Babylon

(Prophet Isaiah's Burden for Babylon)
(Isaiah 13:1-2)

"The burden of Babylon which Isaiah the son of Amoz did see. Lift ye up a banner upon the high mountain, exalt the voice of unto them, shake the hand, that they may go into the gates of the nobles. I have

303

commanded my sanctified ones, I have also called my mighty ones for mine anger, even them that rejoice in my highness. "

Prophet Isaiah

(A People from the North: The Medes & Persians)
(Isaiah 13:17-22)

"Behold, I will stir up the Medes against them, which shall not regard silver; and as for gold, they shall not delight in it.

Their bows also shall dash the young men to pieces; and they shall have no pity on the fruit of the womb; their eye shall hot spare children.

And Babylon, the glory of kingdoms, the beauty of the Chaldees' excellency, shall be as when God overthrew Sodom and Gomorrah.

It shall never be inhabited, neither shall it be dwelt in from generation to generation, neither shall the Arabian pitch tent there; neither shall the shepherds make their fold there.

But wild beasts of the desert shall lie there; and their houses shall be full of doleful creatures, and owls shall dwell there, and satyrs shall dance there.

And the wild beasts of the islands shall cry in their desolate houses, and dragons in their pleasant palaces: and her time is near to come, and her days shall not be prolonged."

(CYRUS: God's Shepherd & Babylon's Executioner)
(Isaiah 44:28; 45:1-3)

"That saith of Cyrus, He is my shepherd, and shall perform all my

pleasure: even saying to Jerusalem, Thou shalt be built; and to the temple, Thy foundation shall be laid.

Thus saith the Lord to his anointed, to Cyrus, whose right hand I have holden, to subdue nations before; him; and I will loose the loins of kings, to open before him the two leaved gates; and the gates shall not be shut;

I will go before thee, and make the crooked places straight: I will break in pieces the gates of brass, and cut in sunder the bars of iron: And I will give thee the treasures of darkness, and hidden riches of secret places, that thou mayest know that I, the Lord, which call thee by thy name, am the God of Israel."

(CYRUS: Did not know Yahweh
But Yahweh knew Cyrus!)
(Isaiah 45:4-6)
"For Jacob my servant's sake, and Israel mine elect, I have even called thee by thy name: I have surnamed thee, though thou hast not known me. That they may know from the rising of the sun, and from the west, that there is none beside me. I am the Lord, and there is none else. I form the light, and create darkness: I make peace, and create evil: I the Lord do all these things."

(CYRUS: Raised in Righteousness!)
(Isaiah 45:13)
"I have raised him up in righteousness, and I will direct all his ways: he shall build my city, and he shall let go my captives, not for price nor reward, saith the Lord of hosts."

(CYRUS: The Righteous Man from the East)
(Isaiah 41:2)
"Who raised up the righteous man [Cyrus] from the east, called him to his foot, gave the nations before him, and made him rule over

305

kings? He gave them as the dust to his sword, and as driven stubble to his bow. He pursued them, and passed safely; even by the way that he had not gone with his feet."

(God's Final Call: Come Out of Babylon)
(Revelation 18:2-8)

*"And after these things I saw another angel come down from heaven, having great power; and the earth was lightened with his glory. And he cried mightily with a strong voice, saying, <u>**Babylon the great is fallen**</u>, and is become the habitation of devils, and the hold of every foul spirit, and a cage of every unclean and hateful bird.*

For all nations have drunk of the wine of the wrath of her fornication, and the kings of the earth have committed fornication with her, and the merchants of the earth are waxed rich through the abundance of her delicacies.

*And I heard another voice from heaven, saying, <u>**Come out of her**</u> [Babylon], my people, that ye be not partakers of her sins, and that ye receive not of her plagues. For her sins have reached unto heaven, and God hath remembered her iniquities.*

Reward her even as she rewarded you, and double unto her double according to her works. In the cup which she hath filled, fill to her double. How much she hath glorified herself, and lived deliciously, so much torment and sorrow give her: for she saith in her heart, I sit a queen, and am no widow, and shall see no sorrow.

*Therefore shall her plagues come in one day, death, and mourning, and famine; and <u>**she shall be utterly burned with fire**</u>: for strong is the Lord God who judgeth her."*

Babylon, the Fallen

The beginning of Babylon's demise starts with the story of king Belshazzar who was the co-regent (*in the absence of his father, Nabonidus*) and the grandson of *king Nebuchadnezzar.*[73] (Jeremiah 27:7) Belshazzar liked showing-off (*because he was a party-king*) and he liked showing off his wives and concubines to his viceroys and lords! For long periods, king Nabonidus would go off to fight various wars and he left behind Mr. Party-man to watch over Babylon. One occasion, Belshazzar had a great feast in a huge ballroom (*recently excavated measuring approximately 60 feet by 172 feet and believed to be the one used for Belshazzar's feast*). There is no definite total on invited guests but there was ONE important person who was not at the party! Answer: The Queen.

(Belshazzar Requested Judah's Sacred Vessels)
The Bible states, ***"Belshazzar the king made a great feast to a thousand of his lords and drank wine before the thousand."*** (Daniel 5:1) In addition to the invited one thousand lords, there were many other guests, ***"Belshazzar whiles he tasted the wine, commanded to bring the golden and silver vessels which his father Nebuchadnezzar*** [in the Chaldean, there is no word for grandfather] ***had taken out of the temple which was in Jerusalem; that the king and his princes, his wives, and his concubines, might drink therein."*** (Daniel 5:2)

(Belshazzar & Guests desecrated the Holy Vessels & honored false gods)
"Then they brought the golden vessels that were taken out of the temple of the house of God which was at Jerusalem and the king, and his princes, his wives, and his concubines, drank in them. They drank wine, and praised the gods of gold, and of silver, of brass, or iron, of wood, and of stone." (Daniel 5:3-4)

---

73   Belshazzar (Means = Bel's prince) was the son of king Nabonidus (the son of king Nebuchadnezzar). However, in the Babylonian language, there is no word for grand-father.

(Laughter Turned into Mourning)

King Belshazzar and his guests had a great time laughing, eating, drinking, singing, dancing, and telling jokes. But very soon, this laughter turned into mourning or better yet *Fright Night*! Something dreadful happened.

(Daniel 5:5-9)

"In the same hour came forth fingers of a man's hand and wrote over against the candlestick upon the plaister of the wall of the king's palace; and the king saw the part of the hand that wrote. The king cried aloud to bring in the astrologers, the Chaldeans, and the soothsayers. And the king spake and said to the wise men of Babylon, Whosoever shall read this writing, and shew me the interpretation thereof, shall be clothed with scarlet and have a chain of gold about his neck, and shall be the third ruler in the kingdom. Then came in the king's wise men: but they could not read the writing, nor make known to the king the interpretation thereof. Then was king Belshazzar greatly troubled, and his countenance was changed in him and his lords were astounded."

Daniel Summoned before king Belshazzar

(Daniel 5:10-16)

"Now the queen by reason of the words of the king and his lords came into the banquet house: and the queen spake and said, O king live for ever: let not thy thoughts trouble thee, nor let thy countenance be changed:

There is a man in thy kingdom, in whom is the spirit of the holy gods; and in the days of thy father light and understanding and wisdom, like the wisdom of the gods, was found in him; whom the king Nebuchadnezzar thy father [grandfather] the king, I say, thy father, made master of the magicians, astrologers, Chaldeans, and soothsayers;

For as much as an excellent spirit, and knowledge, and understanding, interpreting of dreams, and shewing of hard sentences, and dissolving of doubts, were found in the same Daniel, whom the king named Belteshazzar: now let Daniel be called, and he will shew the interpretation.

Then was Daniel brought in before the king. And the king spake and said unto Daniel, Art thou that Daniel, which art of the children of the captivity of Judah, whom the king my father [grandfather] brought out of Jewry?

And now the wise men, the astrologers, have been brought in before me, that they should read this writing, and make known unto me the interpretation thereof: but they could not shew the interpretation of the thing:

And I have heard of thee, that thou canst make interpretations, and dissolve doubts: now if thou canst read the writing, and make known to me the interpretation thereof, thou shalt be clothed with scarlet, and have a chain of gold about thy neck, and shalt be the third ruler in the kingdom."

Prophet Daniel

(The Professor's comments)

The *old Hittite owl* said that king Belshazzar was not humble. Instead, he was lifted up in pride before the **Lord of Heaven.** Also, the Professor said that king Belshazzar had the *audacity* to let his viceroys, other people of rank under him, his wives, and his concubines drink from the holy vessels that the High Priests of Judah had consecrated to the **Lord GOD of Heaven.** They had no rights to

309

put their dirty hands and dirty lips on the things dedicated to **Yahweh!** To make matters worse, they toasted their "gods of silver, and gold, of brass, iron, wood, and stone, which see not, nor hear, nor know..." (Daniel 5:23)

By now, the Professor was hooting and wildly flapping his wings! He said that Belshazzar's behavior was an outrage! The Professor said that Daniel *(still a captive had a high governmental position)* got king Belshazzar told off real good *and the king didn't even know it!* Furthermore, Daniel scolded the king for following in the same steps as his conceited grandfather, king Nebuchadnezzar. The Professor said, *"Listen to what Daniel told the king."*

Daniel's Expository to king Belshazzar)
(Daniel 5:18-25)
"O thou king, the most high God gave Nebuchadnezzar thy father** [grandfather] **a kingdom, and majesty, and glory, and honor:

And for the majesty that he gave him, all people, nations, and languages, trembled and feared before him: whom he would he slew; and whom he would he kept alive; and whom he would he set up; and whom he would he put down.

<u>***But when his heart was lifted up, and his mind hardened in pride, he was deposed from his kingly throne, and they took his glory from him.***</u>

And he was driven from the sons of men; and his heart was made like the beasts, and his dwelling was with the wild asses: they fed him with grass like oxen, and his body was wet with dew of heaven; till he knew that the most high God ruled in the kingdom of men, and that he appointeth over it whomsoever he will.

And thou his son [Belshazzar was Nebuchadnezzar's grandson], ***O Belshazzar has not humbled thine heart, though thou knewest all***

King Nebuchadnezzar

this. But hast lifted up thyself against the Lord of heaven; and they have brought the vessels of his house before thee, and thou, and thy lord thy wives, and thy concubines, have drunk wine in them; and thou hast praised the gods of silver, and gold, of brass, iron, wood, and stone, which see not, nor hear, nor know: and the God in whose hand thy breath is, and whose are all thy ways, hast thou ot glorified: Then was the part of the hand sent from him; and this writing was written. And this is the writing that was written: **MENE, MENE, TEKEL, UPHARSIN.**"

(Daniel Interpreted the Writing to king Belshazzar)
(Daniel 5:26-28)
"*Then was the part of the hand sent from him; and this writing was written. And this is the writing that was written,* MENE, MENE, TEKEL, UPHARSIN.

MENE = God hath numbered thy kingdom and finished it;

TEKEL = Thou art weighed in the balances and art found wanting;

PERES = Thy kingdom is divided and given to the Medes and Persians."

(Daniel Rejected king Belshazzar's Gifts)
Before Daniel read the writing on the wall, he rejected Belshazzar's gifts.

(Daniel 5:17)
"*Then Daniel answered and said before the king,*
(1) *Let thy gifts be to thyself and give thy rewards to another;*
(2) *Yet I will read the writing unto the king, and make known to him the interpretation.*"

(The Professor's comments)

In spite of this fact, Belshazzar commanded gifts to be given to Daniel. This shows Belshazzar's insensitivity, very poor listening and judgmental skills. Obviously, the king was given a terrible omen and he was afraid. However, as the king of Babylon, he must keep up an image. Sometime during his kingship, Belshazzar should have repented and sought Daniels advice. But, Belshazzar didn't know Daniel! Belshazzar was totally out-of-touch with Babylon's daily operations. In fact, the king did not know Daniel. Yahweh's judgment could have been changed to mercy and forgiveness. Unfortunately, we will never know this!

(Regardless, king Belshazzar rewards Daniel)

The *wise old Hittite owl* said, "How dumb can a person be? After Prophet Daniel interpreted the writing on the wall, the king gave Daniel a cape to wear and a gold chain!"

(Daniel 5:29)

"Then commanded Belshazzar, and they clothed Daniel with scarlet and put a chain of gold about his neck, and made a proclamation concerning him that he should be the third ruler in the kingdom."

The Hand Writing Fulfilled

(The Professor's comments)

The *old Hittite owl* said that the Medes and Persians were confederates against the Babylonians and that the Lord GOD used them to punish the Babylonians.

(Daniel 5:30)

"In that night was Belshazzar the king of the Chaldeans slain. And Darius the Median took the kingdom, being about threescore and two years old."

God's Judgment Against Other Nations

(The Professor's comments)

Furthermore, God's anger was directed to twenty nations or more: Jerusalem, Egypt, Uz, Philistines, Ashkelon, Azzah, Ekron, Ashdod, Edom, Moab, Ammon, Tyrus, Zidon, isles beyond the sea, Dedan, Tema, Buz, Arabia, people of the desert, Zimri, Elam, Medes, Sheshach, and all the kingdoms of the world. (Jeremiah 25:18-26)

Chapter 25

God Is

God is **<u>Omniscient</u>** *(having infinite knowledge);* **<u>Omnipotent</u>** *(all powerful);* **<u>Omnipresent</u>** *(present in all places at the same time); Therefore, God can do whatever He likes!*

The All Powerful God: Omniscient

(Isaiah 40:13)
*"**Who hath directed the Spirit of the Lord, or being his counselor hath taught him? With whom took he counsel, and who instructed him, and taught him in the path of judgment, and taught him knowledge, and shewed to him the way of understanding?**"*

(Romans 8:27)
*"**And he that searcheth the hearts knoweth what is the mind of the Spirit, because he maketh intercession for the saints according to the will of God.**"*

(Romans 11:33-36)
*"**O the depth of the riches both of the wisdom and knowledge of God? How unsearchable are his judgments, and his ways past**"*

finding out! For who hath known the mind of the Lord? Or who hath been his counselor? Or who hath first given to him, and it shall be recompensed unto him again? For of him, and through him, and to him, are all things: to whom be glory for ever. Amen."

The All Powerful God: Omnipotent

(Isaiah 40:29-31)

"He giveth power to the faint; and to them that have no might he increaseth strength. Even the youths shall faint and be weary, and the young men shall utterly fall: But they that wait upon the Lord shall renew their strength; they shall mount up with wings as eagles; they shall run, and not be weary; and they shall walk, and not faint."

(Isaiah 45:7-8)

"I formed the light, and create darkness: I make peace, and create evil: I the Lord do all these things.

Drop down, ye heavens, from above, and let the skies pour down righteousness: let the earth open, and let them bring forth salvation, and let righteousness spring up together; I the Lord have created it."

(Isaiah 45:11-12)

"Thus saith the Lord, the Holy One of Israel, and his Maker, Ask me of things to come concerning my sons, and concerning the work of my hands command ye me.

I have made the earth, and created man upon it: I, even my hands, have stretched out the heavens, and all their host have I commanded."

The All Powerful God: Omnipresent

(Psalm 139:7-11)

"Whether shall I go from thy spirit? Or whither shall I flee from thy presence? If I ascend up into heaven thou art there: if I make my bed in hell, behold, thou art there.

If I take the wings of the morning, and dwell in the uttermost parts of the sea; Even there shall thy hand lead me, and thy right hand shall hold me.

If I say, Surely the darkness shall cover me; even the night shall be light about me. Yea, the darkness hideth not from thee; but the night shineth as the day: the darkness and the light are both alike to thee.

For thou hast possessed my reins: thou hast covered me in my mother's womb."

Author's Closing Remarks,

The Well of Souls

The births of many people were foretold in the Bible. For example, the Lord GOD called, sanctified, and ordained Jeremiah before he was born. The Bible states, ***"Then the word of the Lord came unto me, saying, Before I formed thee in the belly I knew thee; and before thou came forth out of the womb, I sanctified thee, and I ordained thee a prophet unto the nations."*** (Jeremiah 1:4-5) This statement proves that souls are immortal and they exist in Heaven in the <u>Well of Souls</u>.

Moreover, the Lord GOD knows every <u>soul</u> by name just as He knows, calls, and numbers every <u>star</u> by name (Psalm 147:4), and the Lord GOD summons every soul at will to place them on Earth according to His plans for every Age and Dispensation right down to the very second!

(Creator of the Universe)
The <u>Bible</u> states, <u>"Great is our Lord, and of great power: his understanding is infinite."</u> (Psalm 147:4)

Amos 5:8 states, "Seek him that maketh the seven stars and Orion[74], and turneth the shadow of death into the morning, and maketh the day dark with night: that calleth for the waters of the sea, and poureth them out upon the face of the earth: The Lord is his name."

---

74   Orion is The Giant or The Hunter (Greek mythology) is a famous constellation located on the celestial equator and seen throughout the world. It includes prominent stars known as the Belt of Orion and in the middle of it is the Orion Nebula.

Job 9:6-10 described God's might as, "Which removeth the mountains…Which shaketh the earth out of her place and the pillars thereof tremble…Which commandeth the sun, and it riseth not; and sealeth up the stars…Which alone spreadeth out the heavens and treadeth upon the waves of the sea…Which maketh Arcturus[75], Orion, and Pleiades[76], and the chambers of the south…Which doeth great things past finding out; yea, and wonders without number."

God told the Children of Israel,

"Behold, I send an Angel before thee, to keep thee in the way, and to bring thee into the place which I have prepared. Beware of him, and obey his voice, provoke him not; for he will not pardon your transgressions: for my name is in him. But if thou shalt indeed obey his voice, and do all that I speak; then I will be an enemy unto thine enemies, and an adversary unto thine adversaries. For mine Angel shall go before thee, and bring thee in unto the Amorites, and the Hittites, and the Perizzites, and the Canaanites, the Hivites, and the Jebusites: and I will cut them off. And ye shall serve the Lord your God, and he shall bless thy bread, and thy water; and I will take sickness away from the midst of thee. There shall nothing cast their young, nor be barren, in thy land: the number of thy days I will fulfil." (Exodus 23:20-23; 25-26)

As a child of God, you have been grafted into the Body of Christ. If

---

75   Arcturus is believed the brightest star (an orange giant) in the constellation Bootes. Arcturus is older and enormously larger than the Earth's Sun. In size comparison, Arcturus is like an elephant to an ant (our Sun). In Greek Mythology, Arcturus forms the left foot of the Bear (in the constellation of Bootes).

76   Pleiades (A.K.A. Seven sisters, the sailing ones, in Greek Mythology) is a cluster of hot blue and shimmering stars in the constellation of Taurus.. However, there are numerous stars in the Pleiades but nine of them are brighter and hotter than the others. Therefore, these nine are given more significance. It is believed that two of the nine are the father and mother and the remaining are their seven daughters! Also, there is a reflecting nebula from the blue light of the stars and its beautiful to look upon.

you are not a child of God, its time for your to make a wise decision. Come in out-of-the rain, out-of-your madness, out-of-confusion, and let the Angel of the Lord guide you. As God promised the Jews, His promises are extended to Gentiles. However, this blessing is conditional.

We must obey the Lord GOD!